NATIONAL SECURITY LAW JOURNAL

VOLUME 1

ISSUE 1

SPRING 2013

National Security Law Journal
George Mason University School of Law
3301 North Fairfax Drive
Arlington, VA 22201

www.nslj.org

© 2013 *National Security Law Journal*. All rights reserved.

ISBN 978-1-300-85920-8

National Security Law Journal

ARTICLES

The Soul of the Chinese Military:
Good Order and Discipline in the People's Liberation Army

Captain Paul A. Stempel

Rules of Engagement:
Balancing the (Inherent) Right and Obligation of Self-Defense
with the Prevention of Civilian Casualties

Christopher Amore

The Advent and Future of International Port Security Law

L. Stephen Cox

COMMENTS & NOTES

Executive Process:
The Due Process of Executive Citizen Targeting
by the Commander-in-Chief

Noah Oberlander

Hinging on Habeas?
The Guantanamo Memorandum of Understanding
and the Detainees' Continued Right to Counsel

Amy M. Shepard

VOLUME 1   SPRING 2013   ISSUE 1

National Security Law Journal

VOLUME 1   SPRING 2013   ISSUE 1

2012-2013 Editorial Board

Editor-in-Chief
Patrick Austin

Executive Editor
Frank Barber

Articles Selection Editor
Alyssa DiGiacinto

Managing Editor
Brendan Cassidy

Senior Articles Editor
Jessica Eddy

Senior Notes Editor
Garrett VanPelt

Senior Research Editor
Samantha Bono

Articles Editors
Jessica Fawson
Miriam Riherd
Armin Tadayon

Notes Editors
Brandon Bierlein
Jessica O'Connell

Research Editors
Emily Gardner
Chaim Mandelbaum

Associate Editors
David Das
Aida Farahani

Candidate Members
Audra Bartels
Brice Biggins
Erica Calys
Jordan Fischetti
Katherine Gorski
Noah Oberlander
Olivia Seo
Michael Sgarlat
Amy Shepard
Stephanie Tan
Linda Tran
Alexander Yesnik

Faculty Advisor
Nathan Sales

NATIONAL SECURITY
LAW JOURNAL

PUBLISHED BY GEORGE MASON UNIVERSITY SCHOOL OF LAW

2012-2013 BOARD OF ADVISORS

STEVEN CASH

ANGELINE CHEN

DENNIS FITZPATRICK

MAJ. GEN. ROBERT HAIRE

GEN. MICK KICKLIGHTER

COL. RICK T. KING

NEOMI RAO

STEVE SHANNON

The NSLJ Editorial Board profoundly appreciates the help and guidance provided by our Board of Advisors as we developed this inaugural issue.

NATIONAL SECURITY LAW JOURNAL

VOLUME 1   SPRING 2013   ISSUE 1

Cite as 1 NAT'L SEC. L.J. ___ (2013)

The *National Security Law Journal* ("NSLJ") is a student-edited legal periodical at the George Mason University School of Law in Arlington, Virginia, published at least two times per year in hard copy and digital form. Our objective is to publish innovative, thought-provoking issues on pressing matters in the field of national security law. Each issue comprises creative, original, groundbreaking articles that appeal to both academia and the practicing legal community.

The Editors of NSLJ can be contacted at:

> *National Security Law Journal*
> George Mason University School of Law
> 3301 North Fairfax Drive
> Arlington, VA 22201
>
> http://www.nslj.org/

Subscriptions: Issues are available online in digital form at www.nslj.org. We also offer a print version of each issue through our print subscription service. Please visit our Web site for details.

Submissions: The NSLJ Editors welcome submissions of scholarly articles and manuscripts. We seek to publish articles and essays that are intended to make a significant and original contribution to the field of national security law. Footnotes should follow the form prescribed in *The Bluebook: A Uniform System of Citation* (19th ed. 2010). Articles are required to be well written and researched at the time of submission.

We incorporate the D.I.M.E. model of national security law and policy when considering scholarly articles for publication. The D.I.M.E. acronym stands for:

> *Diplomacy • Intelligence • Military • Economics*

Articles, manuscripts, and other editorial correspondence should be addressed to the NSLJ Articles Selection Editor at the mailing address above or by e-mail at submissions@nslj.org.

NATIONAL SECURITY LAW JOURNAL

PUBLISHED BY GEORGE MASON UNIVERSITY SCHOOL OF LAW

Acknowledgements

The inception of this journal originated from George Mason University law students, but many individuals contributed to its development and eventual conception. The NSLJ Editorial Board is forever grateful for the support provided by members of the George Mason University School of Law faculty and administration, especially Deans Polsby, Kelsey, and Nields, along with Professor Brandy Wagstaff.

In addition, a very special thanks goes to Professor Nathan Sales, who graciously accepted the position of Faculty Advisor with the journal and was there to help the Editorial Board whenever his guidance was needed. Without the support of these individuals, this inaugural issue would not have been possible.

NATIONAL SECURITY LAW JOURNAL

VOLUME 1　　　　　　　　SPRING 2013　　　　　　　　ISSUE 1

CONTENTS

ARTICLES

1　THE SOUL OF THE CHINESE MILITARY: GOOD ORDER AND DISCIPLINE IN THE PEOPLE'S LIBERATION ARMY
Captain Paul A. Stempel

39　RULES OF ENGAGEMENT: BALANCING THE (INHERENT) RIGHT AND OBLATION OF SELF-DEFENSE WITH THE PREVENTION OF CIVILIAN CASUALTIES
Christopher Amore

77　THE ADVENT AND FUTURE OF INTERNATIONAL PORT SECURITY LAW
L. Stephen Cox

COMMENTS & NOTES

124　EXECUTIVE PROCESS: THE DUE PROCESS OF EXECUTIVE CITIZEN TARGETING BY THE COMMANDER-IN-CHIEF
Noah Oberlander

151　HINGING ON HABEAS? THE GUANTANAMO MEMORANDUM OF UNDERSTANDING AND THE DETAINEES' CONTINUED RIGHT TO COUNSEL
Amy Shepard

THE SOUL OF THE CHINESE MILITARY: GOOD ORDER AND DISCIPLINE IN THE PEOPLE'S LIBERATION ARMY

Captain Paul A. Stempel*

I. INTRODUCTION: THE IMPORTANCE OF STUDYING CHINESE MILITARY LAW

Lieutenant General Richard Harding, a Judge Advocate General of the United States Air Force, published an article in 2010 in which he argued for renewed emphasis on military discipline, which he ranked alongside quality personnel, training, and equipment as one of the four pillars of military strength.[1] "Discipline," he wrote, "is a force multiplier."[2] As Lt. Gen. Harding noted, such sentiments call to mind then-Colonel George Washington's timeless conviction that "discipline is the soul of the army," and the only way to truly understand a military is to study its discipline.[3] Today, few militaries' "souls" capture the

---

* Captain Stempel (B.A., Vanderbilt University; J.D., University of Iowa) wrote this article while Assistant Staff Judge Advocate, Office of the Staff Judge Advocate, Fort George G. Meade, Maryland. He speaks Mandarin Chinese, having lived and worked in the People's Republic of China, and is a member of the Virginia State Bar. The views expressed in this article are those of the author and do not reflect an official position of the Department of the Air Force, Department of Defense or any other government agency or institution.
[1] Lieutenant Gen. Richard C. Harding, *A Revival in Military Justice*, 37 REPORTER 4 (2010).
[2] *Id.* at 5.
[3] *Id.* at 5; *see also* 1 THE WRITINGS OF GEORGE WASHINGTON, 1748-1757, at 470 (Worthington Chauncey Ford ed., New York, G.P. Putnam's Sons 1889).

imagination of the Western world more than that of the People's Republic of China, yet the disciplinary system of China's People's Liberation Army (PLA) remains largely overlooked and misunderstood in Western literature.[4] This article attempts to bridge this knowledge gap, providing an introductory look at good order and discipline in the PLA.

Bridging the Sino-American knowledge gap has received considerable high-level military and diplomatic support in recent years. From the American perspective, the reasons are clearly strategic. Given China's rise as a power broker in the Asia-Pacific theatre and beyond, the future demands that the U.S. military acclimate to a new geopolitical climate, one in which common security threats require Sino-American cooperation and mutual understanding.[5] Both the U.S. and China fight a war on terror; both combat piracy; both purport to desire stability in Central Asia and elsewhere; both seek a peaceful resolution on the Korean peninsula; and both actively participate in humanitarian missions worldwide.[6]

To this end, the two powers held their sixth Defense Policy Coordination Talks in 2009 and their 11th Defense Consultative Talks in 2010.[7] The trend continued in 2011 and 2012, when Admiral Michael

---

[4] For a Cold War-era effort to explain Chinese military law, discussed in greater detail below in Section II, see Captain David C. Rodearmel, *Military Law in Communist China: Development, Structure and Function*, 119 MIL. L. REV. 1 (Winter 1988); *see also* Zhang Chi Sun, *Chinese Military Law: A Brief Commentary on Captain Rodearmel's Article*, 129 MIL. L. REV. 31, 34 (1990).

[5] OFFICE OF THE SEC'Y OF DEF., ANNUAL REPORT TO CONGRESS: MILITARY AND SECURITY DEVELOPMENTS INVOLVING THE PEOPLE'S REPUBLIC OF CHINA 12-14 (2012) [hereinafter ANNUAL REPORT TO CONGRESS: MILITARY AND SECURITY DEVELOPMENTS INVOLVING CHINA], *available at* www.defense.gov/pubs/pdfs/2012_CMPR_Final.pdf.

[6] Info. Office of the State Council of China, China's National Defense in 2010 (2011) [hereinafter China's National Defense in 2010], *available at* http://www.china.org.cn/government/whitepaper/node_7114675.htm ("China and the United States maintain consultations on such issues as non-proliferation, counter-terrorism, and bilateral military and security cooperation."); *see also* ANNUAL REPORT TO CONGRESS: MILITARY AND SECURITY DEVELOPMENTS INVOLVING THE PEOPLE'S REPUBLIC OF CHINA, *supra* note 5 (listing various areas of common interest between U.S. and Chinese militaries).

[7] China's National Defense in 2010, *supra* note 6.

Mullen, the Chairman of the Joint Chiefs of Staff and the highest ranking officer in the U.S. military, visited China, followed by a visit to the U.S. by Defense Minister General Liang Guanglie, China's highest ranking military officer.[8] Both called for combined efforts targeting piracy, medical assistance, and disaster relief.[9] Given such high level efforts at cooperation, it is not unforeseeable that the coming decades will find American troops working side-by-side with their Chinese counterparts.[10]

Such mutual interest prompted American policymakers to study foreign military law in the past. In 2002, the *Air Force Law Review* published an edition dedicated to foreign military law that included articles on the British, Australian, Canadian, Israeli, and Russian military legal systems.[11] In that edition's foreword, the then-Judge Advocate General of the Air Force lamented, "we do not understand enough about how [other countries'] military justice systems operate."[12] He noted that such understanding is "extremely valuable when we are evaluating the opportunities for improving our own system," and can even be "vital when we are working with coalition partners in multinational

---

[8] SHIRLEY A. KAN, CONG. RESEARCH SERV., RL32496, US-CHINA MILITARY CONTACTS: ISSUES FOR CONGRESS 71-72 (2012); Cheryl Pellarin, *Panetta: U.S.-China Relationship One of World's Most Critical*, AM. FORCES PRESS SERV., May 7, 2012, *available at* http://www.defense.gov/News/NewsArticle.aspx?ID=116234 (quoting Chinese Def. Minister Gen. Liang Guanglie: "At present, China-U.S. bilateral relationship is on a new starting line in history . . . to build a new kind of military relationship based on equality, cooperation and mutual benefit.").

[9] *Pellarin, supra* note 8.

[10] Secretary of Defense Robert Gates drove this point home in early 2011, when he travelled to China to meet with Chinese President and Communist Party Secretary Hu Jintao and PLA leadership. *Defense Secretary Robert Gates and Chinese Minister for National Defense Gen. Liang Guanglie Hold a Joint Press Conference from Beijing, China*, CQ Cap. Transcripts, Jan. 10, 2011, *available at* 2011 WLNR 550659. In China, Secretary Gates called for increased cooperation and exchanges to improve mutual understanding. *Id. See also* ANNUAL REPORT TO CONGRESS: MILITARY AND SECURITY DEVELOPMENTS INVOLVING CHINA, *supra* note 5 ("A strong U.S.-China bilateral relationship includes a healthy, stable, reliable and continuous military relationship. . . . This type of engagement enables both militaries to build habits of cooperation and work toward greater mutual understanding.").

[11] 52 A.F. L. REV. i-ii (2002).

[12] *Id.* at v.

operations."[13] In this regard, comparative studies in military law can be understood to serve immediate and tangible national security interests.

Academic interests are served as well. Comparative law scholars are driven by various aims—understanding similarities and differences across cultures, elucidating transcendent principles of justice, even the pursuit of truth itself. Konrad Zweigert and Hein Koetz, whose textbook *An Introduction to Comparative Law* stands as one of the preeminent treatises in the field, wrote of comparative law:

> [B]y the international exchanges which it requires, comparative law procures the gradual approximation of viewpoints, the abandonment of deadly complacency, and the relaxation of fixed dogma. It affords us a glimpse into the form and formation of legal institutions which develop in parallel, possibly in accordance with laws yet to be determined, and permits us to catch sight, through the differences in detail, of the grand similarities and so to deepen our belief in the existence of a unitary sense of justice.[14]

Comparison of U.S. and Chinese systems of military law does indeed reveal certain "grand similarities" that are in- and of-themselves noteworthy, and given the dramatically different lineages of the two militaries, it might come as something of a surprise that the Chinese and American military justice systems have much in common. In many ways, the two systems are, as the Chinese would say, "in harmony," and it can be said that the two share the type of "common core" often sought by scholars in the field of comparative law.[15] At the same time, "differences in detail" do exist. These attributes are explored in this article.

The future might very well bring Chinese and American troops together, for good or ill. And when they meet, they might find that they have more in common than first thought. How better, then, to prepare for an era of increased Sino-American military interaction than by studying the disciplinary system—the "soul"—of the PLA?

---

[13] *Id.*
[14] KONRAD ZWEIGERT & HEIN KÖTZ, AN INTRODUCTION TO COMPARATIVE LAW 3 (Tony Weir trans., 3d rev. ed. 1988).
[15] John Reitz, *How To Do Comparative Law*, 46 AM. J. COMP. L. 617, 625 (1998).

II. THEY STUDY US, WE SHOULD STUDY THEM

Perusing a Chinese language textbook entitled *The Study of Chinese Military Law*—and particularly one published by the Chinese government-sanctioned publishing house China Legal Publishing House—one might be surprised to find a chapter devoted entirely to explaining the *American* system of military justice,[16] particularly amid what is otherwise a survey of *Chinese* military law.[17] The author, legal scholar Yu Enzhi, focuses on the U.S. military's Uniform Code of Military Justice (hereinafter UCMJ), which he lauds as "one of the best in the world" due to its emphasis on procedural justice and the rights of the accused.[18] China, the author contends, would do well to learn from the "scientific and comprehensive" American model of military justice.[19] To put it another way, the Chinese study the "soul" of the American military, and they might borrow its better parts along the way.[20] In short: they study us, we should study them.

In some ways, the Chinese government has sought our attention in recent years. Long a closed society with centralized control over the flow of information, China began a slow thaw in certain areas. Calls by the international community for increased transparency—by the United States in particular—produced preliminary steps in the right direction. One example is the biennial National Defense White Paper, most recently published by the Chinese Information Office of the State Council in March 2011.[21] Insofar as it addresses the military legal system, the white paper serves as something of an advertisement to the world, putting its best and friendliest face forward: this is how we (China) want the world to see us; we (China) have a comprehensive military legal system and our troops obey the law; our system is improving; it will

---

[16] *Zhongguo Junshi Faxue Luncong* [*The Study of Chinese Military Law*], (Xue Gangling ed., 2007) (China).
[17] *Id.* at 21.
[18] *Id.*
[19] *Id.* at 21, 38.
[20] For further discussion of the American military legal system by Chinese military law experts, see *Xin Zhongguo 60 Nian Junshi Fazhi Jianshe* [*60 Years of Military Legal Development in Modern China*] 391-96, (Hu Guangzheng ed., 2009) (discussing the American court-martial system).
[21] China's National Defense in 2010, *supra* note 6.

continue to improve and evolve in the future. The white paper boasts: "the internal security organs, military courts and military procuratorates (attorneys representing the government in criminal cases) of the armed forces have performed their functions to the full, resolutely maintaining justice in punishing various offense [sic] and crimes in accordance with the law."[22] While such pronouncements must be taken with a grain of salt, China's white papers do hold value as invitations, calling on the international community to look deeper, to ask questions, and to hold China to its word. Given an open invitation to study the "soul" of the Chinese military, we should.

We have tried in the past. In 1988, then-Captain (now retired-Lieutenant Colonel) David Rodearmel of the U.S. Army attempted an ambitious, comprehensive study of Chinese military law that was published in the *Military Law Review* (MLR),[23] but he did so at a time when little information about the Chinese military was available to foreigners—and available information was often biased, misleading, or simply incorrect. The Rodearmel article prompted retired PLA General Zhang Chi Sun to publish a constructive critique in *MLR* shortly after.[24] General Sun praised Rodearmel's article as "an informative, objective, and scientific work as a whole," but noted that the inaccessibility of information about the inner-workings of the Chinese military caused the article to contain "errors," "misunderstandings," "disputable [statements]," and "questionable [facts]."[25] General Sun, whose well-intentioned response reads more as an apology than criticism, concluded on a positive note, calling for "further international exchanges of military law research."[26] Unfortunately, perhaps deterred to a degree by the general's comments, Western scholars have not produced much analysis of Chinese military law in subsequent decades.

However, many of the more formidable hurdles that hampered studies like Rodearmel's have diminished in recent years, and what General Sun termed the "blockade of exclusionism" has been

---

[22] *Id.*
[23] Captain David C. Rodearmel, *supra* note 4.
[24] Zhang Chi Sun, *supra* note 4.
[25] *Id.*
[26] *Id.* at 31, 40.

significantly relaxed.[27] Today, publishers like the PLA Publishing House release books on every conceivable subject—military law included. While vast amounts of information remain walled-off from the outside world, pieces of the PLA are slowly beginning to see the light of day (of course, most publications continue to be published only in Chinese). So although Chinese military law remains less than perfectly transparent, this article continues the project Rodearmel and Sun began over two decades ago.

III. THE RULE OF LAW IN CHINA: A BRIEF OVERVIEW

Good order and discipline in the Chinese military is largely enforced internally by the chain of command and without resort to the courts; at times, however, it is enforced pursuant to Chinese criminal law. For this reason, and to offer some context for those less familiar with the Chinese political system, this section briefly introduces the overall Chinese legal system and its position within the Chinese government, before delving more deeply into specifics of Chinese military law in sections to follow.

Founded on a Constitution promulgated in 1982—China's fourth since the 1949 founding of the People's Republic of China—the Chinese legal system follows the civil law tradition of continental European countries, rather than the common law approach found in the United States.[28] The current Constitution can be seen as a repudiation of the prior iterations of 1954, 1975, and 1978, reflecting a shift from the Mao Zedong-era of upheaval and continuous revolution (1949-1976) to the Deng Xiaoping-era and the ongoing march toward modernity (1978-present day). As one expert aptly put it, the 1982 Constitution helped codify that the "energies of the nation would shift from class struggle and political campaigns to economic development and modernization."[29]

---

[27] *Id.* at 39.
[28] JOHN HENRY MERRYMAN & RODELIO PÉREZ-PERDOMO, THE CIVIL LAW TRADITION: AN INTRODUCTION TO THE LEGAL SYSTEMS OF EUROPE AND LATIN AMERICA 4 (noting unique East Asian characteristics distinguishing Chinese civil law from counterparts in Europe and Latin America).
[29] DANIEL C.K. CHOW, THE LEGAL SYSTEM OF THE PEOPLE'S REPUBLIC OF CHINA IN A NUTSHELL 74-75 (2003).

Consequently, over the past three-plus decades a rule of law familiar to Westerners has begun to take shape in China.[30]

The Chinese Constitution provides in its Preamble that "All state organs, *the armed forces*, all political parties and public organizations and all enterprises and institutions must abide by the Constitution and the law."[31] This provision and its explicit endorsement of a rule of law are further codified by statute, such as Articles 6 and 7 of the Military Service Law of the People's Republic of China, which subject members of the armed forces to civilian criminal laws and disciplinary regulations of the military:

> Article 6. The active servicemen and reservists must abide by the Constitution and the law, and shall perform their duties and at the same time enjoy their rights as citizens; their rights and duties resulting from their joining the military service shall be specified separately in military regulations in addition to the provisions of this Law.
>
> Article 7. Active servicemen must abide by the rules and regulations of the army, faithfully discharge their duties and always be ready to fight for the defence of the motherland.[32]

The vast majority of military discipline is enforced pursuant to the "army regulation" provisions of Articles 6 and 7 of the Military Service Law, and is explored below. Serious criminal offenses, however, are prosecuted in the military branch of the national system of "People's Courts," all of which fall under the auspices of the Supreme People's Court in Beijing.

---

[30] Cheng Li & Jordan Lee, *China's Legal System*, 48 CHINA REV. 1 (2009), *available at* http://www.brookings.edu/~/media/research/files/articles/2009/9/autumn%20china%20l egal%20system%20li/autumn_china_legal_system_li.pdf (discussing improvements in the Chinese legal system since 1978).

[31] XIANFA pmbl., para. 12 (China) (italics added). The Preamble also states that the 1982 Constitution is "the fundamental law of the state and has supreme legal authority." *Id.* pmbl.

[32] Military Service Law of the People's Republic of China (promulgated by the President of the People's Republic of China, May 31, 1984, effective Oct. 1, 1984) (China), *available at* http://www.novexcn.com/military_service_law.html.

As a political institution, the Supreme People's Court ranks highly within the national government; but unlike in the United States, it is not considered a coequal branch of government on par with a legislative and executive body. Rather, all entities within the Chinese government—courts included—fall under the singular, centralized authority of the National People's Congress (NPC), an ostensibly representative legislative body consisting of approximately 3,000 members drawn from throughout the country.[33] Within the NPC, a Standing Committee of approximately 155 members carries out most NPC functions, and within the Standing Committee resides a select group of approximately 21 members who together form the Council of Chairmen—the "leading core of the NPC."[34] Among its many functions, the NPC supervises the work of various subordinate government entities, including the Supreme People's Court (and the Central Military Commission, which manages the PLA).[35] The subordinate position of courts is likewise codified in Article 128 of the Constitution, which states that the Supreme People's Court and lower courts are responsible and must report to the NPC and the Standing Committee.[36]

From this relatively constrained political position, Chinese courts are vested with adjudicative powers over civil and criminal cases.[37] Courts work in close coordination with the People's Procuratorate, which functions similar to prosecutors in the United States' system, preparing and bringing criminal cases to trial for prosecution. The Chinese government describes this coordination as follows:

---

[33] XIANFA arts. 2, 57 (1982) (China).
[34] CHOW, *supra* note 29, at 91-95.
[35] XIANFA art. 67 (1982) (China).
[36] XIANFA art. 128 (1982) (China); *see also* Organic Law of the People's Courts (promulgated by the Standing Comm. Nat'l People's Cong., July 1, 1979, amended Sept. 2, 1983) (China) (reaffirming the primacy of the NPC over the courts).
[37] XIANFA art. 126 (1982) (China) ("The people's courts exercise judicial power independently, in accordance with the provisions of the law, and are not subject to interference by any administrative organ, public organization or individual."); *see also* Randall Peerenboom, *Judicial Independence in China: Common Myths and Unfounded Assumptions* (La Trobe Law Sch. Legal Studies Research Paper No. 2008/11, 2008), *available at* http://ssrn.com/abstract=1283179.

The people's court is the judicial organ in China and the People's Procuratorate is the supervisory organ for law enforcement. The people's court and the People's Procuratorate, in accordance with the Constitution, Organic Law of the People's Courts, Organic Law of the People's Procuratorates, Civil Procedure Law, Administrative Procedure Law and Criminal Procedure Law, independently exercise their adjudicative power and supervisory power, respectively, free from any interference of administrative organs, public organizations and individuals.[38]

As indicated, the People's Procuratorate brings criminal cases to trial in accordance with the Criminal Procedure Law of the People's Republic of China. Discussed as it pertains to military courts below, the Criminal Procedure Law governs jurisdiction, appointment of defense counsel, evidence, filing cases with a court, investigation, interrogation, questioning witnesses, searches, seizures, the use of experts, trial procedure, appellate rights, and other standard aspects of criminal procedure.[39]

As is the case in many developing countries, the legal system mapped out by Chinese law does not perfectly comport with the actual state of law and order in China,[40] a point the Chinese government readily acknowledged in a recent publication:

China's legal construction is still facing some problems: The development of democracy and the rule of law still falls short of the needs of economic and social development; the legal framework shows certain characteristics of the current stage and calls for further improvement; in some regions and departments, laws are not observed, or strictly enforced, violators are not brought to justice; local

---

[38] Information Office of the State Council of the People's Republic of China, *China's Efforts and Achievements in Promoting the Rule of Law*, 7 CHINESE J. OF INT'L L. 513 (2008), *available at*
http://www.china.org.cn/government/whitepaper/node_7041733.htm.
[39] Criminal Procedure Law of the People's Republic of China (promulgated by the Nat'l People's Cong., 1979, adopted Jan. 1, 1997), *available at*
http://www.cecc.gov/pages/newLaws/criminalProcedureENG.php [hereinafter Crim. Pro. L. China].
[40] *See* Stanley Lubman, *Looking for Law in China*, 20 COLUM. J. ASIAN L. 1, 33-41 (2006) (listing various factors continuing to undermine the rule of law in China).

protectionism, departmental protectionism and difficulties in law enforcement occur from time to time; some government functionaries take bribes and bend the law, abuse their power when executing the law, abuse their authority to override the law, and substitute their words for the law, thus bringing damage to the socialist rule of law; and the task still remains onerous to strengthen education in the rule of law, and enhance the awareness of law and the concept of the rule of law among the public.[41]

Accordingly, efforts to strengthen the rule of law are a major concern for the Chinese government and the topic appears in official and semi-official media on a regular basis. A recent example entitled "PLA Military Courts Deploy Rule-of-Law Education for New Recruits" appeared in the military's own newspaper, the People's Liberation Army Daily.[42] The article expressed a need for China's military courts to take the lead increasing rule-of-law consciousness within the PLA, and particularly among those just entering the service. It is within this context of an emerging rule of law—both via formal institutions such as the courts and in the minds of Chinese citizens themselves—that good order and discipline in the PLA must be understood.

IV. THE PLA'S "SOUL": A PRIMER ON PLA HIERARCHY AND DISCIPLINE

If the soul of the PLA emanates from one underlying concept, it might be this: *wutiaojian zhixing mingling* or "unconditional obedience."[43] The idea holds special resonance in PLA culture and tradition, and military law textbooks expound on it in considerable detail.[44] Xia Yong, a Chinese professor of military law, provides an

---

[41] *China's Efforts and Achievements in Promoting the Rule of Law*, supra note 38.
[42] Jiefangjun Junshi Fayuan Bushu Jiaoyu Gongzuo [PLA Military Courts Deploy Rule-of-Law Education for New Recruits] Jiefangjun Bao [PLA Daily] (China), Jan. 4, 2012, http://chn.chinamil.com.cn/jsfz/2012-01/04/content_4759484.htm#.
[43] An alternative, more literal translation would be "unconditional execution of orders."
[44] *See* Xu Jiangwei, *Junshifa Jiaocheng* [*The Study of Military Law*], (2003) (China) (describing unconditional obedience as a fundamental principle underlying military discipline); *Junshi Faxue* [*The Science of Military Law*], (Xue Gangling ed., 2006) (China) [hereinafter Gangling 2006] (describing crimes involving failure to obey an order); Gangling, *supra* note 16, at 195-202 (explaining that unconditional obedience "remains the basic requirement of military law in the PLA").

indication of the meaning troops attach to the term in his characterization of unconditional obedience as one of the PLA's "longstanding glorious traditions."[45] The concept is nothing new. Former Chinese President and Party Secretary Deng Xiaoping, himself a decorated military man, once wrote that a military is nothing without discipline, and that disobedience and misconduct cannot go unpunished.[46]

In the Chinese military, obedience begins with allegiance to the ruling Communist Party. This overarching principle is explicitly codified in the Regulation on Discipline in the People's Liberation Army of China (hereinafter Discipline Regulation), which ranks obedience to the Party as the first rule of discipline.[47] An expert on China, Dr. Nan Li has explained the Party's (somewhat convoluted) power position as follows:

> [T]he Chinese Communist Party (CCP) has a monopoly on political power. As a result, the PLA, headed by the [Central Military Commission (CMC)], pledges its allegiance to the CCP .... The CMC ... answers to the CCP Central Committee and the Politburo. The CMC chair, who is the commander-in-chief of the PLA, also comes from among the principal leaders of the Party Central.[48]

At the time of this writing, President Hu Jintao holds several titles, including CMC chairman, commander-in-chief of the PLA, and General Secretary of the Communist Party—thus Party control over the

---

[45] *See* Gangling, *supra* note 16, at 197.
[46] *Id.*
[47] Zhongguo Renmin Jiefangjun Jilu Tiaoling [Regulation on Discipline of the People's Liberation Army of China] arts. 79-80 (2010), *available at* http://chn.chinamil.com.cn/xwpdxw/2010-06/08/content_4234767.htm (hereinafter Discipline Regulation).
[48] Nan Li, *The Central Military Commission and Military Policy in China*, *in* THE PEOPLE'S LIBERATION ARMY AS ORGANIZATION REFERENCE VOL. v1.0 45, 46 (James C. Mulvenon & Andrew N.D. Wang eds., 2002). In practical terms, Party control over the military results in an institution in which maintaining discipline occurs not only for the purpose of promoting the national interest, but also to preserve Party rule. *Id.* The PLA concept of "good order and discipline" consequently implies more than the Western idea of a fighting force loyal to and willing to die for national defense and homeland security. *Id.* In modern Chinese vernacular, a "disciplined" PLA implies a military willing to obey Party policy and guidance as well. *Id.*

PLA is presently at its institutional apex, with one man commanding both.[49] Power flows down from the President and the CMC through the PLA chain of command, which in turn manages a force of over two million troops.[50]

Chain of command in the PLA varies depending on a variety of factors, including whether the country is at war or peace and the type of conflict taking place. The PLA is divided into four branches: the PLA Army, PLA Air Force (PLAAF), PLA Navy (PLAN), and the Second Artillery Force, which controls the country's nuclear and surface-to-surface missile forces. During peacetime, a dual hierarchy exists based on both geography and branch of service. Geographically, China is divided into seven military regions: Shenyang, Beijing, Lanzhou, Nanjing, Guangzhou, Jinan, and Chengdu.[51] Regional commanders control all military operations within their region, but each branch maintains responsibility for training and administration of their forces within the military region.[52] During war, theater commands consisting of one or more regions are established, with theater commanders assuming command over all forces within their assigned theater. Additional nuance is added depending on the nature of the conflict.[53]

To enforce the concept of unconditional obedience within such complex command architecture, the PLA disciplinary system today employs a modern, nuanced code, much like those used by Western

---

[49] As this article goes to press, the positions of President, Chairman of the Central Military Commission, and Communist Party General Secretary are being transferred from Hu Jintao to Xi Jinping.
[50] For a more comprehensive look at the control and command architecture of the PLA, see *id.*
[51] ROGER CLIFF ET AL., SHAKING THE HEAVENS AND SPLITTING THE EARTH: CHINESE AIR FORCE EMPLOYMENT CONCEPTS IN THE 21ST CENTURY, 15 (2011).
[52] An exception to this is the Second Artillery Force, which operates independent of regional command under a "vertical command" system under direct control of the CMC. *See id.* at 23 (explaining this unique command system).
[53] For example, PLAAF literature includes multiple command and control systems that can be implemented where appropriate. *Id.* at 27-31.

militaries—including the United States.[54] The Chinese government offers the following overview of its military legal code:

> As of December 2010, the [National People's Congress] and its Standing Committee has (sic) passed laws and issued law-related decisions on 17 matters concerning national defense and military affairs, the State Council and the [Central Military Commission] have jointly formulated 97 military administrative regulations, the [Central Military Commission] has formulated 224 military regulations, and the general headquarters/departments, Navy, Air Force, Second Artillery Force, military area commands and [People's Armed Police Force] have enacted more than 3,000 military rules and regulations.[55]

Amid this growing library of military laws, three in particular shape discipline within the PLA: the aforementioned Discipline Regulation,[56] the Internal Affairs Regulation of the People's Liberation Army of China (hereinafter Internal Affairs Regulation),[57] and the national criminal code,[58] which includes a number of prohibitions on military-specific conduct.

Each of these laws specifically addresses the conduct expected of PLA troops. Under Internal Affairs Regulation Article 63, subordinates enjoy the right to disagree with their superior and the right to offer

---

[54] The Chinese government published a document in 2011 describing various elements of its military, including the legal system. In pertinent part, the publication states:

> The armed forces of the People's Republic of China abide by the Constitution and laws, implement the guidelines of governing the armed forces according to law, strengthen military legal system building, and guarantee and push forward the building of national defense and armed forces in accordance with the requirements of the legal system.

China's National Defense in 2010, *supra* note 6.
[55] *Id.*
[56] Discipline Regulation, *supra* note 47.
[57] Zhongguo Renmin Jiefangjun Jilu Tiaoling [Internal Affairs Regulation of the People's Liberation Army of China], Jiefangjun Bao [PLA Daily] (China), June 7, 2010, http://chn.chinamil.com.cn/xwpdxw/2010-06/07/content_4233772.htm (last visited Jan. 25, 2013) [hereinafter Internal Affairs]. The Internal Affairs Regulation is primarily aimed at instructing troops on proper etiquette, protocol, appearance, and the like, leaving it to the Discipline Regulation to enumerate punishable offenses. *Id.* Chinese textbooks place greater emphasis on the Discipline Regulation than the Internal Affairs Regulation when explaining troop discipline; this article therefore does the same. *Id.*
[58] Crim. Pro. L. China, *supra* note 39.

suggestions if given an order with which they do not agree, but they may not refuse to execute an order.[59] Similarly, Discipline Regulation Article 4 states as overarching policy *tingcong zhihui, lingxing jinzhi*—every soldier must strictly comply with instructions—and under Article 86 the failure to obey an order constitutes punishable misconduct.[60] Criminal laws such as the Criminal Law Article 421 duty to obey and the Article 425 crime of failure to perform one's duty (discussed in greater detail in Section V) provide additional punitive mechanisms to enforce obedience.[61] While these laws give form and substance to PLA discipline, they too operate within a broader historical context that must be understood to fully appreciate how the PLA conceives of its own soul.

As with much of China today, laws are a fusion of old and new—of ancient tradition and modern thought.[62] Textbooks on military law in China trace concepts of good order and discipline to ancient times.[63] As early as China's first empire, the Qin (pronounced "cheen"), disobedience was punished according to what historian Robin Yates describes as a "complex set of rules to control and manage almost every

---

[59] Internal Affairs, *supra* note 56, art. 63. For discussion of unconditional obedience in the modern PLA, see, e.g., Xun Hengdong, *Xiandai Zhanzheng Zhong de Falu Zhan* [*Legal Warfare in Modern War*], 278 (2005) (China) (explaining the heightened need for unconditional obedience in modern warfare due to evolving definitions of the battlefield, which now arguably includes the cyber domain). The right to offer suggestions to superiors is an integral part of modern PLA command and control strategy. The PLA Air Force, for example, relies on subordinates to "avoid overly centralized and rigid command," even when employing its centralized system of command (other command types include dispersed, hierarchical, and skip-echelon). CLIFF et al., *supra* note 50, at 29 ("They should propose changes to the original plan to the commander unless the situation has fundamentally changed and they are unable to contact their superiors—in which case they should take the initiative to handle the situation and report to the campaign commander later.").
[60] Discipline Regulation, *supra* note 47, arts. 4, 86.
[61] Criminal Law of the People's Republic of China arts. 421, 425 (promulgated by the Nat'l People's Cong., 1979, adopted July. 1, 1997), *available at* http://www.fmprc.gov.cn/ce/cgvienna/eng/dbtyw/jdwt/crimelaw/t209043.htm [hereinafter Crim. L. China].
[62] For an illustration of the fusion of ancient tradition and modern thought in contemporary China, see YAN XUETONG, ANCIENT CHINESE THOUGHT, MODERN CHINESE POWER (Daniel A. Bell & Sun Zhe eds., Edmund Ryden trans., 2011).
[63] *See* Gangling, *supra* note 16, at 68-82.

aspect of military affairs."[64] Commanders ensured obedience by the threat of harsh punishment, which ranged from fines to "mutilating punishments coupled with hard labor."[65] Military disciplinary law proved resilient, surviving in various forms and degrees as Chinese empires rose and fell over subsequent millennia.[66] Eventually, ancient martinet tradition informed the thinking of the architects of modern Chinese military law, many of whom were renowned as historians by nature, warriors by necessity.

Despite its ancient heritage, Chinese legal scholars trace the current disciplinary system back to more modern times and sources—in particular, to the decades preceding the 1949 founding of the communist People's Republic of China. The era was ripe for momentous change: following a devastating war with Japan, the Civil War of the 1940s pitted Mao Zedong's Communists against the Nationalist forces of Jiang Jieshi (a.k.a., Chiang Kai-Shek), when a battle for the hearts and minds of approximately 500 million Chinese citizens played itself out in grand scale.[67]

---

[64] Robin D.S. Yates, *Law and the Military in Early China, in* MILITARY CULTURE IN IMPERIAL CHINA 25, 39 (Nicola Di Cosmo ed., 2009).

[65] *Id.* Punishments in ancient Chinese militaries truly spanned the spectrum: historical records suggest that, in one instance during the late Spring and Autumn Period (8th – 5th centuries BCE), a driver and his horse were both executed for driving at full speed in a military camp; and during the Warring States Period (479 – 221 BCE), soldier misconduct met with the harshest of consequences, as historian Robin Yates explains:

> Execution by beheading was the usual punishment inflicted on a military criminal, although in cases of treachery and collusion with the enemy, relatives of the traitor were also executed, as were, in accordance with the law of collective responsibility, those on his left and right, front and rear. Only accidental arson of a building was punished with cutting off the extremities, hands, feet, ears, nose, although women appear to have been spared this punishment. Intentional arson was savagely punished by the offender being ripped apart by chariots.

Id. at 36-39.

[66] *Id.* at 25.

[67] For a leading account of the Chinese experience during the war against Japan, see IRIS CHANG, THE RAPE OF NANKING: THE FORGOTTEN HOLOCAUST OF WORLD WAR II (1997). For an English language history of the Chinese Civil War as told by a former member of the PLA, see XIAOBING LI, A HISTORY OF THE MODERN CHINESE MILITARY (2007).

As part of his guerilla approach to warfare, Mao sought support of the peasantry through, what would today be termed, psychological warfare.[68] Word was spread throughout the countryside: the Nationalist troops rape, pillage, and debauch the peasantry; the Communists respect and honor the peasantry because they are the party of the masses. To prove Communist commitment to peasant interests, from 1927-1928 Mao wrote and promulgated the framework for what has become a veritable Ten Commandments for PLA troops: the "Three Main Rules of Discipline and the Eight Points for Attention."[69] The Main Rules require solders to "obey orders in all your actions, do not take a single needle or piece of thread from the masses [e.g., do not steal], and turn in everything captured."[70] The Eight Points expand: "speak politely, pay fairly for what you buy, return everything you borrow, pay for anything you damage, do not hit or swear at people, do not damage crops, do not take liberties with women, and do not maltreat captives."[71] Today, the PLA views itself as a force for good, founded on what it perceives to be the firmest of moral bedrock—the words and ethical moorings of then-General Mao Zedong.[72] Indeed, modern PLA disciplinary law draws heavily on Mao's Main Rules. Blending old and new, however, it has been codified into Western-style law. Today, it is not only Mao's fiat, but also Western-style statutory and regulatory provisions—for example

---

[68] MAO ZEDONG, ON GUERILLA WARFARE (Samuel B. Griffith II trans., 1937); *see also* PAUL M.A. LINEBARGER, PSYCHOLOGICAL WARFARE (1948). For more on what is commonly referred to as "unorthodox" warfare in Chinese literature, see RALPH SAWYER, THE TAO OF DECEPTION: UNORTHODOX WARFARE IN HISTORIC AND MODERN CHINA (2007).

[69] Zhang Chi Sun, *supra* note 4, at 37; *see also* XIAOBING LI, *supra* note 66, at 53-54. Today, the Three Main Rules of Discipline and the Eight Points for Attention are codified as attachments to the Regulation on Discipline in the People's Liberation Army of China, *available at* http://chn.chinamil.com.cn/xwpdxw/2010-06/08/content_4234767_23.htm.

[70] He Xiaodong, *The Chinese Humanitarian Heritage and the Dissemination of and Education in International Humanitarian Law in the Chinese People's Liberation Army*, 841 INT'L REV. RED CROSS no. 841 (2001), *available at* http://www.icrc.org/eng/resources/documents/misc/57jqyz.htm (providing an English language translation of the Main Rules and Eight Points).

[71] *Id.*

[72] *Id.* (describing the formative years of the PLA and early efforts to promote humanitarian law). For an example of a Chinese military law scholar tracing the PLA's commitment to humanitarian law back to Mao Zedong, see Jin Huazhi, *Xuezhe Jianyi Jiang Junshifa Zuowei Duli Bumenfa* [*Scholars Recommend Creating an Independent Military Law*], RULE OF LAW DAILY, Oct. 18, 2010, *available at* http://www.chinanews.com/fz/2010/10-18/2594929.shtml.

Criminal Law Article 446 and Discipline Regulation Article 84—that prohibit soldiers from plundering civilian property.[73]

In the eight decades since the Main Rules and Eight Points were first promulgated, China and the PLA have undergone sweeping change. During the Cultural Revolution of the 1960s and 1970s, laws of all kinds were branded bourgeois tools of oppression, and legal institutions of all kinds were dismantled, including those of the PLA.[74] Law and order began its revival following Mao's death in 1976, when Deng Xiaoping and a new generation of leaders took the helm of the state. Military courts resumed operations in 1978 and the military procuratorate followed suit in 1979.[75] A new constitution was passed in 1982, followed by volumes of legislation and administrative regulations. Military law was likewise revived, for example with the passage of the Discipline Regulation in 1990.[76] Today, discipline is firmly enshrined in law and policy—a codified soul.

V.   GOOD ORDER & DISCIPLINE IN THE PLA

Chinese enforcement of good order and discipline might sound familiar to those trained in Western military law.[77] It should, both as a matter of procedure and substantive law. Broadly speaking, like many Western militaries,[78] the PLA imposes two types of punishment for misbehavior: administrative punishment for low-level offenses, and judicially imposed punishment for more egregious offenses that rise to the level of codified crime, with different procedural rules in place for

---

[73] Such rules are similar to U.S. military law, which prohibits looting and pillaging captured or abandoned. Uniform Code of Military Justice ("UCMJ"), 10 U.S.C. § 903, art. 103(b)(3) (2012).
[74] Zhang Chi Sun, *supra* note 4, at 36; *see also* Professor Lu Hui's chapter on the history of court-martials in China in Guangcheng, *supra* note 20, at 275-286.
[75] Zhang Chi Sun, *supra* note 4, at 37.
[76] The Discipline Regulation was first promulgated in 1990. This article elsewhere refers to an amended version promulgated in 2010.
[77] A great deal of military criminal law translates well across countries and cultures. GEORG NOLTE, EUROPEAN MILITARY LAW SYSTEMS (2003) (noting considerable commonalities among European military law systems).
[78] *Id.*

each type of punishment.[79] The vast majority of misconduct is handled either through "indoctrination and political education" or administratively as violations of discipline, rather than criminal law.[80] For instances in which a competent authority deems administrative punishment to be insufficient, however, the Criminal Procedure Law governs subsequent investigations, the rights of the accused, pretrial proceedings, and trial.

This section examines several core aspects of good order and discipline in the PLA: administrative punishment, criminal procedure, and a sampling of military crimes under Chinese law, the latter of which is compared to U.S. law for context. The section concludes with a look at the 1989 Tiananmen Square incident, which illustrates several key aspects of PLA disciplinary law.

A. *Administrative Punishment in the PLA*

PLA rules of discipline derive from a number of sources, including Communist Party policy,[81] national laws such as the Constitution and Criminal Law, administrative regulations promulgated by the Ministry of Defense, lawful orders given by superiors, and the Main Rules and Eight Points discussed above. Ultimately, however, it is the Discipline Regulation that governs day-to-day enforcement of discipline among the PLA rank-and-file.

Guiding principles for the punishment of disciplinary infractions are set forth in Discipline Regulation Article 77 and include maintaining "strict military discipline" (*yanming junji*), educating both violators and

---

[79] General Sun, an expert in Chinese military law profiled above in Section II, contends that "it is [not] precise to classify the process of China's military law and discipline into judicial and nonjudicial punishment categories . . . although that is quite right in the U.S. military system." Zhang Chi Sun, *supra* note 4, at 33. To avoid any confusion, this paper uses the term "administrative punishment" to refer to all forms of punishment not requiring recourse to the judicial process. Thus there are two forms of punishment: those that involve a judge and those that do not.
[80] *Id.*
[81] For an excellent primer on the Chinese Communist Party and its influence over all aspects of Chinese government, including the military, see RICHARD MCGREGOR, THE PARTY: THE SECRET WORLD OF CHINA'S COMMUNIST RULERS (2010).

their units on proper conduct, strengthening unity among the troops, and enhancing combat effectiveness.[82] To ensure constant combat readiness, punishment is intended to be swift—to wit, Article 136 of the Discipline Regulation states that misconduct should generally be investigated and punished within 45 days of the date of discovery.[83] This metric is quite similar to that used by the U.S. military. The U.S. Air Force, for example, attempts to punish relatively serious, but non-criminal misconduct, within 30 days of discovery.[84] Also similar to the U.S. approach, Chinese regulations provide suspects an opportunity to be heard prior to imposition of punishment, and the opportunity to appeal punishment after the fact.[85]

In practical terms, the principles underlying punishment translate into a variety of options available to commanders. Like many Western systems, enforcement can take the form of formal warnings (*jing gao*), "serious" warnings, the creation of a written record of an offense, reduction in rank or grade, and dismissal from a position of command.[86] For particularly grave offenses, including national security crimes and criminal convictions resulting in five or more years imprisonment, soldiers are subject to discharge from military service altogether.[87] Additional punishments are also available for certain offenses. For instance, under the PLA Provisional Regulation on Re-education through Labor, offenders may be sentenced to labor for a

---

[82] Discipline Regulation, *supra* note 47, art. 77.
[83] Discipline Regulation, *supra* note 47, art. 136.
[84] Air Force Instruction 51-202, Procedures for Initiating and Imposing Nonjudicial Punishment ¶ 3.3 (2003), *available at* http://www.e-publishing.af.mil/shared/media/epubs/AFI51-202.pdf.
[85] Discipline Regulation, *supra* note 47, art. 137. For a counterpart regulation in the U.S. military, see, e.g., Air Force Instruction 51-202, *supra* note 83 (governing notice and appellate rules for administrative punishment in the U.S. Air Force).
[86] Discipline Regulation, *supra* note 47, arts. 79-80; *see also* Hengdong, *supra* note 58, at 279. European militaries share many similarities in terms of the range of punishments available to commanders, though they too are far from uniform. Many, but not all, impose fines as punishment. Some permit public admonishments, while others do not. And several do not allow reduction in rank to be imposed as a form of disciplinary punishment. NOLTE, *supra* note 76, at 129-39.
[87] Discipline Regulation, *supra* note 47, art. 120.

number of offenses, including drug offenses, theft, sexual assault, and absence without leave.[88]

The list of offenses punishable as disciplinary violations includes a range of misconduct similar to that punishable in the U.S. military. Traditional offenses such as absence without leave,[89] violent behavior,[90] alcohol-based offenses,[91] sexual assault,[92] and theft[93] are all proscribed under the Discipline Regulation. Having been updated in 2010, the disciplinary code also includes prohibitions on more modern forms of misconduct, such as wrongful use of mobile phones and the "international Internet."[94] In certain circumstances, violations of regulations regarding military and state secrets may likewise be handled as disciplinary infractions.[95] As discussed below, for more serious offenses rising to the level of crime, more formal procedures and trials are required before punishment may be imposed.

B. *Criminal Procedure in the PLA*

As discussed previously, the Chinese system of military criminal law operates within the national criminal justice system, a pyramidal structure atop of which sits the Supreme People's Court (SPC).[96] The Constitution establishes military courts and grants them jurisdiction over cases involving service members and others with a sufficient military

---

[88] *See* Gangling 2006, *supra* note 44. These offenses are also prohibited under the Discipline Regulation, which serves as the primary basis for punishment. For example, absence without leave is a disciplinary violation under Article 94, Discipline Regulation, and carries with it a range of punishments including warnings for minor instances and reduction in rank for more serious offenses.
[89] Discipline Regulation, *supra* note 47, art. 95.
[90] *Id.*, art. 96.
[91] *Id.*, art. 97.
[92] *Id.*, art. 99.
[93] *Id.*, art. 101.
[94] *Id.*, art. 93.
[95] Discipline Regulation, *supra* note 47, art. 93.
[96] Article 2(2), Organic Law of the People's Courts of the People's Republic of China (1983), *available at* http://www.novexcn.com/organic_law.html.

nexus.[97] General Sun, the retired Chinese military attorney discussed in Section II, explains:

> The military courts ... are authorized by the Constitution as an integral part of the State judicial system. They are organized under The Organic Law of the People's Courts ... and are defined as Special People's Courts ... attached to the armed forces.[98]

As part of the state judicial system, both the national Criminal Law and Criminal Procedure Law apply in military courts.[99] As a result, aside from the military status of those involved, the manners in which civilians and service members are tried in Chinese courts are essentially the same.

In this regard, the Chinese and American systems diverge, though the difference is much more as a matter of degree than kind. Court-martialed U.S. service members face an experience similar in many ways to their civilian counterparts due in large part to the fact that constitutional guarantees to a fair and speedy trial apply in both forums. However, American military courts operate in separate venues, under different criminal codes, and pursuant to different procedural rules than civilian criminal trials. In the U.S., misconduct by service members can in some circumstances run afoul of civilian laws, and service members can find themselves haled into civilian courts for prosecution. However, the UCMJ applies to active duty service members at all times and in all locations—whether on or off duty and whether or not in uniform.[100] As a result, civilian authorities often step aside and allow military offenders to

---

[97] State Structure of the People's Republic of China, NATIONAL PEOPLE'S CONGRESS OF THE PEOPLE'S REPUBLIC OF CHINA, http://www.npc.cn/englishnpc/stateStructure/2007-12/06/content_1382076.htm (last updated Dec. 17, 2007) ("The jurisdiction of military courts is restricted to specified criminal cases such as criminal cases committed by army men in active service and by workers on the payroll of the military, and other criminal cases whose trial and judgment are delegated to the military court by the SPC [Supreme People's Court].").
[98] Sun, *supra* note 4, at 34.
[99] Crim. Pro. L. China, *supra* note 39, art. 225 ("The security departments of the Army shall exercise the power of investigation with respect to criminal offences that have occurred in the Army.... The handling of criminal cases by the security departments of the Army ... shall be governed by the relevant provisions of this law.").
[100] UCMJ art. 3, 10 U.S.C. § 803 (2006); UCMJ art. 5, 10 U.S.C. § 805 (2006).

be dealt military justice. For example, a U.S. service member suspected of committing sexual assault outside a base in the U.S. might be handed over to military authorities for prosecution and be charged in a court-martial with violating Article 120 of the UCMJ, rather than the criminal laws of the state where the incident occurred. In the U.S., once a case is referred to court-martial by the appropriate military authority, proceedings are governed by the military's own substantive and procedural laws.

Despite their differences, the Chinese and U.S. systems are in certain ways—to again borrow a distinctly Chinese expression—"harmonious": both recognize the value of keeping military disciplinary matters in-house, yet both acknowledge that criminal conduct sometimes carries with it a societal cost for which civilian prosecution and punishment are appropriate. China strikes this balance by handling most misconduct in-house under the Discipline Regulation, as opposed to criminal trial; and where crimes are sufficiently serious, China refers cases to criminal courts where sanctions intended to serve the public interest can be imposed. The U.S. balances the equation instead by steering suspected military criminals into an independent court-martial system, which operates almost entirely beyond civilian oversight and influence. U.S. courts-martial afford the military considerable autonomy, while simultaneously promoting the social benefits associated with incarceration and rehabilitation of criminals—and, as mentioned, civilian prosecution remains a viable option in appropriate cases.

Once underway, military criminal investigations in China parallel those in the United States. Two players in particular guide proceedings: the military investigator and procuratorate.[101] The Criminal Procedure Law cabins the authority of military investigators and procuratorates, limiting their reach to "internal" military cases—those which directly impact the military or which are committed by service

---

[101] The term procuratorate or *jianchaguan* refers to an attorney representing the government during trial—similar in many ways to a prosecutor in the common law tradition.

members.[102] Within these boundaries, criminal cases play themselves out much as they would in the United States.

A case begins when filed with a court for investigation.[103] For a filed case to go forward, the Criminal Procedure Law requires a showing of both substantive evidence and jurisdiction.[104] As authorized by Articles 3 and 225 of the Criminal Procedure Law, military procuratorates work on behalf of the military court where a case is filed and in concert with military security forces (*baowei*) during the investigatory and charging phase, and responsibilities include conducting interviews and other fact-finding, managing pre-trial detention, and drafting formal charges.[105]

Before a crime is formally charged, a court first applies Article 15 of the Criminal Procedure Law, which lists various grounds for dismissal, including de minimus harm caused, expired statute of limitations, and others familiar to those trained in U.S. law.[106] After a court determines that charging a service member with a crime is appropriate, a charging document is issued, and preparation for trial begins.[107] Crimes forming the basis for criminal trials are the subject of the following section.

C. *Crime and Punishment in the PLA*

1. A Comparative Study: U.S. and Chinese Military Discipline

This section looks at a sampling of crimes for which Chinese service members can be brought to trial and the punishments available for such crimes. As previously discussed, unlike in the U.S., Chinese military courts do not operate under independent criminal laws. Rather, China has one system of criminal law within which military courts operate. Military crimes are prosecuted under provisions of the national Criminal Law, the same comprehensive statute used to prosecute

---

[102] *See* Gangling 2006, *supra* note 44, at 294.
[103] For an in-depth explanation of criminal procedure in the Chinese military, see Gangling 2006, *supra* note 44, at 292-99.
[104] Crim. Pro. L. China, *supra* note 39, art. 86.
[105] *Id.*, arts. 3, 225.
[106] *Id.*, art. 15.
[107] *Id.*, art. 150.

unlawful civilian behavior. However, certain provisions of the Criminal Law apply only to service members and those working in close conjunction with the military.[108] These offenses are contained within Chapter 10 of the Criminal Law and fall under the heading "Crimes of Servicemen's Transgression of Duties." Chapter 10 consists of 32 offenses and applies to "officers, civilian staff, soldiers in active service and cadets with military status of the Chinese People's Liberation Army," as well as members of the "Chinese People's Armed Police, and reservists and other persons performing military tasks."[109]

Much of the conduct prohibited by Chapter 10 likewise runs afoul of the Discipline Regulation. As previously discussed many offenses involving service members are resolved in-house as disciplinary infractions, rather than as criminal conduct warranting trial by judge. As such, cases are referred to the criminal system only for particularly egregious or harmful conduct. So, for instance, sending innocuous but inappropriate information to a friend abroad via email might result in light disciplinary measures under Discipline Regulation Article 92, which prohibits certain wrongful uses of the Internet. However, sending information about military weapons systems in a subsequent email might result in charges under Criminal Law Article 432, which prohibits the leaking of military secrets.[110] While, in both instances, the underlying conduct is the wrongful use of email, the gravity of the offenses differs greatly, making one case appropriate for reprimand or the like, the other appropriate for referral to the courts to be handled as a criminal matter.[111]

---

[108] In addition to the Chapter 10 crimes by service-members, 14 crimes listed in Chapter 7 of the Criminal Law have some military nexus but can be applied to the conduct of civilians. Crim. L. China, *supra* note 60, ch. XII. U.S. law contains similar provisions, such as Chapter 43 of Title 18 of the Federal Code, which lists eight different "Military and Navy" crimes that can be applied to the conduct of civilians. 18 U.S.C. ch. 43 (2006).
[109] Crim. L. China, *supra* note 60, art. 450.
[110] *Id.*, art. 432.
[111] General Sun, discussed above in Section II, used the following example to illustrate the importance of severity when distinguishing between disciplinary violations and crime:

> Disrespect would become [a criminal] offense in a case where the accused not only was disrespectful toward the superior commissioned officer, but also resorted to violence or threat to obstruct the superior in the performance of his duty.

Chapter 10 offenses compare favorably to offenses listed in the U.S. military's criminal code—the UCMJ. On paper at least, in this respect the two systems have more similarities than differences, beginning with several of the more commonly charged offenses under the UCMJ. To illustrate this point, this article compares the following six UCMJ offenses to their Chinese counterparts: Article 86—absence without leave, failure to go, and desertion;[112] Article 92—dereliction of duty and disobeying an order;[113] Article 107—false official statements;[114] Article 112a—wrongful use, possession, etc., of controlled substances;[115] Article 120—rape, sexual assault, and other sexual misconduct;[116] and Article 134—the so-called "general article," under which individuals subject to the UCMJ can be punished for all manner of conduct deemed to be prejudicial to the good order and discipline of the armed forces.[117] Violations of each of these six UCMJ offenses would likely violate Chinese military law as well, and in any case would certainly run afoul of the PLA rules of discipline codified in the Discipline Regulation.

a. Disobedience and Dereliction of Duty

One of the more commonly occurring UCMJ offenses is Article 92, which prohibits disobedience and the failure to obey lawful orders. Chinese law takes a similar tack. Some aggravated forms of dereliction of duty and disobedience could run afoul of Articles 421 and 425 of the Criminal Law, which prohibit disobedience and include anyone "on duty who leaves his post without permission or neglects his duties,"[118] but for run-of-the-mill offenses disciplinary measures can be taken administratively under Discipline Regulation Articles 86 and 89, which require obedience and the performance of one's duty.[119]

SUN, *supra* note 4, at 34.
[112] Manual for Courts-Martial, United States, pt. IV, art. 86 (2008).
[113] *Id.*, art. 92.
[114] *Id.*, art. 107.
[115] *Id.*, art. 112a.
[116] *Id.*, art. 120.
[117] *Id.*, art. 134.
[118] Crim. L. China, *supra* note 60, arts. 421, 425.
[119] Discipline Regulation, *supra* note 47, arts. 86, 89.

In this regard, the two countries' systems are quite similar. In practice, in the U.S. military less severe violations of Article 92 oftentimes result in a service member receiving administrative paperwork such as a letter of counseling, admonishment or reprimand. Only more severe violations result in trial by court-martial. The Chinese approach strikes a similar balance: instances of petty disobedience are handled under the Discipline Regulation and result in administrative punishment, with only aggravated derelictions, such as those satisfying the elements of Criminal Law Articles 421 and 425, finding their way into court.

b. False Statements

False statements are punishable under both U.S. and Chinese military law. In the U.S. military, making a false official statement (e.g., lying) violates Article 107 of the UCMJ, and as with Article 92 less egregious violations often result in administrative paperwork, rather than trial by court-martial. In China, certain false official statements might contravene the Criminal Law Article 422 prohibition on "lying about military intelligence," and Criminal Law Article 433, which makes it a crime to "spread rumors to confuse people,"[120] but ordinary lies can be dealt with administratively as disciplinary violations. For instance, Discipline Regulation Article 90 prohibits various types of deception and misrepresentation,[121] allowing PLA commanders to punish certain false statements in-house without resort to the courts. The end product of the two systems is much the same: in both militaries, only a subset of particularly harmful or aggravated false statements result in trial. Others are a matter for nonjudicial recourse.

c. Absence Offenses: AWOL and Desertion

"Going AWOL" (absence without leave) is one of the classic military offenses; accordingly, its prohibition can be found in both the U.S. and Chinese disciplinary codes. American troops who fail to go to their appointed place of duty, who leave their place of duty, or who "absent" themselves from their place of duty violate Article 86 of the UCMJ. Such offenses occur with relative frequency—commanders in all

---

[120] Crim. L. China, *supra* note 60, arts. 422, 433.
[121] Discipline Regulation, *supra* note 47, art. 90.

services are all too familiar with the subordinate who rolls in 15 minutes late on a regular basis or who manages to stretch every lunch hour into two. In the U.S. military, such offenses generally do not merit trial by court-martial, though exceptions can occur in deployed locations, where repeated reprimands fail to bring the soldier in line, or where the consequences of the absence are particularly serious.

The Chinese system is much the same. Criminal Law Article 425 prohibits AWOL, and as such it can be the basis for a criminal charge. But as Xue Gangling, et al, explain in *The Science of Military Law*, absence offenses should only be charged as a crime if the result of the offense is "serious";[122] otherwise, matters should be handled more quietly as non-criminal disciplinary infractions. For such ordinary offenses, punctuality can be instilled pursuant to Article 95 of the Discipline Regulation, which expressly prohibits AWOL.[123] Both the U.S. and Chinese militaries prefer to handle such misconduct with what the U.S. military informally refers to as "graduated" or "stair-step" punishment, or the practice of giving just enough punishment to correct a soldier's behavior and reserving harsher punishments for recalcitrance or aggravated offenses. An example of this approach is codified in Article 95 of China's Discipline Regulation, which states that "warnings" or "serious warnings" should be given for instances of AWOL totaling seven days or less, demerits for eight to 15 days, demotions for 16 to 30 days, and expulsion from military service for over 30 days.[124]

Like AWOL, both the U.S. and Chinese codes of conduct prohibit the act of desertion, another absence offense. Under Chinese Criminal Law Article 435, desertion carries up to a three-year prison sentence during peace, and up to seven years during war. Similarly, under Article 85 of the UCMJ, desertion, defined to include going or remaining away from one's unit with the intent of remaining away permanently or avoiding hazardous duty, carries different maximum punishments depending on whether committed during peace or war. Interestingly, both countries specifically provide for the death penalty for

---

[122] *See* Gangling 2006, *supra* note 44, at 276.
[123] Discipline Regulation, *supra* note 47, art. 95.
[124] *Id.*

desertion during battle,[125] a reminder that the final aim of both systems of military discipline is to ensure a fighting force willing to fight and die for their country.

d. Drug Offenses

Both militaries have little to no tolerance for drug crimes. Drug offenders in the U.S. military risk a great deal even for relatively mundane offenses. The use of unlawful drugs—such as marijuana or painkillers without prescription—regularly results in administrative punishment followed quickly by discharge from military service. For those caught manufacturing or distributing illegal drugs, criminal charges and court-martial can be expected. Similarly, in China, drug offenses by service members can be punished pursuant to the Criminal Law, and consequences can be severe.[126]

The Chinese government goes to great lengths to combat drug crime, taking part in a number of international efforts to combat drug trafficking and even declaring a "People's War on Drugs" in 2005.[127] Such efforts can be traced back to at least 1997, when amendments to the Criminal Law added numerous drug offenses, including use, possession, trafficking, and manufacturing. Over the decade-plus since the amendments, China's commitment to drug-related law enforcement has been noteworthy, and from 2005 to 2006 its government issued a series of regulations targeting the possession and transportation of precursor chemicals and psychotropic agents, a proactive step similar to that taken in the United States.[128]

Section 7 of China's Criminal Law contains prohibitions on smuggling, trafficking, transportation and manufacturing a broad range of drugs, including "opium, heroin, methylaniline (ice), morphine, marijuana, cocaine and other narcotic and psychotropic substances that

---

[125] Crim. L. China, *supra* note 60, art. 422; UCMJ, art. 85(c), 10 U.S.C. § 885 (2006).
[126] Crim. L. China, *supra* note 60, arts. 347-357 (drug offenses).
[127] Niklas Swanstrom and Yin He, *China's War on Narcotics: Two Perspectives*, SILK ROAD PAPER, Dec. 2006, at 41-47.
[128] *Id.* In the United States, federal drug crimes are enumerated in the United States Code. 21 U.S.C. ch. 13 (2006) (extending prohibitions not only to drugs themselves, but also to various types of precursor materials and paraphernalia).

can make people addicted to their use and are controlled under State regulations."[129] A wide range of drug-related activities are prohibited, allowing for prosecution not only of those principally involved in the trafficking, manufacturing, and the like, but also those who "shield" principals and those involved in drug "gangs" and international trafficking organizations.[130] Drug quantity likewise factors into sentencing. For example, a manufacturer of less than 10 grams of heroin faces up to three years confinement and a fine, but at least seven years confinement for 10 to 50 grams.[131] For those whose involvement does not merit criminal prosecution, punishment under Discipline Regulation provisions like Article 118 for "undisciplined" behavior remains an option for military commanders.

In the U.S. military, offenses such as those prohibited by Section 7 of China's Criminal Law (e.g., smuggling, trafficking, transportation and manufacturing) are punishable under Article 112a of the UCMJ, which authorizes the punishment of anyone who "wrongfully uses, possesses, manufactures, distributes, imports into the customs territory of the United States, exports from the United States, or introduces into an installation, vessel, vehicle, or aircraft used by or under the control of the armed forces" a variety of drugs.[132] The list of prohibited drugs and their precursor chemicals is also similar to those banned under Chinese law, including "opium, heroin, cocaine, amphetamine, lysergic acid diethylamide, methamphetamine, phencyclidine, barbituric acid, and marijuana, and any compound or derivative of any such substance."[133] In sum, both countries take drug crime very seriously, criminalizing not just use, but also manufacturing, distributing and transporting; and both extend prohibitions to precursor chemicals, ensuring that drug-free fighting forces will be available should they be called into action.

---

[129] Crim. L. China, *supra* note 60, art. 357.
[130] *Id.*, art. 347.
[131] *Id.*
[132] UCMJ, art. 112a, 10 U.S.C. § 912(a) (2006).
[133] *Id.*

e. Sex Offenses

The legal regimes of the two countries are likewise similar with regards to sex offenses, though notable differences do exist. Both strictly forbid forcible sex with women and both provide for heightened sentences where aggravating circumstances exist. The Chinese Criminal Law addresses the subject in Articles 236 and 237. Under Article 236, "whoever rapes a woman by violence, coercion or any other means" is guilty of a crime and subject to at least three years in prison.[134] The law provides for lengthier prison sentences where the victim has not reached 14 years of age and for the following aggravators:

(1) [committing rape under] flagrant [circumstances];
(2) raping [multiple] women or girls under the age of 14;
(3) raping a woman before the public in a public place;
(4) raping a woman with one or more persons in succession; or
(5) causing serious injury or death to the victim or any other serious consequences.[135]

Less egregious offenses can be prosecuted under Article 237, which states that "whoever acts indecently against or insults a woman by violence, coercion or any other forcible means" is guilty of a crime.[136] As with Article 236, harsher penalties are available for crimes committed by a group of individuals or where the victim is a child.[137] Additionally, for offenses failing to rise to the level of a criminal sex offense, Article 99 of the Discipline Regulation provides military leadership with an alternate means of punishing sexual misconduct with its prohibition on "molestation, insults, and inappropriate conduct toward women."[138]

The U.S. military approach to sex offenses is similar, with the notable exception that U.S. law does not require the victim of sexual assault to be female for a crime to occur. A 2011 case in China involving a male rape victim made international headlines after a Beijing court

---

[134] Crim. L. China, *supra* note 60, art. 236.
[135] *Id.*
[136] *Id.*, art. 237.
[137] *Id.*
[138] Discipline Regulation, *supra* note 47, art. 99.

convicted a man of intentional injury, but not rape, after the man forced an 18-year-old male to have sex with him.[139] Such an offense assuredly would have resulted in a rape conviction under U.S. law. Aside from this distinction, the U.S. approach to sexual assault in the military is quite similar to China's. Article 120 of the UCMJ goes into considerable detail enumerating impermissible types of sexual conduct. Explicit prohibitions include rape, aggravated sexual assault, aggravated sexual contact, abusive sexual contact, indecent liberty with a child, indecent acts, forcible pandering, wrongful sexual contact, and indecent exposure.[140] Criminal prosecution is the standard response to such offenses and lengthy prison sentences often result.

Less egregious offenses falling outside the scope of Article 120 can result in criminal prosecution, but many are resolved without convening a court-martial. This category of lesser offenses bears considerable resemblance to the category of offenses described in Article 99 of the PLA's Discipline Regulation, which, as mentioned previously, prohibits "molestation, insults, and inappropriate conduct toward women," though "molestation" would potentially be a prosecutable offense in the U.S. military under Article 120's prohibition on "wrongful sexual contact," defined to include "sexual contact with another person without that other person's permission."[141] In China, such lesser sex offenses result in punishments ranging from warnings and reprimands for less serious offenses to demotions for more serious offenses.[142] Similarly, for U.S. service members who commit less serious offenses not meriting trial by court-martial, punishments range from counseling and reprimand for less serious offenses to demotions and fines for more serious offenses.

Overall, the two systems approach sex offenses in substantially similar fashions. While the U.S. approach goes into considerably more detail parsing out the various types of sex offenses in Article 120 of the

---

[139] *Male Rape Case May Be China's First*, UPI.com (Jan 5, 2011, 3:09 PM), http://www.upi.com/Top_News/World-News/2011/01/05/Male-rape-case-may-be-Chinas-first/UPI-12021294258161.
[140] UCMJ, art. 120, 10 U.S.C. § 920 (2006).
[141] *Id.*
[142] Discipline Regulation, *supra* note 47, art. 99.

UCMJ, Chinese law ensures that punishment can be imposed for offenses ranging from "inappropriate conduct toward women" on the low end to rape in the upper extreme. And, like in the U.S., the Chinese system allows for particularly strong punishments where aggravating circumstances exist.

f. Other Misconduct

A sixth offense frequently charged in the U.S. military is Article 134 of the UCMJ, under which conduct that is prejudicial to good order and discipline or service discrediting can be prosecuted. The intentionally vague language of Article 134 equips commanders and prosecutors in the U.S. military with a powerful and flexible charging tool capable of capturing almost any form of misconduct. The Chinese approach is again similar. If misconduct falls outside specific prohibitions listed elsewhere in the Criminal Law or the Discipline Regulation, Article 118 of the Discipline Regulation allows commanders to punish all other "undisciplined" conduct.[143] Likewise, Article 420 of the Criminal Law states that "any act committed by a serviceman in transgression of his duties, an act that endangers the military interests of the State and should therefore be subjected to criminal punishment in accordance with law, constitutes a crime of a serviceman's transgression of duties."[144] Such catch-all prohibitions on poor discipline ensure that PLA commanders—like their U.S. counterparts—have at their disposal the legal tools necessary to punish undisciplined behavior in whatever form it appears.

Thus, while the U.S. and Chinese military justice systems are by no means carbon copies, the two share some fundamental properties. Substantively, the types of crimes that are prohibited in the two militaries are not very different; nor are the options available to commanders for dealing with misbehavior—in both, lack of discipline can result in punishment imposed either administratively or via trial. Procedurally, the two systems are quite different at an institutional level, with no direct parallel to the U.S. court-martial system in the PLA. But examined more

---

[143] Discipline Regulation, *supra* note 47, art. 118.
[144] Crim. L. China, *supra* note 60, art. 420.

closely—at least on paper—suspected criminals can expect significantly similar experiences being brought to justice in either of the two systems.

The Chinese court system remains decades behind international standards, however, and comparisons rightly end on paper. Until Chinese military courts significantly increase transparency and outsiders are permitted to observe firsthand, outside analysis will remain limited to the yet unproven assumption that good order and discipline in the PLA at least resembles that described in the textbooks of its leading practitioners. Unfortunately, at present, Chinese military courts remain enigmatically sealed off from the outside world. As a consequence, publically available case studies are few and far between. Accordingly, to illustrate some of the core disciplinary principles found in PLA law and literature, this article turns to one of the more famous incidents of military discipline—or lack thereof—in PLA history: the 1989 Tiananmen Square incident.

2. Case Study: The 1989 Tiananmen Square Incident

The 1989 Tiananmen Square crackdown helps illustrate several important aspects of the Chinese military justice system. And while the lack of transparency surrounding the incident makes it an imperfect case study at best, the event serves as an excellent vehicle from which to discuss good order and discipline in the PLA. The crisis began with the death of Hu Yaobang, a leading voice in the Communist Party and a man with a reformist reputation thought to favor liberalization of the Chinese government. His death touched a nerve for those seeking change and triggered an outpouring of public mourning—particularly in Beijing, the political and cultural center of China and the home to several of the nation's elite and more politically active universities. As former U.S. Secretary of State Henry Kissinger recently wrote of the incident in his book *On China*, students "took the opportunity to voice their frustration with corruption, inflation, press restrictions, university conditions, and the persistence of Party 'elders' ruling informally behind the scenes."[145] Students were not alone in harboring such grievances—many in the military shared their views. So when crowds of mourners swelled and the

---

[145] HENRY KISSINGER, ON CHINA 409 (2011).

PLA was called in to quell protest, some within the PLA found themselves forced to choose between their military duties and their personal convictions. Some demurred, refusing their orders; many, however, dutifully obeyed.

Images of the resulting carnage have come to be seen somewhat singularly as the embodiment of arbitrary and brutal authoritarianism.[146] Yet the incident can be mined for additional insight as well. In particular, Tiananmen offers context to better understand the PLA disciplinary system. Here, two points are worth noting: first, when called upon to use force against Chinese citizens deemed to be threats to public order, the Chinese military largely obeyed and successfully carried out orders assigned them; second, those who did not obey were punished.

Chinese military historian Li Xiaobing writes that, after being ordered to clear the square, a group of generals signed a letter addressed to Deng Xiaoping and the [Central Military Commission]:

> "We request that troops not enter the city and that martial law not be carried out in Beijing." . . . Deng sent top military leaders to visit these generals, and Yang Shangkun, the PRC president, made some phone calls. Thereafter . . . the mini-revolt was pacified.[147]

As explained previously in Section III, under Chinese military law an order may be questioned and alternatives may be suggested, but a subordinate may not refuse to execute an order.[148] At least insofar as current military law would have applied to what is known about the Tiananmen Square incident, the initial reluctance exhibited by certain elements within the PLA conformed to the letter of the law—that is, it was the exercise of the right to disagree guaranteed by Chinese law. The same cannot be said for those who, in the end, refused to use force against the student protesters.

---

[146] *See id.*, at 411 (explaining that following Tiananmen Square the Chinese government "emerged in the media of the world as an arbitrary authoritarian state crushing popular aspirations to human rights").
[147] XIAOBING LI, *supra* note 66, at 265.
[148] *See supra* note 36.

Refusing an order violates several provisions of both the Chinese Criminal Law and the PLA Discipline Regulation, as previously explained. General Xu Qinxian, who feigned illness to avoid commanding his troopers against the demonstrators on the eve of battle, ran afoul of several laws—including for example Criminal Law article 428 (disobedience by a commander, "flinching before a battle," or remaining inactive during a military operation)—was court-martialed and imprisoned in a massive crackdown following the incident.[149] By one account, well over 3,000 PLA soldiers were investigated for disciplinary violations—in the aftermath, a great many troops were punished administratively or brought to trial.[150]

Only so much can be gleaned from a case study like the Tiananmen Square incident, about which we admittedly have limited knowledge. We learn nothing, for example, about what (if any) legal procedures were followed before punishments were meted out, and we are left to speculate about punishments imposed. But the incident does help drive home a larger point: calls by Western governments for greater transparency by the PLA should extend to its disciplinary system as well.

VI.   CONCLUSION

What difference does it make how the Chinese military maintains discipline—how well its troops fall in line? Does a deeper threat lie beneath the obvious point recently made by Guo Boxiong, Vice Chairman of China's Central Military Commission, that the discipline of a combat unit determines how efficiently and how rapidly warfighting capabilities can be mobilized?[151] Chinese leadership appears to believe it does.

---

[149] When recently interviewed about his decision to defy orders during the Tiananmen Square incident, former General Xu Qinxian expressed no regret, despite the career-ending implications of his decision. Verna Yu, *No Regrets for Defiant Tiananmen General*, S. CHINA MORNING POST, Feb. 15, 2011, at 5, *available at* http://www.scmp.com/article/738185/no-regrets-defiant-tiananmen-general.
[150] XIAOBING LI, *supra* note 66, at 268.
[151] Guo Boxiong Inspects Shenyang Theatre, Stressing Grassroots Building, PEOPLE'S LIBERATION ARMY DAILY (May 26, 2011), http://eng.mod.gov.cn/DefenseNews/2010-06/12/content_4165318.htm.

One of the more remarkable chapters of the Arab democratic revolution of 2011 occurred in Egypt, where a world-class military maintained continuity of operations as it transferred its loyalties to a new government. What would the Egyptian revolution have been had discipline and the command and control architecture of the Egyptian military collapsed? At the very least, it would have been much different. One might likewise ask: what would happen in a future Tiananmen Square incident? How would the Chinese military respond amid wide-scale domestic uprising? The answer is far from certain, and not only for those outside China—clearly concerned, the Chinese government reportedly censored media coverage of the Egyptian revolution.[152]

Such questions serve as a reminder of the difficulties of studying the PLA, which, for all its professed efforts to increase transparency, remains an enigmatic institution to the outside observer.[153] Moreover, the answers to such questions are heavily informed by the character and culture of the PLA itself, an area difficult to quantify and therefore an area for which it remains difficult to draw any firm conclusions. Yet, such challenges need not deter outsiders from analyzing presently available information. However limited such inquiries may be due to deficits in reliable information, they are nonetheless important: as discussed in Section I, common security interests have the potential to bring Chinese and U.S. service members to the same table, if not the same team, at a not-so-distant point in the future. What level of discipline can U.S. troops expect from a Chinese partner? For that matter, in the event cooperation does not materialize and the U.S. and

---

[152] *See, e.g.*, Jeremy Page, *China Co-Opts Social Medial to Head Off Unrest*, WALL ST. J., Feb. 22, 2011, at A8.

[153] In its 2010 annual report to Congress on the Chinese military, the United States Department of Defense stated the following regarding PLA transparency:

> The PLA has made modest improvements in the transparency of China's military and security affairs. However, many uncertainties remain regarding how China will use its expanding military capabilities. The limited transparency in China's military and security affairs enhances uncertainty and increases the potential for misunderstanding and miscalculation.

OFFICE OF THE SEC'Y OF DEF., ANNUAL REPORT TO CONGRESS: MILITARY AND SECURITY DEVELOPMENTS INVOLVING THE PEOPLE'S REPUBLIC OF CHINA I (2010), *available at* http://www.defense.gov/pubs/pdfs/2010_CMPR_Final.pdf.

China find themselves on different sides of armed conflict—what level of discipline can U.S. troops expect from a Chinese adversary?

Additional reasons exist for continuing the project begun decades ago by Rodearmal and Sun. One example comes from the cyber domain and questions of attribution. Outside assessments about the robustness and integrity of PLA command and control architecture within its cyber warfighting elements would be an important variable when responding to a cyber attack emanating from PLA computer networks.[154] For example, an attack from an element known to have lax discipline might be more likely to be deemed a rogue attack not attributable to the Chinese government than one emanating from a unit where subordinates could be presumed to act only in accordance with the orders of their superiors.[155]

In the end, the importance of studying PLA discipline is captured in the words of Lt. Gen. Harding, who observed that "discipline is a force multiplier."[156] The converse, also captured by Lt. Gen. Harding, is likewise true: "Without discipline, a fighting force is little more than a dangerous mob."[157] Whatever direction PLA discipline takes in the coming years, it will be a direction tethered to an ancient and proud tradition. Both George Washington and Mao Zedong led underequipped forces against technologically superior foes. They passed on legacies of courage under fire and commitment to a cause. What they left behind is a loyalty—a discipline. In this institutionalized discipline, their souls live on.

---

[154] David E. Sanger, David Barboza & Nicole Perlroth, *China's Army Seen as Tied to Hacking Against U.S.*, N.Y. TIMES, Feb. 19, 2013, at A1.

[155] For a discussion of command and control infrastructure in the PLA as it relates to cyber activities, see BRYAN KREKEL, NORTHROP GRUMMAN CORP., CAPABILITY OF THE PEOPLE'S REPUBLIC OF CHINA TO CONDUCT CYBER WARFARE AND COMPUTER NETWORK EXPLOITATION (2009), *available at* http://www.au.af.mil/au/awc/awcgate/china/uscesc_prc_cyber_capab_16oct2009.pdf (prepared for the U.S.-China Econ. & Sec. Rev. Comm'n).

[156] *See supra* note 1.

[157] *Id.*

Rules of Engagement:
Balancing the (Inherent) Right and Obligation of Self-Defense with the Prevention of Civilian Casualties

Christopher D. Amore*

> "Stand your ground; don't fire unless fired upon, but if they mean to have a war, let it begin here."[1]

Introduction

On September 15, 2011, Marine Corps Sergeant (Sgt.) Dakota Meyer was awarded the Congressional Medal of Honor for his actions

---

* Christopher Amore is a graduate of Brooklyn Law School and an associate at the law firm of Mound Cotton Wollan & Greengrass in New York. Prior to law school, he was a Captain in the United States Army and served as a platoon leader in Iraq from November 2005 to October 2006. The professionalism and discipline of the Soldiers he served with inspired this article. It is dedicated to those who have come under enemy fire and bravely endured to protect their brothers in arms. He would like to thank Ms. Chelsea Hathaway and MAJ R.J. Hughes for their commentary and support throughout the drafting process. The opinions and views expressed in this article, as well as the mistakes, are solely those of the author and do not reflect the views of Mound Cotton Wollan & Greengrass or the United States Army.

[1] Rule of engagement attributed to Captain Jonas Parker at the Battle of Lexington, April 19, 1775.

during an ambush in the village of Ganjgal in Kunar Province, Afghanistan on September 8, 2009.[2] His citation reads:

> Corporal Meyer maintained security at a patrol rally point while other members of his team moved on foot with two platoons of Afghan National Army and Border Police into the village of Ganjgal for a pre-dawn meeting with village elders. Moving into the village, the patrol was ambushed by more than 50 enemy fighters firing rocket propelled grenades, mortars, and machine guns from houses and fortified positions on the slopes above. Hearing over the radio that four U.S. team members were cut off, Corporal Meyer seized the initiative. With a fellow Marine driving, Corporal Meyer took the exposed gunner's position in a gun-truck as they drove down the steeply terraced terrain in a daring attempt to disrupt the enemy attack and locate the trapped U.S. team. Disregarding intense enemy fire now concentrated on their lone vehicle, Corporal Meyer killed a number of enemy fighters with the mounted machine guns and his rifle, some at near point blank range, as he and his driver made three solo trips into the ambush area. During the first two trips, he and his driver evacuated two dozen Afghan soldiers, many of whom were wounded. When one machine gun became inoperable, he directed a return to the rally point to switch to another gun-truck for a third trip into the ambush area where his accurate fire directly supported the remaining U.S. personnel and Afghan soldiers fighting their way out of the ambush. Despite a shrapnel wound to his arm, Corporal Meyer made two more trips into the ambush area in a third gun-truck accompanied by four other Afghan vehicles to recover more wounded Afghan soldiers and search for the missing U.S. team members. Still under heavy enemy fire, he dismounted the vehicle on the fifth trip and moved on foot to locate and recover the bodies of his team members. Corporal Meyer's daring initiative and bold fighting spirit throughout the 6-hour battle significantly disrupted the enemy's attack and inspired the members of the combined force to fight on. His unwavering courage and steadfast devotion to his U.S. and Afghan comrades in the face of almost certain death reflected great credit

---

[2] *See* C.J. Chivers, *Top Medal for Marine Who Saved Many Lives*, N.Y. TIMES, Sept. 15, 2011.

upon himself and upheld the highest traditions of the Marine Corps and the United States Naval Service.[3]

Unfortunately, Sgt. Meyer's citation does not tell the whole story. Omitted from the narrative is how the Rules of Engagement (ROE) and the misapplication of the law of armed conflict almost cost him his life, and contributed to the death of his fellow soldiers.

A few days after receiving the medal, Sgt. Meyer appeared on the CBS Television Network show "60 Minutes" and told a more complete version of the events that unfolded that day in Ganjgal. He recounted how First Lieutenant (1st Lt.) Michael Johnson, one of the Marines who was surrounded by enemy fire, used his radio to request artillery support by sending in coordinates of the enemy positions, but that lawful request was denied by commanders back at the operations center on base.[4] Meyer commented, "[t]hey denied it. The Army denied it and told [Johnson] it was, it was too close to the village. . . . And [Johnson] said, 'Too close to the village?' And the last words I heard him say was, 'If you don't give me these rounds right now I'm going to die.'"[5] 1st Lt. Johnson and the three other Marines trapped in Ganjgal never received artillery or air support. All four Marines died.

According to Army Colonel (Col.) Richard Hooker, the officer who conducted the AR 15-6 investigation[6] into the events of September 8, 2009, when 1st Lt. Johnson fell silent on the radio Army Captain (Cpt.) Will Swenson, who was trapped by the insurgents just outside Ganjgal, continued the request for artillery and air support. Col. Hooker found that "Captain Swenson probably made nine or ten different calls for fire before he probably gave up in frustration."[7] Based on the evidence that Col. Hooker uncovered, Cpt. Swenson "was very, very insistent in his

---

[3] *Medal of Honor Recipients: Afghanistan*, U.S. ARMY CENTER OF MILITARY HISTORY, http://www.history.army.mil/html/moh/afghanistan.html (last updated Jan. 5, 2012).
[4] *See 60 Minutes* (CBS television broadcast Sept. 18, 2011).
[5] *Id.*
[6] DEP'T OF THE ARMY, ARMY REGULATION 15-6, PROCEDURES FOR INVESTIGATING OFFICERS AND BOARDS OF OFFICERS (2006) (providing the procedures for conducting investigations in the military and conferring authority upon the investigating officer to make findings and recommendations that are warranted by the facts of the incident being investigated).
[7] *Id.*

calls for help. No question about that."[8] It would be another forty-five minutes into the battle before the first helicopters arrived with the much-needed air support. During the "60 Minutes" interview, Col. Hooker opined: "If we'd gotten supporting aviation on station early in the fight we . . . wouldn't be sitting here having this conversation. That's my firm belief."[9]

The findings and recommendations of Col. Hooker's AR 15-6 investigation were published, with redactions, on November 25, 2009. As a result of the investigation, two Army officers received general letters of reprimand for their failure to act appropriately on September 8, 2009.[10] Col. Hooker concluded that "[d]uring mission execution on 8 September 2009, the actions of key leaders at the battalion level were inadequate and ineffective, contributing directly to the loss of life which ensued."[11] He noted: "the fire support NCO [non-commissioned officer] on duty . . . took action to provide immediate support to the units in the Ganjgal valley early in the engagement. The USAF JTAC [Air Force Joint Terminal Attack Controller] acted similarly. However, both were overruled by higher echelons."[12] Col. Hooker concluded: "[t]he perception by [U.S. Marine Corps] and U.S. Army leaders engaged in the Ganjgal valley on 8 September 2009 that . . . elements did not adequately support the mission is accurate. Timely aviation and indirect fire support [were] not provided."[13] Although one unnamed officer who received a general letter of reprimand stated that he did not feel constrained by the ROE in Afghanistan at that time, Col. Hooker's investigation revealed that "that perception clearly existed in the minds of . . . leaders during and after the battle."[14] This tragic incident is a harsh

---

[8] *Id.*
[9] *Id.*
[10] *See* Dan Lamothe, *2 Officers Reprimanded Over Ganjgal Mistakes*, MARINE CORPS TIMES, Feb. 21, 2011, *available at* http://www.marinecorpstimes.com/news/2011/02/army-officers-reprimanded-over-ganjgal-022111w/.
[11] AR 15-6 Report of Investigation into Operations in the Ganjgal Valley, Konar Province, Afghanistan, 8 September 2009 (Nov. 25, 2009), *available at* http://www.captainsjournal.com/2010/02/19/ar-15-6-investigation-of-marine-deaths-in-kunar-province/.
[12] *Id.*
[13] *Id.*
[14] *Id.*

reminder of the chaos of war, and demonstrates that the law of armed conflict often offers imperfect solutions in its attempt to prevent unnecessary deaths of both soldiers and civilians. The events of September 8, 2009 underscore the dichotomy that exists between enforcing the ROE while at the same time not depriving the war fighter of his lawful right to self-defense on the battlefield. It brings to light a debate that arises in most cases of armed conflict – how to balance the prevention of civilian casualties with the humanitarian and legal right to self-defense. It will be demonstrated throughout this article that commanders and staff officers who draft the policies implementing the ROE have the ability to shift the balance one way or another.

Part I of this article will explore the humanitarian and legal right to self-defense and will show how the lawful use of self-defense is recognized in both domestic and international law. Part I will also address how the U.S. military has interpreted and applied this right through the standing rules of engagement (SROE).

Part II of this article analyzes the history of ROE up through the modern era, allowing this article to identify which factors military leaders consider in the development of the ROE. Additionally, Part II will examine the tactical directives and counterinsurgency (COIN) guidance of Generals Stanley McChrystal and David Petraeus to compare how they adjusted the ROE within the same military campaign at different times and analyze what factors were considered in making those adjustments.

Focusing on the need for U.S. soldiers to defend themselves and their fellow soldiers, this article endorses General Petraeus's directives that allowed soldiers to protect themselves without violating international or domestic law. It will illustrate that while the SROE are designed to balance the achievement of national strategic objectives with the inherent right to self-defense, military leaders can tailor the theater-specific ROE to achieve specific military objectives, but should never do so at the expense of the right to self-defense.

I. SELF-DEFENSE

A. *The Inherent Right to Self-Defense*

The concept of self-defense has long been a part of most legal systems.[15] For example, the Bible endorses the principle of self-defense in its recognition of the right of the homeowner to kill the unlawful intruder.[16] The Talmud acknowledges a right to use force against aggressors who threaten human interests, or threatened to kill.[17] Saint Thomas Aquinas, a thirteenth century Italian Catholic priest and philosopher, reasoned that the purpose of using deadly force in self-defense was not to kill, but rather to repel the attacker. "[The] force had to be directed against the attack, not the attacker. The death was a side effect of the legitimate purpose rather than the goal itself."[18]

In 1688, English lawmakers, affirming the natural right for people to defend themselves, codified the right to bear arms in the Declaration of Right: "the Subjects which are Protestants may have Arms for their Defence suitable to their Conditions and as allowed by Law."[19] The Convention Parliament, the legislative body responsible for the drafting of the Declaration of Right, believed that the right to bear arms for the purpose of self-defense was one of the "true auntient and indubitable Rights and Liberties of the People."[20] England's recognition of the inherent right to self-defense in the seventeenth century would be echoed over three hundred years later by the United States Supreme Court. Interpreting this provision of the Declaration of Right in the landmark Second Amendment case *District of Columbia v. Heller*,[21] the Court explained that "the right of having and using arms for self-

---

[15] GEORGE P. FLETCHER & JENS DAVID OHLIN, DEFENDING HUMANITY: WHEN FORCE IS JUSTIFIED AND WHY 26 (2008) ("[T]he contours of the idea [of self-defense] have engaged the imaginations of lawyers and philosophers for thousands of years.").

[16] "If the thief is found breaking in, and he is struck so that he dies, there shall be no guilt for his bloodshed." Exodus 22:2.

[17] FLETCHER & OHLIN, *supra* note 15, at 27.

[18] *Id.* at 26-27.

[19] Bill of Rights, 1688, 1 W. & M., c. 2 (Eng.).

[20] *Id.*; *see also* David B. Kopel, *The Natural Right of Self-Defense:* Heller*'s Lesson for the World*, 59 SYRACUSE L. REV. 235, 236 (2008).

[21] District of Columbia v. Heller, 554 U.S. 570 (2008).

preservation and defence" was necessary in order to protect "the natural right of resistance and self-preservation."[22]

References to the right of self-defense in the United Stated prior to *Heller* can be found in the Federalist Papers, state constitutions, and case law. In the eighteenth century, Alexander Hamilton commented that the "original right of self-defense . . . is paramount to all positive forms of government."[23] Throughout the history of the nation, at least thirty-seven states have agreed with Hamilton by affirming a right to self-defense in their constitutions.[24] The state courts have also contributed to the discussion. In 1832, a Kentucky court held that not only was killing in self-defense justified, but that the right to do so was derived from nature.[25]

> [T]he right of necessary defence, in the protection of a man's person or property, is derived to him from the law of nature, and should never be unnecessarily restrained by municipal regulation. . . . [T]he right of self-defence . . . is founded in the law of nature, and is not, nor can be superceded by the law of society. Before societies were formed, the right of self-defence resided in individuals, and since, in case of necessity, individuals incorporated into society, can not resort for protection to the law of society, that law with great propriety and strict justice considereth them as still, in that instance, under the protection of the law of nature.[26]

Similar findings have been made, for example, by the state of Ohio: "[b]y universal consent self-defense is recognized as a natural right of every individual and of every collection of individuals;"[27] by Oregon: "[t]he law upon that subject is the same as it was 500 years ago. The right

---

[22] *Id.* at 594 (2008) (citing 1 Blackstone 136, 139-40, 144 (1765)).
[23] THE FEDERALIST NO. 28, at 128 (Alexander Hamilton) (Terence Ball ed., 2003).
[24] *See* David B. Kopel, Paul Gallant & Joanne D. Eisen, *The Human Right of Self-Defense*, 22 BYU J. PUB. L. 43, 101-02, 128 (2007).
[25] *See* Gray v. Combs, 30 Ky. (7 J.J. Marsh.) 478 (1832).
[26] *Id.* at 481 (internal quotation omitted).
[27] R.R. Comm'n of Ohio v. Hocking Valley Ry. Co., 91 N.E. 865, 866 (Ohio 1910).

of self-defense is a natural right, inherent in mankind;"[28] and by Washington: "[t]he plea of self-defense rests on the natural right."[29]

The first documented interpretation in the United States of the legal principle of self-defense in the context of law of armed conflict can be traced back to 1837 and the Caroline Doctrine.[30] The Caroline was a U.S. steamboat that came under attack by British ships while it was attempting to deliver supplies to Canadian rebels fighting against the British.[31] Daniel Webster, U.S. Secretary of State at the time of the Caroline incident, condemned the act and declared that it was not justifiable self-defense. Specifically, he stated that self-defense is only justified "if the necessity of that self-defense is instant, overwhelming, and leaving no choice of means, and no moment for deliberation."[32] Webster's definition came to be known as the Caroline Doctrine, and was recognized as a standard in international law until the United Nations presented a competing definition of self-defense in Article 51 of the U.N. Charter.[33]

B. *Codified Self-Defense*

Article 51 of the Charter of the United Nations, signed on June 26, 1945, states: "Nothing in the present Charter shall impair the inherent right of individual or collective self-defence if an armed attack occurs against a Member of the United Nations . . . ."[34] By referring to this right as "inherent" the Charter acknowledges that the right to self-defense

---

[28] Konigsberger v. Harvey, 7 P. 114, 115 (Or. 1885).
[29] State v. McGonigle, 45 P. 20, 22 (Wash. 1896).
[30] *See* Amos Guiora, *Targeted Killing as Active Self-Defense*, 36 CASE W. RES. J. INT'L L.. 319, 323 (2004).
[31] *Id.*
[32] *Id.* ("According to Webster, Britain could have dealt with the Caroline in a more diplomatic manner. He limited the right to self-defense to situations where there is a real threat, the response is essential and proportional, and all peaceful means of resolving the dispute have been exhausted.").
[33] *Id.*
[34] United Nations Charter art. 51 (emphasis added).

predates the drafting of the Charter, and is fundamental to international humanitarian law.[35]

In the United States, the Chairman of the Joint Chiefs of Staff Instruction ("CJCSI") 3121.01B,[36] which contains the current SROE for the U.S. military, describes the "Inherent Right of Self-Defense" as the empowerment of commanders "with the inherent right and obligation to exercise unit self-defense" and authorizes "military members [to] exercise individual self-defense in response to a hostile act or demonstrated hostile intent."[37] "Hostile act" is defined in CJCSI 3121.01B as "[a]n attack or other use of force against the United States, US forces or other designated persons or property."[38] It can also be "force used directly to preclude or impede the mission and/or duties of US forces, including the recovery of US personnel or vital [US government] property."[39] "Hostile intent" refers to "[t]he threat of imminent use of force against the United States, US forces or other designated persons or property."[40] As noted in CJCSI 3121.01B, "[i]mminent does not necessarily mean immediate or instantaneous."[41] The drafters of CJCSI 3121.01B recognize that on the battlefield this determination is not always a bright-line scenario. Whether the use of force against U.S. forces is imminent, thus allowing U.S. forces to invoke their inherent right to self-defense, "will be based on an assessment of all facts and circumstances known to US forces at the time and may be made at any level."[42]

Despite the apparent inherency of the right to self-defense, a closer examination of the current SROE reveals that the U.S. military

---

[35] *See* Nicole Deller & John Burroughs, *Jus ad Bellum: Law Regulating Resort to Force*, 30 HUM. RTS. MAG. 8 (2003).

[36] The current SROE for US Forces are published by the Chairman of the Joint Chiefs of Staff (CJCS) in Instruction 3121.01B, and approved by the Secretary of Defense. CHAIRMAN OF THE JOINT CHIEFS OF STAFF, INSTRUCTION 3121.01B, STANDING RULES OF ENGAGEMENT/STANDING RULES FOR THE USE OF FORCE FOR U.S. FORCES (June 13, 2005) [hereinafter CJCSI 3121.01B].

[37] *Id.*, A-2.
[38] *Id.*, A-3.
[39] *Id.*
[40] *Id.*
[41] *Id.*
[42] CJCSI 3121.01 B, *supra* note 36.

may not view the right to be inherent at all levels. Prior to the publication of the current SROE in 2005, the Department of Defense categorized self-defense into four levels: (i) national self-defense, (ii) collective self-defense, (iii) unit self-defense, and (iv) individual self-defense.[43] National self-defense is retained at the Presidential or Secretary of Defense (SECDEF) level and is defined as "[d]efense of the United States, U.S. forces, and, in certain circumstances, U.S. persons and their property, and/or U.S. commercial assets from a hostile act or demonstration of hostile intent."[44] Collective self-defense, also applicable at the Presidential and SECDEF level, is "[d]efense of designated non-U.S. military forces and/or designated foreign nationals and their property from a hostile or demonstrated hostile intent."[45] The definitions of national self-defense and collective self-defense remained unchanged in CJCSI 3121.01B.

This article focuses on unit and individual self-defense; neither of which is explicitly defined in the current SROE. However, the language used in the SROE in place prior to the publication of the current SROE reveals how the U.S. military's position has changed with respect to unit and individual self-defense. The previous SROE were published in CJCSI 3121.01A on January 15, 2000, prior to both the Afghanistan and Iraq wars, and prior to September 11, 2001. It defined unit self-defense as "[t]he act of defending a particular US force element, including individual personnel thereof, and other US forces in the vicinity, against a hostile act or demonstrated hostile intent."[46] Individual self-defense was described as follows:

> The inherent right to use all necessary means available and to take all appropriate actions to defend oneself and US forces in one's vicinity from a hostile act or demonstrated hostile intent is a unit of self-defense. Commanders have the obligation to ensure that individuals

---

[43] *See* CHAIRMAN OF THE JOINT CHIEFS OF STAFF, INSTRUCTION 3121.01A, STANDING RULES OF ENGAGEMENT FOR U.S. FORCES, at A-4 (Jan. 15, 2000) [hereinafter CJCSI 3121.01A].
[44] CJCSI 3121.01 B, *supra* note 36, A-3.
[45] *Id.*
[46] CJCSI 3121.01A, *supra* note 43.

within their respective units understand and are trained on when and how to use force in self-defense.[47]

Although CJCSI 3121.01B, and therefore the current SROE, do not expressly define unit or individual self-defense, both are discussed. As commented on in the Operation Law Handbook, published by Judge Advocate General's Legal Center and School, the 2005 SROE refined the definitions of the prior SROE, merging the definitions of "unit" and "individual" self-defense into the general definition of "inherent right of self-defense" suggesting, as further discussed below, that individual self-defense is no longer recognized by the U.S. as absolute.[48] Under the Policy section of CJCSI 3121.01B, unit self-defense is addressed as follows: "Unit commanders always retain the inherent right and obligation to exercise unit self-defense in response to a hostile act or demonstrated hostile intent."[49] Therefore, not only may commanders act in self-defense of their units, but they must act in self-defense if such situation presents itself. Although commanders must often adjust the ROE in response to the various military, political, or legal concerns they are presented with on the battlefield, these concerns, as addressed in the OPLAW Handbook, should "have NO impact on a commander's right and obligation of self-defense."[50]

Additionally, as stated above, individual self-defense is discussed in the current SROE's definition of "Inherent Right of Self-Defense":

> Unless otherwise directed by a unit commander as detailed below, military members may exercise individual self-defense in response to a hostile act or demonstrated hostile intent. When individuals are assigned and acting as a part of a unit, individual self-defense should be

---

[47] *Id.* (emphasis added).
[48] JUDGE ADVOCATE GEN.'S LEGAL CTR. & SCH., OPERATIONAL LAW HANDBOOK 75 (2008) [hereinafter OPLAW HANDBOOK].
[49] CJCSI 3121.01 B, *supra* note 36, A-2 (emphasis added). For some nations, unit self-defense is only a right. In other nations, "the concept of unit self-defence is both a right and an obligation.... Some nations permit the right of unit-defence to be limited by orders from higher authority." INT'L INST. OF HUMANITARIAN LAW, RULES OF ENGAGEMENT HANDBOOK 3 (2009) [hereinafter ROE HANDBOOK].
[50] OPLAW HANDBOOK, *supra* note 48, at 75.

considered a subset of unit self-defense. As such, unit commanders may limit individual self-defense by members of their unit.[51]

Not only does the current SROE lack an explicit declaration that individual self-defense is an inherent right, but they also provide that self-defense measures may be further limited by unit commanders. The plain language of the current SROE empowers commanders with the inherent right to unit self-defense, but does not provide individuals with the same inherent right. Enclosure I of CJCSI 3121.01B, which establishes the process for the development of supplemental measures to the ROE, states:

> [U]nit commanders may issue supplemental measures to limit self-defense by members of their units. The use of force for mission accomplishment may sometimes be restricted by specific political and military goals that are often unique to the situation.[52]

These limitations did not exist in the previous SROE published in CJCSI 3121.01A. This was not an oversight. The prior SROE stated that the "purpose of these SROE [was] to provide implementation guidance on the application of force for mission accomplishment and the exercise of the inherent right and obligation of self-defense."[53] In comparison, the current SROE state that the "purpose of the SROE is to provide implementation guidance on the application of force for mission accomplishment and the exercise of self-defense."[54] The language between the two is nearly identical except for use of the phrase "inherent right and obligation" in the latter.

This change in the current SROE is a dramatic departure from the prior SROE, as well as from the foundational principles of law recognizing an inherent right to self-defense. While the SROE do not prevent individuals from exercising self-defense, there is a clear shift of responsibility to commanders to ensure self-defense measures are exercised appropriately. When a commander invokes the right to self-defense in fulfilling his obligation to defend the unit, this action may

---

[51] CJCSI 3121.01 B, *supra* note 36, A-2 (emphasis added).
[52] *Id.*, I-1.
[53] *Id.*, A-1 (emphasis added).
[54] *Id.*

often clash with mission objectives. As the International Institute of Humanitarian Law notes, "[b]ecause national laws and policies differ, there will not always be consistency . . . as to when the right to use force in self-defence ends and the use of force for mission accomplishment begins."[55] As will be discussed below, military leaders in Afghanistan were faced with this challenge when drafting the ROE for soldiers conducting operations against insurgent and Taliban forces.

II. THE RULES OF ENGAGEMENT[56]

A. *Early Rules of Engagement*

Like the right to self-defense, the ROE have long been recognized as an element of international humanitarian law. During the Middle Ages, certain norms regulating warfare were tacitly agreed upon.[57] "The canonistic doctrine of privilege was rooted in the notion that the public welfare could be promoted in certain circumstances by granting special rights to groups who served the general interests of the community . . . ."[58] Attempts were made to civilize warfare by granting immunity to non-combatants, even though immunity was not an accepted practice.[59] Groups such as clerics, monks, other religious clergy, travelers, merchants and peasant farmers were spared from harm or death and

---

[55] ROE HANDBOOK, *supra* note 49, at 3.

[56] Under International Law, *jus in bello* ("justice in war") is the set of laws that regulate actions during the war once it has begun. ROE fall under *jus in bello* since they guide conduct during war. Although the phrase "rules of engagement" was not used formally until the 1950s, the principles embodied in ROE have been used in warfare for hundreds of years. *See* Karma Nabulsi, *Jus ad Bellum/Jus in Bello*, CRIMES OF WAR, *available at* http://www.crimesofwar.org/a-z-guide/jus-ad-bellum-jus-in-bello/; *see also* Mark S. Martins, *Rules of Engagement for Land Forces: A Matter of Training, Not Lawyering*, 143 MIL. L. REV. 1, 36 (1994) ("Contemporaneous dogfights between American and Soviet aircraft . . . probably provided the impetus for the Pentagon to coin the term 'ROE.'. . . These highly charged confrontations likely prodded the [Joint Chiefs of Staff] to issue, on November 23, 1954, a set of 'Intercept and Engagement Instructions,' which Air Force and Navy staffers termed ROE. In 1958, the JCS formally adopted and defined the term 'rule of engagement.'").

[57] *See generally* THEODOR MERON, HENRY'S WARS AND SHAKESPEARE'S LAWS, PERSPECTIVE ON THE LAW OF WAR IN THE LATER MIDDLE AGES 91-93 (1993).

[58] *Id.* at 91.

[59] *Id.*

were even afforded some protection for some of their property.[60] The primary reason for being spared was that their position in society precluded their participation in war.[61]

Although women, children, and the elderly were not precluded for the same reasons, they were protected by the secular code of chivalry.[62] The code of chivalry afforded protection to broader groups of people, typically defined by weakness or innocence: women, children, the elderly, the sick, and other persons who traditionally would not engage in warfare.[63] Despite the presumption of innocence granted to these individuals, they would lose their protected status if they took part in the hostilities.[64] For example, the "chivalric presumption" that women were not strong enough to carry weapons and engage in combat was clearly rebuttable.[65] Women could, and frequently did, engage in warfare, usually to aid in the defense of cities under siege.[66] These women who partook in warfare would lose their immunity.[67]

Long before the modern ROE era, the doctrine of privilege and the code of chivalry prevented those engaged in combat from killing at will. Restrictions were placed on combatants to prevent the deaths of the innocent and attempt to promote civility during war.

In 1625, the renowned Dutch philosopher, lawyer, and writer, Hugo Grotius[68] wrote *De Jure Belli ac Pacis* [On the Law of War and

---

[60] *Id.* at 91-92.
[61] *Id.* at 92.
[62] *See id.*
[63] MERON, *supra* note 57, at 92.
[64] *Id.* at 93.
[65] *Id.* at 95.
[66] *Id.*
[67] *Id.* at 95-96.
[68] Grotius began his studies at eleven years old at Leiden University. *Hugo Grotius*, GROTIUS CTR. FOR INT'L LEGAL STUDIES (2010), http://www.grotiuscentre.org/page1182911.aspx. After graduation, he worked as a lawyer in the Netherlands until his arrest and imprisonment in 1618 when a political group adverse to his ideas took power. *Id.* After escaping to Paris in 1621, he wrote DE JURE BELLI AC PACIS, in which "he expounded his ideal of a system of laws, rules and treaties for all nations, and moral duties of nations to strive for altruism in relations with other states." *Id.* (leading many to consider him the "father of international law.").

Peace]. In Book III, Chapter IV, The Right of Killing Enemies in a Solemn War, and of Other Hostilities Committed Against the Person of the Enemy, an extensive list is given of scenarios where killing is both justifiable and legal.[69] Grotius imparts impunity on those who kill another through acts of war:

> [I]t is lawful for one Enemy to hurt another, both in Person and Goods, not only for him that makes War on a just Account, and does it within those Bounds which are prescribed by the Law of Nature, as we have said in the beginning of this Book, but on both Sides, and without Distinction; so that he cannot be punished as a Murderer, or a Thief, tho' he be taken in another Prince's Dominion, neither can any other make War upon him barely upon this Account.[70]

Though it may seem that Grotius extends the right to kill to almost any scenario,[71] Chapter XI, Moderation Concerning the Right of Killing Men in a Just War, explains that killing is not always justified in war. For example, those who are unfortunate enough to have been made the subjects of the enemy cannot be justly killed.[72] Additionally, according to Grotius, all care must be taken to ensure those who are innocent are not killed.[73] Special protection should be given to women, children, priests, scholars, merchants, and captives to ensure they are spared from the violence of war.[74] These Medieval principles would have a lasting effect on the development of the law of war.

B. *The Rules of Engagement in the Modern Era*

Although it may seem apparent that throughout history the primary purpose of the ROE was to regulate the use of force by military personnel, the ROE actually serve three purposes: (1) political, (2)

---

[69] *See* 3 HUGO GROTIUS, THE RIGHTS OF WAR AND PEACE (Richard Tuck ed., Jean Barbeyrac trans., Liberty Fund 2005) (1625).
[70] *Id.*
[71] Grotius even gives approval for killing prisoners, women, and children in some circumstances. *See generally id.* (throughout the entire book there are discussions of such killings.).
[72] *Id.* ("They are to be esteemed unfortunate who happen to be in the party of one of the Enemies, without and hostile Disposition towards the other party . . . .").
[73] *Id.*
[74] *Id.*

military, and (3) legal.[75] The ROE serve a political purpose by ensuring the policies and objectives of a nation are reflected in the actions of the military conducting operations abroad, particularly under circumstances where communication with senior level authority is not possible.[76] The military purpose of the ROE is to establish parameters within which commanders in the field must operate to accomplish a unit's assigned mission.[77] This includes placing limitations on military units or limiting the use of certain weapon systems so that undesired escalation of hostilities does not occur.[78] The ROE serve a legal purpose by ensuring that a commander's actions are consistent with both domestic and international law.[79] Using the ROE to serve all three purposes simultaneously helps provide a framework to assist the United States in achieving its objectives associated with military operations.[80]

The United States Department of Defense defines the ROE as the "[d]irectives issued by competent military authority that delineate the circumstances and limitations under which United States forces will initiate and/or continue combat engagement with other forces encountered."[81] They are disseminated in a variety of forms. The ROE may be encompassed in U.S. military doctrine, execution orders, operation orders, deployment orders, or standing directives that are issued by military commanders to combat troops carrying out an assigned mission.[82] "Whatever their form, they provide authorization for and/or limits on, among other things, the use of force, the positioning and posturing of forces, and the employment of certain specific capabilities."[83]

---

[75] OPLAW HANDBOOK, *supra* note 48, at 73-74.
[76] *Id.*
[77] *Id.* at 74.
[78] *Id.*
[79] *Id.*
[80] *Id.* at 73.
[81] JOINT CHIEFS OF STAFF, JOINT PUB. 1-02: DEPARTMENT OF DEFENSE DICTIONARY OF MILITARY AND ASSOCIATED TERMS 317 (Nov. 8, 2010).
[82] ROE HANDBOOK, *supra* note 49, at 1.
[83] *Id.*

1. Standing Rules of Engagement

The SROE for U.S. Forces are published by the Chairman of the Joint Chiefs of Staff (CJCS) and approved by the SECDEF.[84] These rules apply to all U.S. forces "during all military operations and contingencies and routine Military Department functions."[85] The SROE establish fundamental policies and procedures that regulate the actions of military personnel engaged in armed conflict. Their primary purpose is "to provide implementation guidance on the application of force for mission accomplishment and the exercise of self-defense."[86] According to the Purpose paragraph of CJCSI 3121.01B "it is imperative to keep in mind these two purposes . . . as a clear understanding of the differences between the two is critical to the proper understanding and implementation of the SROE."[87] The Policy section of CJCSI 3121.01B further emphasizes the objectives of self-defense and mission accomplishment by noting: "Unit commanders always retain the inherent right and obligation to exercise unit self-defense in response to a hostile act or demonstrated hostile intent."[88] The self-preservation goals of U.S. national security policy are also addressed. The SROE allow the U.S. to conduct military operations in order to "ensure the survival, safety, and vitality of our nation and to maintain a stable international environment consistent with US national interests."[89] The SROE serve as the foundation for further development of the ROE for a specific military operation or campaign.[90] When a unit embarks on a specific operation or campaign, the SROE will be in effect until commanders publish theater-specific ROE.

---

[84] *See* CJCSI 3121.01 B, *supra* note 36.
[85] *Id.*, A-1.
[86] *Id.*
[87] Richard J. Grunawalt, *The JCS Standing Rules of Engagement: A Judge Advocate's Primer*, 42 A.F. L. Rev. 245, 247 (1997).
[88] *Id.*
[89] *Id.*
[90] *See* Major Paul E. Jeter, *What Do Special Instructions Bring to the Rules of Engagement? Chaos or Clarity*, 55 A.F. L. Rev. 377, 384, 387-88 (2004) ("The starting point for all ROE should be the SROE. As a crisis forms which may require military action, staffs at the strategic level evaluate and coordinate how the ROE fits into the mission.").

It should also be underscored that these rules are standing – i.e., they are in effect at all times and not just limited to peacetime operations.[91] Although wartime or theater-specific ROE may be enacted after the outbreak of armed conflict, the SROE are designed to work effectively in prolonged operations as well.[92]

2. Theater-Specific Rules of Engagement

Theater-specific ROE are developed by staff officers at the strategic level[93] during the initial stages, or Crisis Action Phase, of an operation.[94] Developers of the ROE, and the appropriate authorities, will review the military's objectives and strategies in order to develop the ROE applicable to the mission.[95] Additionally, theater-specific ROE reflect "political guidance from higher authorities, the tactical considerations of the specific mission, and [the law of armed conflict]."[96] Therefore, military planners are faced with the challenge of implementing the ROE that enable the warfighter to accomplish the mission, but do not conflict with national objectives or lead to fratricide.[97] Officers on the planning staff should incorporate development of the ROE into mission analysis in order to "review higher headquarters planning documents for political, military, and legal considerations that affect ROE [and] [a]ssess ROE requirements throughout pre-conflict, deterrence, conflict and post-conflict phases of an operation."[98] ROE developers must ensure that the ROE support achievement of the desired end state of the mission.[99]

---

[91] Grunawalt, *supra* note 87, at 248.
[92] *Id.*
[93] CJCSI 3121.01 B, *supra* note 36, J-1 ("Due to the operational nature of ROE, the Director of Operations (J-3) and his staff are responsible for developing ROE during crisis action planning. Likewise, the Director for Strategic Plans and Policies (J-5) should play a large role in ROE development for deliberate planning.").
[94] Jeter, *supra* note 90, at 388.
[95] *Id.*
[96] ROE HANDBOOK, *supra* note 49, at 6.
[97] Jeter, *supra* note 90, at 388 (citing U.S. DEP'T OF AIR FORCE, 12TH AIR FORCE, JUDGE ADVOCATE OFFICE, *Supplement to 612 COS/DOOCOS Operations Duty Officer Guide for an Air Operations Center* S1-30).
[98] CJCSI 3121.01B, *supra* note 36, J-2.
[99] *Id.*

Because theater-specific ROE are dependent on mission objectives, the CJCS recognizes the need to allow for changes to the ROE just as mission objectives often change. While conducting course of action (COA) analysis, ROE developers should identify any ROE-making authority normally retained by a higher echelon that must be delegated to subordinate units.[100] This includes refining the ROE to support the different phases of a proposed COA.[101] As stated in CJCSI 3121.01B: "[t]he ROE process must anticipate changes in the operational environment and modify supplemental measures to support the assigned mission. Commanders and their staffs must continuously analyze the ROE and recommend modifications required to meet changing operational parameters."[102]

Enclosure I of CJCSI 3121.01B provides guidance on the development of supplemental measures which enable a commander to alter the SROE in order to accomplish a specific mission.[103] There are two types of supplemental measures: (1) those that require approval from the SECDEF, and (2) those that allow a commander to place restrictions on the use of force.[104] Generally, those that fall into the first category are permissive; meaning the "particular operation, tactic, or weapon is generally restricted, and either the President [or the] SECDEF . . . implements the supplemental measure to specifically permit the particular operation, tactic, or weapon."[105] All other supplemental measures (those in the second category) are restrictive in nature, and are delegated to subordinate commanders. Restrictive measures can be implemented by a subordinate commander without having to first get permission from superior officers. Using restrictive measures, a commander may place further restrictions on the use of force despite being authorized to use any weapon or tactic permitted under the ROE or the law of war.[106] A subordinate commander who seeks to restrict the

---

[100] *Id.*
[101] *Id.*, J-3.
[102] *Id.*
[103] *Id.*, I-1.
[104] OPLAW HANDBOOK, *supra* note 48, at 76.
[105] *Id.*
[106] *Id.*

SECDEF-approved ROE must notify the SECDEF as soon as possible.[107] From the perspective of subordinate commanders, supplemental measures only allow them to further restrict the SROE. There is no mechanism in place that allows a subordinate commander to broaden the use of force under the ROE, even if he or she believes that doing so is necessary to accomplish the assigned mission. This is problematic since subordinate commanders, who are often most aware of the conditions on the battlefield, essentially play no part in theater-specific ROE development.

If a commander believes "that the existing ROE are unclear, too restrictive, or otherwise unsuitable for his or her particular mission . . . he or she may request additional ROE."[108] Drafting the request message[109] will be a combined effort between the Judge Advocate (JA) and the operations (J/G/S-3) staff.[110] When drafting a ROE request, the subordinate commander and those advising him or her must be mindful of the supplemental measures that require SECDEF approval. A request of this magnitude is rarely approved since ROE developers have already given these items significant consideration.[111] For the subordinate unit to succeed in getting its ROE request granted, it must provide the requisite justification for the supplemental measure.[112] According to the OPLAW Handbook, this can be achieved by demonstrating that the unit has a mission "that earlier ROE planners could not have foreseen, and that the ROE do not quite fit."[113]

The numerous levels of command that a ROE request must go through before reaching the final approval authority further contributes to the difficulty of the process. Prior to finalization, the request may be disapproved by intermediate commands.[114] It is therefore recommended

---

[107] *See* CJCSI 3121.01B, *supra* note 36, A-2.
[108] OPLAW HANDBOOK, *supra* note 48, at 78.
[109] The format for an ROE request message can be found in Appendix F to enclosure I of CJCSI 3121.01B.
[110] OPLAW HANDBOOK, *supra* note 48, at 76 (discussing how Enclosure J of CJCSI 3121.01B goes a step further and suggests creation of an ROE Planning Cell).
[111] *Id.* at 78.
[112] *Id.*
[113] *Id.*
[114] *Id.*

that subordinate commanders keep close contact with the JAs at their higher headquarters in order to facilitate the process.[115] Having a liaison with higher headquarters "may prove instrumental in having close cases approved, and in avoiding lost causes."[116] The process will arguably be most difficult for the subordinate commander who operates out of a small remote forward operating base with limited access to the higher headquarters where the unit's JA would be located. This commander, who best understands how the ROE are limiting the unit's ability to accomplish its mission, will likely have no recourse for getting a change to the ROE. When the force requirements stated by a subordinate commander are at odds with the force that higher command believes is necessary to accomplish the mission, the ROE may provide more confusion than clarity on the battlefield.

C. *Rules of Engagement in Afghanistan*

1. The Rules of Engagement under General Stanley McChrystal

General (Gen.) Stanley McChrystal was commander of the Joint Special Operations Command (JSOC) from September 2003 to August 2008.[117] After a successful career as a special operations commander, Gen. McChrystal was nominated by President Obama to command all conventional forces in Afghanistan, and was confirmed by the Senate in June 2009.[118] His command included responsibility for all U.S. military forces, as well as all NATO[119] operations.[120]

---

[115] *Id.*
[116] OPLAW HANDBOOK, *supra* note 48, at 76.
[117] COUNCIL ON FOREIGN RELATIONS, *Biography of General Stanley McChrystal* (2010), http://www.cfr.org/afghanistan/biography-general-stanley-mcchrystal/p19396 [hereinafter *Gen. McChrystal Bio*].
[118] *Id.*
[119] "The North Atlantic Treaty Organization (NATO) is an alliance of 28 countries from North America and Europe committed to fulfilling the goals of the North Atlantic Treaty signed on 4 April 1949. In accordance with the Treaty, the fundamental role of NATO is to safeguard the freedom and security of its member countries by political and military means." Frequently Asked Questions, NATO, http://www.nato.int/cps/en/natolive/faq.htm (last updated Mar. 11, 2009).
[120] *Gen McChrystal Bio., supra* note 117.

Shortly after taking command, Gen. McChrystal published his Tactical Directive[121] for NATO's International Security Assistance Force (ISAF) in Afghanistan.[122] Although much of the Directive is classified, portions of it were released to the public "to ensure a broader awareness of the intent and scope of Gen. McChrystal's guidance to ISAF and [U.S.] forces" on the ROE and the use of force in Afghanistan.[123] Despite the fact that some portions of the Tactical Directive are classified, the purpose and intent of Gen. McChrystal's ROE are clear.

The focus of the Tactical Directive was the reduction of civilian casualties (CIVCAS). Noting the importance of winning the support of the Afghanistan population, Gen. McChrystal stated: "[g]aining and maintaining that support must be our overriding operational imperative – and the ultimate objective of every action we take."[124] Although he recognized the fact that the military must be able to use the weapons at its disposal, winning would not be based on increasing "the number of Taliban we kill, but instead on our ability to separate insurgents from the center of gravity – the people."[125] According to Gen. McChrystal this would be achieved by reducing civilian casualties, avoiding excessive collateral damage, and respecting and protecting the local populace from violence in order to gain their support.[126] Specific restrictions in the Tactical Directive included limiting the use of close air support (CAS) in residential areas, using air-to-ground munitions and indirect fires in residential areas in only very limited and prescribed scenarios, forbidding

---

[121] A "directive" is defined as:

> 1. A military communication in which polity is established or a specific action is ordered.
> 2. A plan issued with a view to putting it into effect when so directed, or in the event that a stated contingency arises.
> 3. Broadly speaking, any communication which initiates or governs action, conduct, or procedure.

JOINT CHIEFS OF STAFF, JOINT PUB. 1-02: DEPARTMENT OF DEFENSE DICTIONARY OF MILITARY AND ASSOCIATED TERMS 162 (amended through Oct. 31, 2009).
[122] Gen. Stanley McChrystal, *Tactical Directive*, NATO/ISAF UNCLASS (July 6, 2009), *available at* http://www.nato.int/isaf/docu/official_texts/Tactical_Directive_090706.pdf [hereinafter *Tactical Directive*].
[123] *Id.*
[124] *Id.*
[125] *Id.*
[126] *Id.*

entry into an Afghan home without the participation of Afghan National Security Forces (ANSF), and an absolute prohibition of ISAF forces on entering, firing upon, or firing into a "mosque or any religious or historical site except in self-defense."[127] Further, any searches or entries into such a structure would only be conducted by ANSF.[128] The ROE also prevented troops from firing at Taliban members if it presented a risk of causing civilian casualties.[129] Under Gen. McChrystal's ROE, troops were forbidden from shooting in these situations even if it meant allowing the enemy to escape.[130]

Gen. McChrystal's Tactical Directive contained the following note: "This directive does not prevent commanders from protecting the lives of their men and women as a matter of self-defense where it is determined no other options (specific options deleted due to operational security) are available to effectively counter the threat."[131] So, while Gen. McChrystal seemed to recognize a commander's right to unit self-defense, the Tactical Directive contained no indicia of a *soldier's right* to individual self-defense.

Within a month of publishing his Tactical Directive, Gen. McChrystal issued his ISAF Commander's Counterinsurgency (COIN) Guidance.[132] His key points were to embrace the people of Afghanistan,

---

[127] *Id.*
[128] *Tactical Directive, supra* note 122.
[129] Karl Gotthardt, *New Rules of Engagement Issued to NATO Forces by Gen McChrystal*, NOWPUBLIC, (July 2, 2009, 2:10 PM) http://www.nowpublic.com/world/new-rules-engagement-issued-nato-forces-gen-mcchrystal.
[130] *Id.*
[131] *Tactical Directive, supra* note 122.
[132] Counterinsurgency, or COIN, is a military doctrine employed to defeat an insurgency. DEP'T OF ARMY, FIELD MANUAL 3-24, COUNTERINSURGENCY x (2006) ("COIN campaigns are often long and difficult. Progress can be hard to measure, and the enemy may appear to have many advantages. Effective insurgents rapidly adapt to changing circumstances. They cleverly use the tools of the global information revolution to magnify the effects of their actions. They often carry out barbaric acts and do not observe accepted norms of behavior. However, by focusing on efforts to secure the safety and support of the local populace, and through a concerted effort to truly function as learning organizations, the Army and Marine Corps can defeat their insurgent enemies."); *see also* Michael T. Hall and Stanley A. McChrystal, *ISAF Commander's Counterinsurgency Guidance*, ISAF (Aug. 2009), http://www.nato.int/isaf/docu/official_texts/counterinsurgency_guidance.pdf.

partner with the ANSF, help develop the government's capacity and accountability, and to "get better every day."[133] Building on the strategy laid out in his Tactical Directive, Gen. McChrystal reiterated the importance of winning the support of the Afghan people with every action taken by the military.[134] "Protecting the Afghan people is the mission."[135] He stressed the need for the military to see things through the eyes of the people, to protect them from violence and intimidation, while operating in a way that respected their religion and culture.[136]

According to Gen. McChrystal, to succeed in a COIN fight, the military would have to abandon a conventional approach which he believed could be self-defeating.[137] Because insurgents hide amongst the Afghan people, taking the fight to them with aggressive offensive tactics significantly raises the risks of civilian casualties and collateral damage.[138] These secondary effects increase support for the insurgents and even "create[] more willing recruits" to the insurgency.[139] Gen. McChrystal noted that the U.S. could "not win simply by killing insurgents."[140] He recognized the challenges of changing the mindset of how military personnel typically think.

Perhaps one of the more illustrative examples of the impact of Gen. McChrystal's ROE was the ambush in the village of Ganjgal in September 2009. Four Marines, eight Afghan troops, and an interpreter were killed in eastern Afghanistan during that firefight, which lasted several hours.[141] A U.S. journalist embedded with the Marines reported

---

[133] DEP'T OF ARMY, FIELD MANUAL 3-24, COUNTERINSURGENCY x (2006).
[134] Id.
[135] Id.
[136] Id.
[137] Id.
[138] Hall & McChrystal, *supra* note 132.
[139] Id.
[140] Id.
[141] *Report: Marines Killed in Ambush Denied Support*, MARINE CORPS TIMES (Sept. 10, 2009, 9:53 AM), http://www.marinecorpstimes.com/news/2009/09/marine_ambush_090909w/; *see also* Bill Roggio, *4 Marines, 9 Afghan Troops Killed in Kunar Ambush*, THREAT MATRIX: A BLOG OF THE LONG WAR JOURNAL (Sept. 9, 2009, 12:49 PM), http://www.longwarjournal.org/threat-matrix/archives/2009/09/4_marines_9_afghans_troops_kil.php ("Yesterday's ambush in

that the unit "walked into a trap, a killing zone of relentless gunfire and rocket barrages from Afghan insurgents hidden in the mountainsides and in a fortress-like village where women and children were replenishing their ammunition."[142] The Marines requested artillery support to counter the enemy ambush, but the requests were repeatedly denied by their commanders who feared the artillery would inflict civilian casualties.[143] Although the Pentagon refuted the idea that artillery support was denied because of Gen. McChrystal's Tactical Directive, during the investigation of the incident, one of the officers under investigation stated that fire support was denied "for various reasons including: lack of situational awareness of locations of friendly elements [and] proximity to the village."[144]

This was not an isolated incident. In another situation, a unit was being hit with mortar fire while conducting a nighttime mission.[145] A request was made for a 155 millimeter illumination artillery round[146] in order to reveal the location of the enemy.[147] The unit reported that the request was denied "on the grounds that it may cause collateral

---

the eastern Afghan province of Kunar will certainly raise additional questions about the restrictive rules of engagement (ROE).... The Afghan and US troops were denied artillery and air support that could have suppressed the heavy Taliban fire that was raining down from the slopes.").

[142] Jonathan S. Landay, *'We're Pinned Down:' 4 U.S. Marines Die in Afghan Ambush*, McCLATCHY (Sept. 8, 2009) [hereinafter *4 U.S. Marines Die in Afghan Ambush*], http://www.mcclatchydc.com/2009/09/08/75036/were-pinned- down-4-us-marines.html.

[143] *Report: Marines Killed in Ambush Denied Support*, supra note 141; *see also 4 U.S. Marines Die in Afghan Ambush*, supra note 142 ("U.S. commanders, citing new rules to avoid civilian casualties, rejected repeated calls to unleash artillery rounds at attackers dug into the slopes and tree lines – despite being told repeatedly that they weren't near the village.").

[144] Jonathan S. Landay, *Officers Blamed in Afghan Ambush that Killed 5 U.S. Troops*, McCLATCHY (Feb. 17, 2010), http://www.mcclatchydc.com/2010/02/17/85883/xxxx.html.

[145] George F. Will, *An NCO Recognizes a Flawed Afghanistan Strategy*, WASH. POST June 20, 2010.

[146] U.S. DEP'T OF ARMY, FIELD MANUAL 3-09 p. 2-16, *available at* http://armypubs.army.mil/doctrine/DR_pubs/dr_a/pdf/fm3_09.pdf. An illumination artillery round detonates in the air and is designed to emit light in order for soldiers on the ground to observe people or objects obscured by the darkness. It is not designed to be used as an offensive weapon.

[147] Will, *supra* note 145.

damage."[148] One non-commissioned officer from the unit was baffled since "the only thing that comes down from an illumination round is a canister, and the likelihood of it hitting someone or something was akin to that of being struck by lightning."[149]

The same NCO also recalled a mission where his unit again came under heavy gunfire and was attacked with rocket-propelled grenades (RPGs). When the unit sent a radio request for artillery support, they were asked by higher command where the closest civilian structure was.[150] Having been denied the request, the NCO later commented, "[j]udging distances . . . can be difficult when bullets and RPGs are flying over your head."[151] The unit then requested smoke artillery rounds to be fired to screen their position. Higher command granted this request. However, fearful of collateral damage, they had the round deliberately aimed one kilometer away from the requested site, rendering the "smoke mission useless and leaving [them] to fend for [them]selves."[152]

Despite initial reports of success in reducing CIVCAS,[153] Gen. McChrystal faced much criticism for imposing ROE that many felt were too restrictive and placed troops at greater risk of harm.[154] Criticism also

---

[148] Id.
[149] Id.
[150] See id.
[151] Id.
[152] Id.
[153] Laura King, *New Tactics Cut Afghan Fatalities*, L.A. TIMES, Aug. 28, 2009, at A20 ("Western troops have killed far fewer Afghan civilians since the top U.S. general imposed strict new rules of engagement aimed at addressing one of the contentious issues of the conflict . . . . Military officials credit the marked decrease to a tactical directive issued July 2 by Gen. Stanley A. McChrystal . . . .").
[154] C.J. Chivers, *Warriors Vexed by Rules for War*, N.Y. TIMES, June 23, 2010, at A11 [hereinafter *Warriors Vexed by Rules for War*]. Indicative of the sentiment of many of the troops, a soldier being interviewed for the article stated the following: "I wish we had generals who remembered what it was like when they were down in a platoon . . . . Either they never have been in real fighting, or they forgot what it's like." Id. See also Marc Schenker, *Under Obama, Rules of Engagement in Afghan War Are Extreme Political Correctness Which Slow Down US Troops*, ASSOCIATED CONTENT, Feb. 10, 2010, http://www.associatedcontent.com/article/2719863/under_obama_rules_of_engagement_in.html?cat=75 (reporting statements from service members that the rules of engagement are overly restrictive and cause "[t]he problem [of] isolating where the enemy is").

came from those who believed the ROE were a product of "extreme political correctness" from the Obama administration.[155]

Another criticism of Gen. McChrystal's strict ROE was that by reducing the risks to civilians, the Taliban gained a strategic advantage.[156] One Army Major observed that prior to the ROE being constricted by Gen. McChrystal, firefights were often brief, typically lasting thirty minutes.[157] The Taliban would ambush U.S. forces and quickly flee the area knowing that additional firepower would likely be called in.[158] Under the ROE implemented by Gen. McChrystal, however, the process for requesting fire support or CAS became more difficult, and was only authorized under very limited conditions. The Taliban became aware of this and "seem[ed] noticeably less worried about an American response" to their ambush attacks.[159] As a result, firefights became considerably longer in duration, increasing exposure of troops to Taliban small arms fire.[160] When CAS was available, it was often of little help because pilots were also bounded by the ROE restrictions regardless of what ground troops were communicating to the pilots.[161] Pilots were prohibited from attacking fixed targets unless they could visually confirm from their aircraft the enemy firing on U.S. or Coalition Forces.[162] In some of these situations, patrol leaders adopted the absurd tactic of having their soldiers briefly expose themselves to the enemy in an attempt to draw fire

---

[155] Schenker, *supra* note 154 ("Retired Major General Scales ... [made] the long-overdue point that the rules of engagement under Obama are 'overly restrictive' and that they go too far ....").

[156] *Warriors Vexed by Rules for War*, *supra* note 154 ("Some rules meant to enshrine counterinsurgency principles into daily practices, they say, do not merely transfer risks away from civilians. They transfer risks away from the Taliban.").

[157] *Id.*

[158] *Id.*

[159] *Id.*

[160] *Id.* ("One Marine infantry lieutenant ... said he had all but stopped seeking air support while engaged in firefights. He spent too much time on the radio trying to justify its need, he said, and the aircraft never arrived or they arrived too late or the pilots were reluctant to drop their ordnance.").

[161] *Id.*

[162] *Warriors Vexed by Rules for War*, *supra* note 154.

from the enemy.[163] Only after a visual confirmation of attacking insurgents could the pilot then engage the enemy.[164]

The principle espoused in Gen. McChrystal's Tactical Directive and COIN Guidance has been referred to as "courageous restraint." Those who support these policies argued that soldiers "[should] refrain from using lethal force, even at risk to themselves, in order to prevent possible harm to civilians."[165] In April 2010, the NATO commander of troops in southern Afghanistan, British Maj. Gen. Nick Carter, suggested the creation of a new medal to be awarded to troops who demonstrate "courageous restraint" on the battlefield.[166] In his opinion, "courageous restraint" should be viewed as "an act of discipline and courage not much different than those seen in combat actions."[167] Some viewed Maj. Gen. Carter's proposal as an effective way of reducing CIVCAS by providing an incentive for troops to "think twice before calling in an airstrike or firing at an approaching vehicle if civilians could be at risk."[168] Others, however, responded with an immediate negative reaction, believing that the creation of such a commendation could place soldiers in even more danger.[169] Lt. Gen. Sir Nick Parker, the United Kingdom's top general in Afghanistan at the time, acknowledged that the rules for engaging Taliban insurgents needed to be "re-examined" following protests from soldiers that the rules were too restrictive.[170] In an interview, he

---

[163] *Id.*

[164] *Id.*

[165] Chris Carter, *NATO's Contemptible "Courageous Restraint" Medal*, HUMAN EVENTS, May 18, 2010, *available at* http://www.humanevents.com/article.php?id=37012.

[166] Sebastian Abbot, *A Medal for 'Courageous Restraint'? NATO Seeks To Avoid Killing Afghan Noncombatants*, ASSOCIATED PRESS, May 4, 2010 *available at* http://www.cleveland.com/world/index.ssf/2010/05/a_medal_for_courageous_restrai.html.

[167] *Id.*

[168] J.P. Freire, *NATO Rewarding "Courageous Restraint" Awards*, WASH. EXAMINER, May 9, 2010, *available at* http://washingtonexaminer.com/article/3997.

[169] *See* William H. McMichael, *Hold Fire, Earn a Medal*, MARINE CORPS TIMES, May 11, 2010, *available at* http://www.marinecorpstimes.com/news/2010/05/military_restraint_medal_051110mar; Chris Carter, *NATO's Contemptible "Courageous Restraint" Medal*, HUMAN EVENTS, May 18, 2010, *available at* http://www.humanevents.com/article.php?id=37012.

[170] Thomas Harding, *Britain's Top General in Afghanistan Admits "Courageous Restraint" Must Change*, THE TELEGRAPH (July 11, 2010),

suggested that troops in more hostile regions should be able to use "all the tools at their disposal."[171] Critical of "courageous restraint," Lt. Gen. Parker noted that with regards to the ROE policy, NATO leadership had "over-corrected" and now the ROE should be brought back in line without alienating the population.[172] He recognized the importance of ensuring that troops "have the right degree of manouevre on operations to deal with the circumstances they face."[173] As discussed in the next section, at least one other general shared Lt. Gen. Parker's concerns.

2. The Rules of Engagement under General David Petraeus

In June 2010, after one year of command, President Obama relieved Gen. McChrystal of his command in Afghanistan.[174] Gen. McChrystal was replaced by his boss and mentor, Gen. David Petraeus.[175] Prior to taking command in Afghanistan, Gen. Petraeus commanded Multi-National Force-Iraq. Prior to that command, he was the commander of the U.S. Army Combined Arms Center at Fort Leavenworth, where he oversaw the development of the Army/Marine Corps Counterinsurgency Manual.[176]

Like Gen. McChrystal, Gen. Petraeus also issued Tactical Directives shortly after assuming command in Afghanistan.[177] Gen. Petraeus's Tactical Directives are also classified; however, the unclassified portions reveal that the central concept of his Tactical Directive was "disciplined use of force" and not "courageous restraint".[178] Gen.

---

http://www.telegraph.co.uk/news/worldnews/asia/afghanistan/7884017/Britains-top-general-in-Afghanistan-admits-courageous-restraint-must-change.html.
[171] Id.
[172] Id.
[173] Id.
[174] Helene Cooper & David E. Sanger, *Obama Fires Afghan Commander, Citing Need for Unity in the War*, N.Y. TIMES, June 24, 2010, at A1.
[175] Id.
[176] Thom Shankner, *Win Wars? Today's General Must Also Meet, Manage, Placate, Politick and Do P.R.*, N.Y. TIMES, Aug. 13, 2010, at A11.
[177] *General Petraeus Issues Updated Tactical Directive: Emphasizes "Disciplined Use of Force"*, ISAF RELEASES, Aug. 1, 2010, *available at* http://www.isaf.nato.int/article/isaf-releases/general-petraeus-issues-updated-tactical-directive-emphasizes-disciplined-use-of-force.html.
[178] Id.

Petraeus's Directive does not suggest that there is any downside to killing the enemy. He noted that "[p]rotecting the Afghan people does require killing, capturing, or turning the insurgents."[179] Coalition forces must continue to pursue the Taliban tenaciously, so long as the fight is conducted "with great discipline and tactical patience."[180] Gen. Petraeus added that all assets must be used to protect military personnel and the Afghan security forces.[181] Troops must be given the confidence to "take all necessary actions when it matters most."[182] More importantly, unlike Gen. McChrystal, Gen. Petraeus alluded to the inherent right of individual self-defense: "All commanders must reinforce the right and obligation of self-defense of coalition forces, of our Afghan partners, and of others as authorized by the rules of engagement."[183] This strong language promoting the use of force to defeat the enemy and the right of self-defense was balanced with renewed efforts to prevent civilian casualties.

Gen. Petraeus articulated to his subordinates the need to balance the "relentless pursuit of the Taliban and others who mean Afghanistan harm . . . [with] compassion for the Afghan people."[184] Believing the Afghan people to be the "center of gravity in this struggle," he emphasized that "[e]very Afghan civilian death diminishes our cause."[185] He noted the "moral imperative both to protect Afghan civilians and . . . bring all assets to bear to protect our men and women in uniform."[186] Gen. Petraeus believed that the best way to accomplish this was by partnering Coalition Forces with Afghan forces. Noting that "[s]ome civilian casualties result from a misunderstanding or ignorance of local customs and behaviors," Gen. Petraeus believed that partnering with Afghan forces could help generate greater situational awareness and improve relations between coalition forces and the Afghan populace.[187]

---

[179] *Id.* (emphasis added).
[180] *Id.*
[181] *Id.*
[182] *Id.*
[183] *General Petraeus Issues Updated Tactical Directive: Emphasizes "Disciplined Use of Force"*, *supra* note 177.
[184] *Id.*
[185] *Id.*
[186] *Id.*
[187] *Id.*

To sum up his goal of combining an aggressive pursuit of the enemy with a reduction of civilian casualties, Gen. Petraeus concluded: "Take the fight to the enemy. And protect the Afghan people and help our Afghan partners defeat the insurgency."[188]

The only specific Rule of Engagement published in the unclassified version of Gen. Petraeus's Tactical Directive pertained to the use of artillery:

> Prior to the use of fires, the commander approving the strike must determine that no civilians are present. If unable to assess the risk of civilian presence, fires are prohibited, except under [one] of the following two conditions (specific conditions deleted due to operational security; however, they have to do with the risk to ISAF and Afghan forces).
>
> (NOTE) This directive, as with the previous version, does not prevent commanders from protecting the lives of their men and women as a matter of self-defense where it is determined no other options are available to effectively counter the threat.[189]

It is apparent that Gen. Petraeus was concerned with a repeat of the fatal situations discussed earlier, where troops were denied support and could not defend themselves. The verbiage in Gen. Petraeus's Tactical Directive demonstrated his commitment to balancing protection of the force with protection of the civilian population. The Directive also demonstrated that it sought to prevent conflicts in the interpretation of the ROE experienced under Gen. McChrystal. Although the conditions for the use of artillery was redacted in the unclassified version of the Tactical Directive, one can infer that commanders now had greater authority to use fire support assets during operations if the risk to the force caused troops to invoke their inherent right to self-defense.

In conjunction with his Tactical Directive, Gen. Petraeus also published his COIN Guidance for all NATO, ISAF, and U.S. Forces in

---

[188] *Id.*
[189] *General Petraeus Issues Updated Tactical Directive: Emphasizes "Disciplined Use of Force", supra* note 177.

Afghanistan.[190] Gen. Petraeus reiterated his objective of protecting the Afghan people, again referring to them as the "center of gravity."[191] This was the first objective listed among several and clearly the most important. However, he also realized the importance of empowering the warfighter to use force to achieve these objectives. "Pursue the enemy relentlessly . . . get our teeth into the insurgents and don't let go. When the extremists fight, make them pay. Seek out and eliminate those who threaten the population."[192] As long as soldiers and Marines were fighting with discipline, Gen. Petraeus encouraged the use of force if it was vital to mission accomplishment. "Fight hard and fight with discipline. Hunt the enemy aggressively, but use only the firepower needed to win a fight. We can't win without fighting, but we also cannot kill or capture our way to victory."[193]

3. Differences between Gen. Petraeus's and Gen. McChrystal's Rules of Engagement Policies

Although Gen. Petraeus clearly endorsed the importance of preventing civilian casualties, the language in his Tactical Directive and his COIN Guidance differs from Gen. McChrystal's in several aspects. While Gen. McChrystal downplayed the importance of killing the enemy, Gen. Petraeus recognized the importance of pursuing the enemy with a controlled aggression – aggression that could be balanced with achieving the military objectives of winning the support of the Afghan people. A British officer who worked with Gen. Petraeus compared the two approaches as follows: "Gen. McChrystal imposed courageous restraint as a mantra whereas the big theme of Gen. Petraeus was a strategic patience."[194] This is more than just semantics. While "courageous restraint" was interpreted as a passive approach that placed troops in considerable danger, Gen. Petraeus's message was to use a slow strategic

---

[190] Gen. Petraeus, *COMISAF's Counterinsurgency Guidance*, (Aug. 1, 2010), *available at* http://graphics.nytimes.com/packages/pdf/world/2010/COMISAF-MEMO.pdf.
[191] *Id.*
[192] *Id.*
[193] *Id.*
[194] Toby Harnden & Damien McElroy, *Gen. David Petraeus To Review "Courageous Restraint"*, THE TELEGRAPH, June 24, 2010, http://www.telegraph.co.uk/news/worldnews/northamerica/usa/barackobama/7852684/Gen-David-Petraeus-to-review-courageous-restraint.html.

build up to get all elements in place, while at the same time prizing the importance of momentum by taking the fight to the insurgents hiding amongst the people.[195]

From a legal perspective, both Generals' ROEs complied with CJCSI 3121.01B, which bestows upon commanders, not individuals, the inherent right and obligation to exercise unit self-defense. However, Gen. McChrystal's command prevented troops from shooting the enemy if there was a risk to civilians and promoted a sense of restricted use of force. These factors combined to create an environment that encouraged commanders to violate the rule that required them to implement self-defense measures when no other options existed to counter the threat to the unit. Even though Gen. McChrystal's Tactical Directive was not intended to deprive commanders of their right to protect the lives of the men and women in their unit, as demonstrated above, numerous situations arose where legitimate requests for air support and artillery were denied by commanders despite the fact that troops requesting it were in harm's way and there was little or no threat to civilians on the battlefield.

The ROE under Gen. Petraeus were consistent with the general principles of self-defense as recognized by case law and U.S. policy in place since the time of Daniel Webster.[196] Gen. Petraeus's Tactical Directive and COIN Guidance, which allowed troops to "take all necessary actions when it matters most," and authorized the use of "firepower needed to win a fight," resonates with Webster's position that the principle of necessity should be applied to all actions in self-defense when the defensive act must be "instant, overwhelming, and leaving no choice of means, and no moment for deliberation."[197] Therefore, as long as the commanders on the battlefield made a determination based on all facts and circumstances known on the battlefield that the use of force was necessary to defend their units, their actions would be deemed legal under the ROE and the law of war.

---

[195] *See id.*
[196] Letter of Secretary of State Daniel Webster to Lord Ashburton (Aug. 6, 1842), *available at* http://avalon.law.yale.edu/19th_century/br-1842d.asp.
[197] *Tactical Directive, supra* note 122; Gen. Petraeus, *COMISAF's Counterinsurgency Guidance, supra* note 190 (emphasis added).

The military leaders in charge in Afghanistan on September 8, 2009, either failed in their assessment or felt the ROE prevented them from providing the necessary response. Although Gen. McChrystal's ROE endorsed the commander's right and obligation of self-defense, the commanders in Ganjgal that day exercised what they believed was their right to deny troops needed support, despite numerous request from lower ranking troops, even though CJCSI 2121.01B specifically states that the assessment of whether or not force is required for unit self-defense "may be made at any level."[198] Unfortunately, a commander's right to exercise self-defense, as described in Gen. McChrystal's ROE, was overshadowed by the idea that holding fire was a better approach. The examples discussed in this paper suggest that military leaders had taken "courageous restraint" too far and denied troops CAS and artillery support when it was clearly necessary. Gen. Petraeus recognized this shortcoming and adjusted the ROE appropriately.

Both Gen. McChrystal and Gen. Petraeus believed that preventing civilian casualties was critical to the success of the mission in Afghanistan. COIN doctrine requires winning the support of the people in order defeat an insurgency. If civilians are constantly being killed, it will be difficult to win that support. To help minimize the impact of the Afghan war on civilians, the Human Rights Unit of the United Nations Assistance Mission in Afghanistan (UNAMA HR) compiled a report on CIVCAS in Afghanistan to "monitor the situation of civilians, to coordinate efforts to ensure their protection, to promote accountability and to assist in full implementation of the fundamental freedoms and human rights provisions of the Afghan Constitution and international treaties to which Afghanistan is a State party."[199]

From July 2008 to April 2009, ISAF caused twenty-eight percent of civilian deaths in Afghanistan.[200] This was the highest rate of ISAF

---

[198] CJCSI 3121.01 B, *supra* note 36.
[199] United Nations Assistance Mission in Afghanistan (UNAMA), *Afghanistan: Report on Protection of Civilians in Armed Conflicts, Mid Year Report 2010* (Aug. 2010), *available at* http://www.unhcr.org/refworld/docid/4c6120382.html.
[200] Anthony H. Cordesman & Arleigh A. Burke, *The Afghan-Pakistan War: Status in 2009*, CTR. FOR STRATEGIC & INT'L STUDIES, Apr. 12, 2009, *available at* http://csis.org/files/090701_status_of_2009.pdf.

caused civilian deaths for the prior two years[201] and a likely contributor to the issuance of Gen. McChrystal's Tactical Directive in July 2009. If the goal of the Tactical Directive was simply to reduce CIVCAS numbers, then it was a success. By June 2010, civilian casualties caused by Pro-Government Forces (PGF) decreased by thirty percent compared to the first six months of 2009.[202] Additionally, civilian deaths attributed to PGF aerial attacks had decreased by sixty-four percent compared to the same period in 2009.[203] These numbers did not, however, lead to a more stable Afghanistan, nor was life safer for civilians as one might erroneously conclude.

By June 2010, despite the successes of ISAF in lowering CIVCAS-related incidents, overall injuries and deaths to civilians had actually increased by thirty-one percent compared with the same period in 2009.[204] This was due to the increased activity of Anti-Government Elements (AGEs).[205] More than seventy-five percent of all civilian casualties were caused by AGEs, a fifty-three percent increase from 2009.[206] Where PGF-caused deaths had decreased by twenty-nine percent from 2009, AGEs increased their killings to 920 in the first half of 2010—a forty-nine percent increase from the prior year.[207] There was also a sharp increase in AGE-caused deaths of women and children.[208]

---

[201] *Id.*
[202] Pro-Government Forces (PGF) is a term used by the United Nations to describe all Afghan Government forces, including Afghan Army and Afghan National Police, as well as all International Military Forces, including US and NATO forces. *Afghanistan: Report on Protection of Civilians in Armed Conflicts, Mid Year Report 2010, supra* note 199.
[203] *Id.* at i.
[204] *Id.*
[205] Anti-Government Elements "encompass all individuals and groups currently involved in armed conflict against the Government of Afghanistan and/or International Military Forces. They include those who identify as 'Taliban' as well as individuals and groups motivated by a range of objectives and assuming a variety of labels." *Id.*
[206] *Id.*
[207] *Id.*
[208] "UNAMA HR recorded 39 women and 74 child deaths as a result of both IED explosions and suicide attacks in the first half of 2010. This is a 44 per cent increase in deaths of women and 155 per cent increase in child deaths compared to the same period in 2009." *Afghanistan: Report on Protection of Civilians in Armed Conflicts, Mid Year Report 2010, supra* note 199, at 10.

Taliban and insurgent forces increased their use of improvised explosive devices (IEDs),[209] suicide attacks,[210] and intimidation tactics.[211]

Not only was Afghanistan less safe for civilians in 2010 compared to 2009, but Coalition Forces also suffered greater casualties. For the first six months of 2010, NATO troops suffered 323 fatalities.[212] That was a 105% increase from the same period in 2009.[213] For the entire year of 2010, there were 711 fatalities, up from 521 in all of 2009.[214] While the ROE adjustments may have decreased CIVCAS incidents caused by Coalition Forces, overall civilian casualties were up due to increased Taliban and insurgent activity. Troop fatality rates increased as well. The stricter ROE were ineffective at reducing civilian casualties, and seem, instead, to have increased them by allowing the enemy to exploit an over-disciplined force.

CONCLUSION

Since the early days of American military combat, the principle of self-defense has been recognized as an inherent right, rooted in nature and impervious to societal influences. Many States have acknowledged this right in their own courts and constitutions, and as a nation it has been adopted as a standard in the U.S.'s understanding of international law. Although the U.S. Military seems to have limited the right at the individual level, at the unit level it is not only the right of a commander, but it is an obligation to be exercised in defense of the unit. This right and obligation have become critical elements to the ROE, and only

---

[209] "IEDs kill and injure more civilians than any other tactic used in the conflict. . . . IEDS accounted for 374 (29 per cent) of the total number of civilian deaths in the first six months of 2010 . . . ." *Id.* at 2.

[210] "In the first six months of 2010, 183 civilians died as a result of suicide attacks . . . . These figures reflect an increase of 20 percent from the same period in 2009 and an increase of 43 per cent from the last half of 2009." *Id.* at 3.

[211] "AGEs greatly intensified their intimidation campaign against supporters, or those perceived to be supportive of the Government and the international community. The campaign included abductions, assassinations and executions of civilians and Government officials." *Id.* at 6.

[212] *Operation Enduring Freedom, Fatalities by Year and Month*, ICASUALTIES.ORG, http://icasualties.org/OEF/ByMonth.aspx (last visited Dec. 29, 2012).

[213] *Id.*

[214] *Id.*

through adherence to the foundational principles of the law of war can the ROE be implemented to ensure the safety of troops on the battlefield and serve to prevent civilian casualties.

In the COIN environment of Afghanistan, the ROE were altered in an attempt to reduce civilian casualties. In retrospect, it is apparent that this unfortunately was done at the expense of the troops' ability to defend themselves. Gen. McChrystal's ROE minimized the inherent right of self-defense as defined by the United Nations and prior versions of the SROE, and that are supported by the foundational principles of the law of war. While the strict ROE and the concept of "courageous restraint" were initially successful at reducing civilian casualties caused by U.S. and NATO forces, the total number of civilian casualties actually increased due to greater insurgent activity. Additionally, soldiers and Marines, like those in Ganjgal, consistently found themselves in positions of greater danger while their commanders refrained from providing them with the necessary support in order to uphold the ROE. As seen in the incidents discussed in this article, artillery support and CAS were often denied to troops attempting to invoke their inherent right to self-defense and lives were lost as insurgents won small victories in prolonged firefights.

In the summary of his investigation into the ambush in Ganjgal, Col. Hooker stated: "[t]he events of 8 September 2009 . . . reinforce the principle that when in doubt, our bias must be to support troops in contact."[215] Under the command of Gen. Petraeus, implementation of the ROE that ensured compliance with the law of war and protected innocent civilians from the violence of armed conflict was attainable without depriving warfighters of their right to self-defense. By partnering with Afghan forces, pursuing the enemy aggressively, and renewing efforts to reduce civilian casualties through tactical patience, Gen. Petraeus was able to use the ROE to achieve military objectives. Furthermore, he was able to accomplish this while also allowing the U.S. to achieve its political and legal objectives during combat operations

---

[215] AR 15-6 Report of Investigation into Operations in the Ganjgal Valley, Konar Province, Afghanistan, 8 September 2009 (Nov. 25, 2009), *available at* http://www.captainsjournal.com/2010/02/19/ar-15-6-investigation-of-marine-deaths-in-kunar-province/.

without compromising the safety of the troops responsible for executing the mission.

THE ADVENT AND FUTURE OF INTERNATIONAL PORT SECURITY LAW

L. Stephen Cox[*]

Awakened to the inherent vulnerability of ships and seaports to the twenty-first century brand of terrorism, the global seafaring community is largely putting aside regional, political, and ideological differences to devise a new international legal framework to safeguard world shipping interests, protect coastal populations from the threat of surreptitious seaborne attack, and to assure trading partners of ship and cargo security. The first iteration of the world-wide effort to regulate port security is codified in a document authorized by amendment to the 1974 United Nations Convention on Safety of Life at Sea ("SOLAS"),[1] called the International Ship and Port Facility Security ("ISPS") Code.[2] Originally adopted to promote mariners' welfare, SOLAS set forth rules for the construction and navigation of ships engaged in international

---

[*] L. Stephen Cox, United States Coast Guard International Port Security Program; LL.M - Admiralty, Tulane University School of Law; J.D., Loyola University New Orleans School of Law; M.A., University of South Florida; B.A., University of South Florida. The opinions expressed in this Article are solely the views of the author and do not reflect the position of the United States Coast Guard.
[1] International Convention for the Safety of Life at Sea, Nov. 1, 1974, 32 U.S.T. 47, 1184 U.N.T.S. 276 (entered into force May 25, 1980) [hereinafter SOLAS].
[2] *See*, IMO Doc. SOLAS/CONF.5/34, annex 1 (Dec. 12, 2002) [hereinafter ISPS Code] (providing resolution 2 of the Dec. 2002 conference containing the ISPS Code). The ISPS Code is implemented through chapter XI-2 of SOLAS. *See* SOLAS, *supra* note 2, at ch. XI-2.

trade.[3] Pursuant to a 2002 amendment, SOLAS signatories were required to implement the provisions of the Code and self-certify compliance by July 1, 2004.[4] Since then, as participating nations recognize opportunities to improve upon ISPS Code's basic tenets, they continue to refine the regulations in their own bodies of laws. Participating governments have established programs to coordinate the international application of ISPS regulations. Using a wide array of legislative devices such as treaties, statutes, regulations, rules, executive orders, and royal decrees, the world's maritime nations have spontaneously created an entire field of international maritime law—where none existed before.

This article considers the conditions giving rise to international port security law and the subsequent and future legislative and regulatory evolution of international port security law. This article weighs the regulatory influence of the ISPS Code from the United States' perspective and will consider five main issues of port security law. First, to what degree is global port security constrained by self-imposed regulatory gaps in the ISPS Code? Second, how have SOLAS signatory nations addressed and corrected regulatory deficiencies arising from these gaps? Third, how has the United States addressed the jurisdictional challenges resulting from the ISPS Code and from maritime law in general? Fourth, to what extent have ISPS Code regulation protocols given rise to unforeseen legal uncertainties involving jurisdictional infringement, trade agreement adherence, evidentiary procedures, criminal prosecutions, contractual obligations, and tort litigation? Finally, how can maritime nations continue to improve and strengthen the international port security legal regime?

In order to enhance the international port security legal regime, this article then proposes that the United Nation's International Maritime Organization ("IMO") develop an advanced international port security regulatory model. This advanced port security regulatory model will promote international cooperation, facilitate information sharing, and elevate the global port security regulatory discussion above and

---

[3] SOLAS, *supra* note 2, preamble.
[4] *Id.*

beyond the existing ISPS Code minimum standard. This, in turn, will improve global security.

I. BACKGROUND

Marine insurance giant Lloyd's of London estimates that approximately 112,000 merchant vessels comprising the contemporary maritime shipping industry[5] link the world's 11,892 international port facilities in 155 coastal nations, dependent territories, and island states. Roughly half a billion containers are dispatched to the seas each year and one in nine of these containers are bound for the United States.[6] Annually, U.S. ports handle in excess of 50,000 international vessel arrivals, receiving almost ten million containers by sea transport, along with hundreds of millions of tons of liquid and bulk cargo.[7] Due to the sheer size and complexity of maritime transit based commerce, the U.S. Transportation Security Administration and Federal Bureau of Investigation have identified the global shipping network as the most viable and logistically feasible conduit to move a terrorist organization's weapons and operatives to the United States.[8]

The overwhelming flow of container cargo entering the United States by sea makes unilateral security oversight virtually impossible. Security checks of marine imports at U.S. points of entry are negligible

---

[5] Peter Chalk, *Maritime Terrorism: The Threat to Container Ships, Cruise Liners, and Passenger Ferries, in* LLOYD'S MIU HANDBOOK OF MARITIME SECURITY 117, 118 (Rupert Herbert-Burnes et al., eds., 2009).

[6] BUREAU OF TRANSP. STATISTICS, U.S. DEP'T OF TRANSP., AMERICA'S CONTAINER PORTS: DELIVERING THE GOODS (2007), *available at*
http://www.rita.dot.gov/bts/sites/rita.dot.gov.bts/files/publications/americas_container_ports/2007/pdf/entire.pdf. The American portion of world maritime trade is close to twenty percent. The American portion of world maritime trade is close to twenty percent. *See* Maritime Commerce Security Plan for the National Strategy for Maritime Security, June 28, 2005, pp 3-4.

[7] *The State of Maritime Security: Hearing Before the S. Comm. on Commerce, Science & Transp.*, 108th Cong. 2 (2004) (statement of Admiral Thomas H. Collins, Commandant, U.S. Coast Guard, Robert C. Bonner, Comm'r, Customs & Border Protection & Admiral David M. Stone, Acting Adm'r, Transp. Sec. Admin.).

[8] *Security Challenges for Transportation of Cargo: Hearing Before the S. Subcomm. of the Comm. on Appropriations.*, 107th Cong. (2002) (prepared statement of John MaGaw, Undersecretary of Transp. for Sec.).

and only about ten percent of containers and bulk cargos are subject to scrutiny.[9] Even then, a security "screening" may consist only of the computer reconciliation of cargo manifests and bills of lading. Further compounding the issue, the supply chain is frighteningly porous. Stretching from manufacturer to consumer, the supply chain winds through a frequently unvetted shipper, then exporter, importer, freight forwarder, customs broker, excise inspector, an uncleared dock worker, and a truck driver, a harbor feeder craft, an ocean carrier, and finally, it reaches the consumer. This long chain presents a myriad of opportunities for exploitation by terrorist groups. For example, terrorist groups are adept at defeating the rudimentary container locks and seals in current use by the shipping industry—and access to these containers are made easier by the porous nature of the chain.[10]

A. New Threats to International Maritime Security

The world is a different place than it was when the nineteenth century naval historian Alfred Thayer Mahan theorized that "(a)s a nation . . . launches forth from its own shores, the need is soon felt of points upon which the ships can rely for peaceful trading, for refuge and supplies. In the present day friendly, though foreign, ports are to be found all over the world; and their shelter is enough while peace prevails."[11] With the dawn of the twenty-first century, many maritime nations find this friendly shelter threatened by terrorists.

Evidence of the security challenges inherent to the modern shipping industry is plentiful. In October 2001, dockworkers in the southern Italian port of Gioia Tauro investigated unusual noises coming from a Canadian-bound container and found Rizik Amid Farid ("Farid") inside a well-appointed box. Farid, an Egyptian national and suspected al Qaeda member, was bearing communications devices, computers, maps, and an airline mechanic's certificate. The airline mechanic's certificate was valid for New York's JFK, Newark, Los Angeles

---

[9] Robert Block, *Security Gaps Already Plague Ports*, WALL ST. J., Feb. 23, 2006, at A12.
[10] Joshua Ho, *Managing Port and Ship Security in Singapore*, in LLOYD'S MIU HANDBOOK OF MARITIME SECURITY 307, 307-09 (Rupert Herbert-Burnes et al., eds., 2009).
[11] ALFRED THAYER MAHAN, THE INFLUENCE OF SEA POWER UPON HISTORY 27 (Dover Publications 1987) (1890).

International, and O'Hare Airports. After his arraignment and release on bond, the stowaway disappeared.[12] Soon after the September 11th attacks, Abdul Qadeer Khan ("Khan"), the founder of Pakistan's nuclear development program, stepped up covert nuclear assistance to known state sponsors of terrorism. Having previously provided clandestine technical assistance to Iran, Libya, and North Korea, Khan secretly arranged for the transport of nuclear production components by container ship to those countries from 2002 to 2003. When one of the ships was intercepted, Khan confessed his involvement, but the extent of the illicit container shipments remains unknown.[13] In December 2002, covert North Korean ballistic missile shipments were intercepted en route to Yemen.[14] In April 2005, Chinese human traffickers set up a fraudulent import/export company and outfitted a container with food, water, blankets, sleeping bags, circulation fans, and pre-cut egress holes. Twenty-nine people boarded the container and transited to the Port of Los Angeles, remaining undetected until they attempted to exit the port facility.[15]

Even when not specifically targeted, the global maritime supply chain can be profoundly impacted by terrorism. This was illustrated in the days following the September 11th attacks when the U.S. Customs Service ratcheted the standing port security posture to such a level that all ports of entry were effectively closed.[16] This halted import/export operations, severely impacted time sensitive manufacturing operations,

---

[12] John-Thor Dahlburg, *Guarding the Coast, and More; Already Protecting 95,000 Miles of Shoreline, the Smallest U.S. Military Branch Found Itself on the Homeland Defense Front Lines After Sept. 11*, L.A. TIMES, Apr. 13, 2002, at A1.

[13] Michael Laufer, *A.Q. Khan Nuclear Chronology*, 8 CARNEGIE ENDOWMENT FOR INTERNATIONAL PEACE 1, 7-8 (2005).

[14] Robert Marquand & Peter Ford, *A New Doctrine and a Scud Bust*, CHRISTIAN SCIENCE MONITOR, Dec. 12, 2002, at 1.

[15] MICHAEL MCNICHOLAS, MARITIME SECURITY: AN INTRODUCTION 184 (2008).

[16] *The Container Security Initiative and the Customs-Trade Partnership Against Terrorism: Securing the Global Supply Chain or Trojan Horse?: Hearing Before the Permanent Subcomm. On Investigations of the S. Comm. on Homeland Security & Governmental Affairs*, 109th Cong. (2005) (statement of Robert C. Bonner, Comm'r, Customs & Border Protection, U.S. Dep't of Homeland Security).

substantially hindered output in the heavy industrial sector, and disrupted a wide range of international commerce.[17]

Mirroring the U.S.'s reaction to September 11th, the international community immediately took action. The IMO's responsive development and imposition of maritime security requirements was conducted at a pace described as "mind-boggling."[18] In November 2001, the IMO scrambled to close the gaps in ship-to-port security made painfully obvious by the previous month's terrorist attacks. Seizing upon the malleable and already widely accepted SOLAS[19] as the speediest device to improve security, the IMO chose it as a means to standardize and give effect to a uniform list of ship and port facility security measures.[20] The twenty-seven year old SOLAS Convention was amended on December 12, 2002 to incorporate the ISPS Code, a newly minted set of maritime transportation security standards that could respond better to the threats posed by international terrorism.[21]

The stated objective of the ISPS Code was to "establish the new international framework of measures to enhance maritime security and through which ships and port facilities can co-operate to detect and deter acts which threaten security in the maritime transport sector."[22] The ISPS Code imposes basic security obligations upon international port

---

[17] Joseph L. Parks, *The United States-Canada Smart Border Action Plan: Life in the FAST Lane*, L. & BUS. REV. AM. 395, 399 (2004); *State of Maritime Security Hearing*, supra note 9 ("[A] terrorist incident against our marine transportation system would have a devastating and long-lasting impact on global shipping, international trade, and the world economy. Based on a recent unscheduled port security closure incident, a maritime terrorist act was estimated to cost up to $2 billion per day in economic loss to the United States.").
[18] Dennis L. Bryant, *Historical and Legal Aspects of Maritime Security*, 17 U.S.F. MAR. J.L. 1, 24 (2005).
[19] The United Nations Convention for the Suppression of Unlawful Acts Against Maritime Navigation also afforded means to address this issue. Convention for the Suppression of Unlawful Acts Against the Safety of Maritime Navigation, arts. 3-4, Mar. 10, 1988, 1678 U.N.T.S. 221 (defining a panoply of offenses pertaining to the terroristic use of ships either international transit, or ships in port and scheduled to be in international transit).
[20] ISPS Code, *supra* note 3, preamble, para 5.
[21] ISPS Code, *supra* note 3, foreword, p. iii.
[22] ISPS Code, *supra* note 3, part B, 1.1.

facilities and shipping interests of contracting governments and supplements those obligations with optional implementation guidance. Addressing the security responsibilities of the shipper and the port facility, the ISPS Code mandates: (1) security threat assessment; (2) the establishment of ship-to-port communications; (3) physical access restriction; (4) weapons and explosives interdiction; (5) security threat notification; (6) ship and port facility security assessment and planning; and (7) the performance of security training, drills, and exercises.[23] Complementing the mandatory provisions, the ISPS Code envisions more specific measures and arrangements needed to achieve and maintain compliance with the mandatory requirements,[24] particularly with respect to the protection of ships berthed within port facilities (i.e., the ship-to-port interface).[25]

B. *ISPS Code Limitations*

Though conceptually ambitious, the ISPS Code suffers from a number of built-in limitations[26] that undermine its ultimate effectiveness. First, as noted above, the ISPS Code is only partially mandatory. The mandatory portion constitutes only about a third of the Code, rendering it more of a port security primer lacking the application of meaningful port security measures. ISPS Code's optional portion delves into greater detail on the mechanics of security, but its implementation cannot be compelled. Second, even the mandatory security measures are restricted to ship-to-port interface.[27] Beyond the immediate boundaries of regulated wharves and piers, the international community makes no

---

[23] ISPS Code, *supra* note 3, part A, 1.3.
[24] ISPS Code, *supra* note 3, part B, 1.2, 1.4-1.5.
[25] ISPS Code, *supra* note 3, part B, 1.4 ("There could, however, be situations when a ship may pose a threat to the port facility, e.g. because, once within the port facility, it could be used as a base from which to launch an attack.").
[26] ISPS Code, *supra* note 3, preamble para. 5 ("[I]t was ... agreed that the provisions relating to port facilities should relate solely to the ship/port interface. The wider issue of security of port areas will be the subject of further joint work between the International Maritime Organization and the International Labour Organization. It was also agreed that the provisions should not extend to the actual response to attacks or to any necessary clean-up activities after such an attack.").
[27] *Id.*

demands.[28] Sprawling industrial zones immediately adjacent to many of the world's port facilities remain unregulated. Furthermore, the IMO specifically declined to address incident response procedures in the ISPS Code[29], which is of little help to developing nations and, by design, also completely fails to provide enforcement guidance. Standing alone, the ISPS Code is limited in scope because it is mostly suggestive, lacks meaningful security guidance, and is, as a practical matter, unenforceable.

C. *SOLAS 74: International Responses*

Enforceability issues aside, the philosophy behind the ISPS Code's universal port security scheme is based on twin precepts: to be effective, security measures must be initiated at the beginning of the supply chain (the production/loading phase) and it is easier to prevent a terrorist device from entering the supply chain than to detect it once it is there.[30] This modern cargo security methodology employs a chain-of-custody approach similar to the start-to-finish control of evidence in a criminal investigation.[31] In order to have the chain-of-custody approach within the global maritime trade, previously unheard of levels of international cooperation fostering heightened maritime security awareness are required. To this end, SOLAS's 2002 amendment pertaining to port security required all of the Convention's one hundred and fifty-five signatories to promulgate the individually applicable laws, decrees, orders, and regulations necessary to fully implement the fledgling ISPS Code[32] in their jurisdiction by July 1, 2004.[33] Although this initiative is meeting varying degrees of success, it promotes a compelling common objective, coupled with significant commercial incentives, and most maritime states have complied to the best of their respective abilities.

---

[28] *Id.*
[29] *Id.*
[30] MICHAEL MCNICHOLAS, MARITIME SECURITY: AN INTRODUCTION 135(2008).
[31] *Id.* at 137.
[32] SOLAS, *supra* note 2, art. I(b).
[33] ISPS Code, *supra* note 3.

The global family of water-bordering states is as diverse as its constituents. Illustrating this, the maritime community employs a wide array of legislative tools to implement the ISPS Code.[34] The most basic form of compliance is implementation by citation. By this method, some SOLAS signatories opt to adopt the entire ISPS Code as written, without expansion.[35] Other signatories restate the ISPS Code language in full or in part in their own legislative traditions.[36] While technically sufficient to comply with standing international obligations, these methods of implementation automatically adopt the ISPS Code's built-in shortcomings, rendering the subject government powerless to respond to security incidents or to enforce security standards in the absence of supplemental legislation. Though nations may rise to independently address this challenge,[37] the potential impact upon the effectiveness of port security in developing nations may be significant. Worse, some SOLAS signatories rely upon aging general port regulations that fail to address security altogether[38] and others neglect to report any effort at compliance.[39]

Anticipating the challenges to developing nations, the Convention, by resolution, strongly urged signatories and member states to "provide, in co-operation with the organization, assistance to those

---

[34] See Annex A for a comprehensive list of national legislation that implements the ISPS Code.
[35] See, e.g., Annex A, supra note 35 (including Argentina, Cameroon, Equatorial Guinea, and Iceland).
[36] See, e.g., Annex A, supra note 35 (including Bangladesh, Dominica, Ghana, Guatemala, and Honduras).
[37] Annex A, supra note 35 (including Cambodia and Fiji).
[38] See, e.g., Annex A, supra note 35 (including Benin, Chile, Gambia, and India).
[39] SOLAS, supra note 2, art. I(b) ("The Contracting Governments undertake to promulgate all laws, decrees, orders and regulations and to take all other steps which may be necessary to give the present Convention full and complete effect ...."); id. art. III(b) (requiring Contracting Governments to deposit with the IMO Secretary-General "the text of laws, decrees, orders and regulations which shall have been promulgated on the various matters within the scope of the present Convention ...."). To date, the following countries have yet to promulgate or deposit applicable port security laws or regulations as required: Benin, Comoros, Cote d'Ivoire, Curacao, Djibouti, Egypt, Eritrea, Guinea, Guinea-Bissau, Haiti, India, Iran, Kiribati, Lebanon, Libya, Maldives, Micronesia, Namibia, Nauru, Nicaragua, Nigeria, North Korea, Oman, Pakistan, Qatar, Senegal, Seychelles, Sierra Leone, Solomon Islands, Somalia, Sri Lanka, St. Maarten, Syria, Timor-Leste, Tuvalu, United Arab Emirates, and Western Sahara.

States which have difficulty in implementing or meeting the requirements of the adopted amendments or the ISPS Code...."[40] To further this, the IMO initiated the Global Program on Maritime and Port Security in 2002 to assist developing countries in improving SOLAS and ISPS Code compliance.[41]

D. *The United States' Approach to Port Security*

The United States was motivated to significantly contribute to the development of the international port security infrastructure to counter the most spectacular terrorist attentions in modern history. U.S. port security legislation took a truly innovative turn in the international realm post-9/11. Taking what is arguably the most vigorous approach to port security, the United States' domestic port security implementation strategy relies on U.S. Coast Guard officers appointed as port captains[42] who have authority to establish security zones,[43] command incident response efforts,[44] and to otherwise enforce port security laws and regulations.[45] By late 2002, the U.S. stood ready to proactively implement its own port security legislation and adopt regulations with verbiage remarkably similar to the international effort.[46] Not content to rely upon the efficacy of the fledgling ISPS international maritime security scheme for the protection of the American seaports, Congress took unprecedented measures to push the boundaries of the U.S. maritime transportation system all the way to the ports of origin around the world. Signed into law almost a month before the ISPS Code's

---

[40] ISPS Code, *supra* note 3.
[41] Press Release, Int'l Mar. Org., Security Compliance Shows Continued Improvement (Aug. 6, 2004).
[42] 14 U.S.C. § 634(a) (2006).
[43] 33 C.F.R. §1.05-1(f) (2012).
[44] 46 U.S.C. §70107A(d) (2010).
[45] 33 C.F.R. §§1.01-30 (2007); 33 C.F.R. §§101-106 (2003).
[46] Maritime Transportation Security Act of 2002, Pub. L. No. 107-295, 116 Stat. 2067 (2002) ("It is in the best interests of the United States... to have a free flow of interstate and foreign commerce and to ensure the efficient movement of cargo.... The International Maritime Organization and other similar international organizations are currently developing a new maritime security system that contains the essential elements for enhancing global maritime security. Therefore, it is in the best interests of the United States to implement new international instruments that establish such a system.").

adoption, the U.S. Maritime Transportation Security Act[47] ("MTSA") granted the U.S. Coast Guard[48] sweeping powers to regulate domestic and international shipping within U.S. ports and territorial waters.

Similar in theme but far more specific than the ISPS Code, MTSA established detailed new regulatory authority in maritime governance,[49] shipping,[50] port facility[51] and outer continental shelf security.[52] Given the United States' influence as a global economic power, MTSA effectively codified maritime transportation security protocols not only for the U.S., but also for every seafaring nation seeking to trade along her shores because the party must comply with the MSTA.[53]

In 2004, the U.S. Coast Guard established the International Port Security ("IPS") Program to meet MTSA's foreign port assessment mandates.[54] IPS Program representatives, who are primarily junior officers below the rank of Commander, are dispatched around the world to meet with key government and port authorities to verify compliance with international security standards and assess the effectiveness of anti-terrorism measures in facilities that service U.S.-bound vessels.[55]

---

[47] *Id.*
[48] 46 U.S.C. § 70101(5) (2006).
[49] 33 C.F.R. §§ 101, 103 (2011).
[50] 33 C.F.R. § 104 (2011).
[51] 33 C.F.R. § 105 (2011). In concept, "ports" are much more expansive than "port facilities," which are generally limited to the ship-to-port interface. Accordingly, depending on the geography and nature of commerce in a coastal area, a single port may contain several separate and distinct port facilities, each with its own owner/operator and cargo specialty (i.e. petroleum, container, bulk, passenger, etc.).
[52] 33 C.F.R. § 106 (2011).
[53] Similarly influential, Australia, Canada, and the European Community soon followed with similar maritime security legislation that further solidified international ship and port facility security standards.
[54] US COAST GUARD, Navigation & Vessel Inspection Circular No. 06-03 (2007); Edward H. Lundquist, *International Port Security Program: Coast Guard's Watchful Eye Monitors Security Problems Overseas*, COAST GUARD OUTLOOK 136, 137 (2011) (quoting U.S.C.G. Commandant ADM Robert J. Papp and Commander Tanya Schneider).
[55] US COAST GUARD, Navigation & Vessel Inspection Circular No. 06-03 (2007); Lundquist, *supra* note 55, at 136, 137 (quoting Commander Tanya Schneider).

The IPS Program prefers to take a cooperative, bi-lateral approach, inviting foreign maritime trading partners to the United States to observe how the U.S. Coast Guard implements port security on a reciprocal basis.[56] Since its inception, the IPS Program finds the policy of reciprocity sufficient to overcome most jurisdictional hurdles. The U.S. Coast Guard has visited the port facilities of more than 150 maritime trading partners, and more than half of the world's coastal nations have accepted the invitation to view U.S. port facilities in return.[57]

In addition to defining domestic port security obligations and establishing a policy of reciprocity, the MTSA requires the U.S. Coast Guard to evaluate the effectiveness of anti-terrorism measures in the ports of foreign trading partners,[58] notify those governments of noted lapses,[59] provide technical assistance to correct security deficiencies which could potentially affect U.S. port security, and to prescribe conditions of entry for any vessel arriving from a foreign port that does not maintain effective anti-terrorism measures.[60]

In the event of an adverse determination, the U.S. Coast Guard, in cooperation with the U.S. Department of State, must issue a formal demarche to the trading partner outlining the noted deficiencies and recommending steps for improvement.[61] A foreign government has

---

[56] Lundquist, *supra* note 55, at 137 (quoting Commander Tanya Schneider). Private port owners in the United States are under no statutory or regulatory obligation to cooperate with the Coast Guard to allow foreign port security delegations access their facilities. While the Coast Guard enjoys domestic port facility access by virtue of its numerous law enforcement and regulatory authorities, that power does not extend to authorizing access to third parties and foreign powers. *See* 33 C.F.R. §§ 101-106 (2011). Should the Coast Guard ever seek to force the issue, a reluctant port owner could potentially object on the ground that the U.S. sponsored inspection of a facility by a foreign power constitutes a violation of the Fourth Amendment prohibition against unreasonable searches and seizures. U.S. CONST. amend. IV. Furthermore, such an involuntary inspection would violate regulatory prohibitions on divulging the proprietary information and trade secrets of U.S. entities. 49 C.F.R. § 1520.7 (2011).

[57] Dan Orchard, *International Port Security – A Global Challenge*, 68 U.S. COAST GUARD PROCEEDINGS 34 (2011).

[58] 46 U.S.C. § 70108 (2011).

[59] 46 U.S.C. § 70109 (2006).

[60] 46 U.S.C. § 70110 (2006).

[61] 46 U.S.C. § 70109(a) (2006) (stating that unless the Secretary "[finds]" that a port in a foreign country does not maintain effective antiterrorism measures, the Secretary shall

ninety days from the date of notification to remedy major security deficiencies within its port facilities.[62] After the ninety days, if the trading partner remains unresponsive, the U.S. Coast Guard must notify the public of the insufficiency of security measures within the ports of that country.[63] This notice, known as a Port Security Advisory ("PSA"), is published in the Federal Register and alerts U.S. Coast Guard units and the maritime industry at large to the security deficiencies and the control measures prescribed for ships coming from non-compliant ports.[64] Vessels arriving in the U.S. that have visited any country on the PSA list during their five most recent port calls are normally boarded or examined by the U.S. Coast Guard to ensure the vessel implemented sufficient security measures while in those ports.[65] If the Captain of the Port is not satisfied with the vessel's security posture, the Captain may impose conditions of entry[66] and then deny entry if the vessel does not meet those conditions.[67] If the government of a foreign trading partner refuses to cooperate or otherwise obstructs the assessment process, the U.S. Coast Guard is empowered by statute to formally conclude non-compliance with international port security standards by virtue of its inability to complete the assessment due to the lack of cooperation.[68]

---

notify the appropriate authorities of the government of the foreign country of the finding and recommend the steps necessary to improve the antiterrorism measures in use in the port.").

[62] 46 U.S.C. § 70110(b); Mike Brown, *International Port Security Program - Implementation of International Regulations*, 63 U.S. COAST GUARD PROCEEDINGS 45, 47 (2006).

[63] 46 U.S.C. § 70110(b) (2006).

[64] *See, e.g.*, Notification of the Imposition of Conditions of Entry for Certain Vessel Arriving to the United States from the Democratic Republic of Sao Tome and Principe, 75 Fed. Reg. 18,871 (Apr. 13, 2010).

[65] Lundquist, *supra* note 55, at 137.

[66] Conditions of entry may include, but are not limited to, the imposition of enhanced security measures, declaration of security, daylight transit, security sweeps, armed security, vessel escorts, offshore lightering, and underwater hull surveys. *See, e.g.*, Notification of the Imposition of Conditions of Entry for Certain Vessel Arriving to the United States from the Democratic Republic of Sao Tome and Principe, 75 Fed. Reg. 18871 (Apr. 13, 2010).

[67] 46 U.S.C. §70110(b) (2006).

[68] 46 U.S.C. §70108(e) (2006).

In theory, if foreign port security measures are similar to U.S. MTSA standards,[69] the respective trading partners could enter into cooperative agreements recognizing this to satisfy mutual assessment requirements. The obvious benefits of such an arrangement include freeing personnel to concentrate assessment efforts in areas of genuine need, reduced costs to all parties, and an enhanced atmosphere of cooperation and partnership between signatories. However, such an agreement will require an adjustment to existing U.S. law, which currently imposes a positive obligation on the U.S. Coast Guard Commandant to reassess the effectiveness of antiterrorism measures in foreign ports not less than once every three years.[70] To allow for bilateral security agreements in this context, the statute must first be amended to allow the U.S. Coast Guard to rely upon PSAs performed by approved third parties. While under discussion, this idea has not advanced legislatively.

II. PORT SECURITY LAW

To date, there are no legal challenges against the United States' policy and procedure for assessing anti-terrorism measures in foreign ports and imposing conditions on ships arriving from foreign ports. However, the rapid domestic and international progression of the body of port security regulation gives rise to the potential for repercussions in other areas of public and private law. In the absence of extant case or controversy, the student of international port security law is not afforded the benefit of authoritative deliberation and guidance. Nevertheless, certain avenues for legal debate are obvious in the areas of jurisdictional authority, trade obligations, contracts, torts, criminal law, evidence and international convention.

---

[69] *See, e.g.*, Regulation 725/2004 of the European Parliament and of the Council of 31 March 2004 on Enhancing Ship and Port Facility Security, 2004 O.J. (L 129) 6 (EC); Council Directive 2005/65 of the European Parliament and of the Council of 26 October 2005 on Enhancing Port Security, 2005 O.J. (L 310) 28 (EC); *Maritime Transport and Offshore Facilities Security Act 2003* (Cth) (Austl.); *Maritime Transport and Offshore Facilities Security Regulations 2003* (Cth) (Austl.); Maritime Transportation Security Act, S.C. 1994, c. 40 (Can.); Marine Transportation Security Regulations, SOR/2004-144 (Can.).

[70] 46 U.S.C. § 70108(d) (2006).

A. Public Law

To the extent that port security law frequently invokes intergovernmental interaction, the body of public law is perhaps most sensitive to the emanations of these regulations. Political, ideological, or nationalistic differences may spark criticism of America's unrepentant regulatory focus on port security even though global maritime trade arguably benefits from the increased security environment promoted by U.S. law and foreign policy. In some quarters, the United States is derided as the self-assumed guardian of the world order writ large,[71] especially by countries with more complex hostilities hard wired into the national, tribal, or religious psyche.

1. State Sovereignty

Addressing Congress in 2004, Admiral Thomas Fargo, the former commander of U.S. Forces in the Pacific, suggested the deployment of special operations forces in high-speed vessels to protect U.S. shipping against the threat of terrorism in the Strait of Malacca and approaches to the Port of Singapore.[72] Malaysia rejected the proposal out of hand, noting that they could look after their own area and that "the use of forces in Southeast Asia to fight terrorism will only serve to fuel Islamic Fundamentalism."[73] Likewise, the Indonesian Foreign Ministry balked at U.S. participation in the region on the ground, stating "[i]t is the sovereign responsibility and right of the coastal states of Indonesia and Malaysia to maintain safety and security of navigation in the Malacca Strait."[74]

---

[71] Chris Rahman, *Evolving U.S. Framework for Global Maritime Security from 9/11 to the 1000-ship Navy*, in LLOYD'S MIU HANDBOOK OF MARITIME SECURITY 39 (Rupert Herbert-Burnes et al., eds., 2009).

[72] David Rosenberg, *Dire Straits: Competing Security Priorities in the South China Sea*, ASIA-PACIFIC JOURNAL: JAPAN FOCUS, (Apr, 13, 2005), http://www.japanfocus.org/-David-Rosenberg/1773.

[73] Sudha Ramachandran, *Divisions Over Terror Threat in Malacca Straits*, ASIA TIMES, June 16, 2004.

[74] *Indonesia Joins Malaysia in Shunning U.S. help in Malacca Straits*, ASSOCIATED PRESS, Apr. 12, 2004 (quoting Foreign Ministry spokesman, Marty Natalegawa); Ramachandran, *supra* note 75.

The precept of state sovereignty is enshrined by the United Nations Charter[75] and embraced by international courts.[76] Pursuant to the United Nations Convention on the Law of the Sea[77] this sovereignty is also applicable to the territorial seas,[78] harbors within,[79] and roadsteads beyond.[80] In the United States, the commitment to the sanctity of national sovereignty is perhaps most evident with regard to the protection of her shores.[81] The U.S. Supreme Court has long held that territorial waters are "subject to the complete sovereignty of the nation, as much as if they were a part of its land territory, and the coastal nation has the privilege even to exclude foreign vessels altogether."[82] Thus, Congress has "the power . . . to condition access to our ports by foreign-owned vessels upon submission to any liabilities it may consider good American policy to exact."[83] In application, the Third Restatement of the Foreign Relations Law of the United States notes that "in general, maritime ports are open to foreign ships on condition of reciprocity, . . .

---

[75] U.N. Charter art. 2.
[76] Military and Paramilitary Activities in and Against Nicaragua (Nicar. v. U.S.), 1986 I.C.J. 14, 112 (June 27).
[77] United Nations Convention on the Law of the Sea, Dec. 10, 1982, 1833 U.N.T.S. 397 [hereinafter UNCLOS].
[78] UNCLOS, *supra* note 78, art. 2 ("The sovereignty of a coastal State extends, beyond its land territory and internal waters . . . to an adjacent belt of sea, described as the territorial sea.").
[79] UNCLOS, *supra* note 78, art. 11 ("For the purpose of delimiting the territorial sea, the outermost permanent harbour works which form an integral part of the harbour system are regarded as forming part of the coast. ").
[80] UNCLOS, *supra* note 78, art. 12 ("Roadsteads which are normally used for the loading, unloading and anchoring of ships, and which would otherwise be situated wholly or partly outside the outer limit of the territorial sea, are included in the territorial sea.").
[81] The United States is, by history and geography, a maritime nation and its national security is inextricably linked with seaport security and the control of territorial waters and its approaches. Haig v. Agee, 453 U.S. 280, 307 ("It is 'obvious and unarguable' that no governmental interest is more compelling than the security of the Nation.") (quoting Aptheker v. Secretary of State, 378 U.S. 500, 509 (1964)).
[82] United States v. Louisiana, 394 U.S. 11, 22 (1969).
[83] Lauritzen v. Larsen, 345 U.S. 571, 592-93 (1953). This authority derives from the enumerated powers of Congress under the U.S. Constitution. *See* U.S. CONST. art. I, § 8 ("The Congress shall have power … [t]o regulate Commerce with foreign Nations ….").

but the coastal State may temporarily suspend access in exceptional cases for imperative reasons . . . ."[84]

In 1986, the International Court of Justice echoed U.S. jurisprudence and set a precedent more specifically applicable to the discussion of ISPS Code implementation and enforcement in light of public law state sovereignty. In an attempt to deter Nicaragua from launching guerilla attacks against its Central American neighbors in the early 1980's, the U.S. imposed sanctions against the regime of Manuel Noriega, closing American ports to vessels of Nicaraguan registry. The sanctions were challenged in the International Court of Justice by the Nicaragua Mining Company. Supporting U.S. policy, the court held that internal waters are subject to the sovereignty of the particular port state and that it is "by virtue of its sovereignty that the coastal State may regulate access to its ports."[85] Considerations of state sovereignty[86] naturally lead to jurisdictional discussions.[87]

2. U.S. Jurisdiction Over International Waters

This paper will not delve into the intricacies of jurisdiction, except to note the exceptional circumstances under which U.S. courts occasionally adjudicate on extraterritorial matters with no traditional

---

[84] Restatement (Third) of Foreign Relations Law § 512 cmt. c (1987).
[85] Military and Paramilitary Activities in and Against Nicaragua (Nicar. v. U.S.), 1986 I.C.J. 14, 111 (June 27).
[86] As an aside on the general issue of Sovereignty, ISPS Code Part B, section 4.3 allows contracting governments to authorize a Recognized Security Organization (RSO) to undertake certain security related activities, including: (1) approval of Ship Security Plans, or amendments thereto, on behalf of the Administration; (2) verification and certification of compliance of ships with the requirements of chapter XI-2 and part A of this Code on behalf of the Administration; and (3) conducting Port Facility Security Assessments required by the Contracting Government. Although it is incumbent upon each SOLAS signatory to identify and qualify its own RSOs, there are many companies which provide international RSO services. Where such services are rendered, the RSOs are arguably exercising regulatory authority over that country's shipping and port infrastructure, thus suggesting that the contracting governments have ceded certain of their sovereign powers to the foreign companies.
[87] The general concept of "jurisdiction" encompasses not only the traditional exercise of adjudicative and regulatory power by courts and law enforcement agencies, but also describes the constitutional powers of Congress to exert extraterritorial authority to promote the interests of U.S. foreign policy in the form of legislative jurisdiction.

jurisdictional nexus. One such avenue for jurisdiction is territorial, which arises from the location of an offense.[88] If no territorial connection exists, a nation may still create that nexus on the high seas or in foreign territorial waters through bi-lateral enforcement agreements or by obtaining the consent of any other affected states.[89] Long employed by the U.S. Coast Guard to greatly extend the bounds of general maritime law enforcement authority, bi-lateral and consent agreements are supported by U.S. courts, which have held that nothing prevents two nations from agreeing that the domestic laws of one nation shall be extended onto the high seas or into the territorial waters of the other.[90]

3. Congressional Authority

By contrast, the extraterritorial reach of Congress in matters of foreign policy has nothing to do with the jurisdiction of the courts. The Constitution grants Congress broad powers to "regulate Commerce with foreign Nations,"[91] and the Supreme Court upholds the Congressional power to "make laws applicable to persons or activities beyond our territorial boundaries where United States interests are affected."[92] Congress is generally presumed not to have exceeded the limits of customary international law.[93] [94] However, that is not to say that Congress is absolutely bound by international law.[95] Although acts of Congress do not normally have extraterritorial application, that presumption may be overcome if such intent is clearly manifested, particularly with regard to the application of treaties and circumstances

---

[88] United States v. Smith, 680 F.2d 255, 257 (1st Cir. 1982).
[89] United States v. Cardales, 168 F.3d 548, 553 (1st Cir. 1999).
[90] United States v. Gonzales, 776 F.2d 931, 938 (11th Cir. 1985).
[91] U.S. CONST. art. I, § 8, cl. 3.
[92] Hartford Fire Ins. Co. v. California, 509 U.S. 764, 813-14 (1993) (citing Ford v. United States, 273 U.S. 593, 621-23 (1927)).
[93] *See* Hartford Fire Ins. Co., 509 U.S. at 814 (stating that under one of the fundamental tenets of statutory construction, "an act of congress ought never to be construed to violate the law of nations if any other possible construction remains.") (quoting Murray v. Schooner Charmer Baby, 6 U.S. 64, 81 (1804)).
[94] *Hartford Fire Ins. Co.*, 509 U.S. at 814-15.
[95] *Hartford Fire Ins. Co.*, 509 U.S. at 814-815; Rainey v. United States, 232 U.S. 310, 316 (1914); Whitney v. Robertson, 124 U.S. 190, 194 (1888).

that involve foreign and military affairs.[96] Accordingly, if it chooses to do so, Congress may legislate with respect to conduct outside the United States in excess of the limits imposed by international law.[97] Where the presumption against extraterritoriality is overcome or is otherwise inapplicable, Congress is deemed to have asserted its "legislative jurisdiction" or "jurisdiction to prescribe."[98] Establishing adjudicative or legislative jurisdiction to govern port security on a public law state sovereignty basis is only the first step towards affecting enhanced international port security protocols.

4. Enforcement

Whether implemented by international agreement or through unilateral assertion of legislative jurisdiction, the efficacy of port security standards abroad ultimately rests on the enforcing nation's power to punish non-compliance, typically through the influence or manipulation of market forces. In fact, the U.N.'s IMO takes the general position that while it has no direct power to enforce the ISPS Code, it anticipates that market forces and economic factors will either drive compliance or quickly force non-cooperative shippers and facilities out of the market.[99] In U.S. ports, conditions of entry designed to safeguard against terrorist attacks also tend to subject non-compliant vessels to increased scrutiny, delay, and additional costs.[100] PSAs serve to deter passenger traffic to non-compliant countries.[101] Given the commercial strength of the United States, the issuance of conditions of entry and public security warnings ultimately has the potential to affect shipping rates, increase insurance premiums, deter tourism, and cause the diversion of cargo to

---

[96] *Hartford Fire Ins. Co.*, 509 U.S. at 814 (Scalia, J., dissenting); Sale v. Haitian Centers Council, Inc., 509 U.S. 155, 188 (1993).
[97] *Hartford Fire Ins. Co.*, 509 U.S. at 814-16.
[98] *Id.* at 813; RESTATEMENT (FIRST) OF CONFLICT OF LAWS § 60 (1934); RESTATEMENT (THIRD) OF FOREIGN RELATIONS LAW OF THE UNITED STATES §§ 401, 403 (1987).
[99] *FAQ on ISPS Code and Maritime Security*, IMO, http://www.imo.org/OurWork/Security/FAQ/Pages/Maritime-Security.aspx (last visited Nov. 5, 2012).
[100] Brown, *supra* note 63, at 48.
[101] *See, e.g.*, Notification of the Imposition of Conditions of Entry for Certain Vessels Arriving to the United States from the Democratic Republic of Sao Tome and Principe, 75 Fed. Reg. 18,871, 18,872 (Apr. 13, 2010).

more security-conscious countries. In theory, the threat of such business losses should be incentive to promote port security measures sufficient to the higher standards of more security-conscious nations. The willingness of most maritime states to cooperate with the U.S. Coast Guard in ensuring the efficacy of those measures seems to bear out this theory.[102]

5. Trade Agreements

From the perspective of government liability, international trade agreement prohibitions could also be a consideration in the application of trans-national security related regulatory requirements. Adopted by the international community in increments,[103] the General Agreement on Tariffs and Trade ("GATT")[104] sets international trade guidelines and dispute resolution procedures. It also guarantees freedom of maritime transit and forbids member states from discriminating against vessels because of the vessel's flag, origin, or destination.[105] To that end, GATT encourages member states to reduce the complexity of import formalities and documentation requirements, so as to avoid unnecessary administrative delay.[106] However, GATT also recognizes that it is the maritime state's sovereign right to take any measures necessary to ensure the national security.[107]

---

[102] Brown, *supra* note 63, at 48; Lundquist, *supra* note 66, at 137.
[103] With the most recent iteration finalized in 1994 at the Uraguay round of talks. Uraguay Round Agreements Act, Pub. L. No. 103-465, 108 Stat. 4809 (1994).
[104] General Agreement on Tariffs and Trade, Oct. 30, 1947, 61 Stat. A-11, 55 U.N.T.S. 194 [hereinafter GATT]; Marrakesh Agreement Establishing the World Trade Organization, Apr. 15, 1994, 1867 U.N.T.S. 154 [hereinafter Marrakesh Agreement].
[105] GATT, *supra* note 105, art. V.
[106] GATT, *supra* note 105, art. VIII.
[107] GATT, *supra* note 105, art. XXI(b) ("Nothing in this Agreement shall be construed ... (b) to prevent any contracting party from taking any action which it considers necessary for the protection of its essential security interests (i) relating to fissionable materials or the materials from which they are derived; (ii) relating to the traffic in arms, ammunitions and implements of war and to such traffic in other goods and materials as is carried on directly or indirectly for the purpose of supplying a military establishment; (iii) taken in time of war or other emergency in international relations.").

6. Current Port Security Regulations in Practice

The convergence of obligation and authority observed in treaties, GATT, U.S. domestic law, and public law is illustrated in the general provisions of SOLAS which empower contracting governments to subject arriving ships to control measures, but grants those ships an entitlement to compensation for damages incurred as a result of undue detention or delay.[108] If a port authority has clear grounds to suspect that an arriving vessel or its port of origin are not security compliant, the authority may impose control measures,[109] including the requirement of additional security-related information, inspection of the ship, delaying the ship, detention of the ship, restriction of operations and movement within the port or expulsion of the ship from port.[110] However, SOLAS tempers this clause, warning that denial of entry or expulsion from a port is only appropriate where a ship poses an *immediate* security threat.[111] Thus, under the terms of the Convention, port authorities must make every effort to avoid undue delay or detention, or face civil liability for any loss or damage suffered.[112]

7. U.S. Liability Arising From Distinctions Between MTSA and ISPS Code

The U.S. is in a unique situation because the vigorous port security standards prescribed by MTSA [113] far exceed ISPS Code minimums. Accordingly, an inconvenienced shipper whose voyage originated in the port of a PSA country, that is, a country found by the U.S. Government to have ineffective anti-terrorism measures, may be able to mount challenges after MTSA's application. If the country has self-certified ISPS Code compliance as required by SOLAS, it could arguably maintain that a non-contemporaneous sampling by the U.S. Coast Guard does not constitute "clear grounds" or indicate an

---

[108] SOLAS, *supra* note 2.
[109] SOLAS, *supra* note 2, ch. XI-2, reg. 9.
[110] SOLAS, *supra* note 2, ch. XI-2, reg. 9.
[111] SOLAS, *supra* note 2, ch. XI-2, reg. 9, 3.3.
[112] SOLAS, *supra* note 2, ch. XI-2, reg. 9, 3.5.
[113] Maritime Transportation Security Act of 2002, Pub. L. No. 107-295, 116 Stat. 2064 (2002).

"immediate security threat". If the claimant can convince the court that the port authority subjected the vessel to undue detention or delay, the U.S. Government may be indebted to the shipper and other affected parties for commercial loss and cargo damage arising from the port authority's actions.

Such an assertion is not without comparative precedent, as seen in *Canadian Transport Co. v. United States*.[114] In *Canadian Transport*, a foreign company based out of a foreign port filed a lawsuit due to the U.S. government's attempts to administer domestic port regulations. In April 1974, the Canadian-chartered coal carrier M/V TROPWAVE attempted to enter the port of Norfolk, Virginia. The Coast Guard denied entry on the ground that the ship's master and several of its officers were Polish nationals and so the ship diverted to Baltimore, disembarked the Communist Bloc personnel and returned to Norfolk.[115] It was alleged by Canadian Transport Co. that the detour caused the company to suffer $93,000 in damages.[116] The company filed a claim against the U.S. Government alleging intentional interference with contract rights under the Suits in Admiralty Act,[117] violation of U.S. treaty obligations, and deprivation of property without due process of law in violation of the Fifth Amendment.[118] On motion for summary judgment, the U.S. argued that the U.S. Coast Guard was engaged in the performance of a "discretionary function," thereby rendering the U.S. immune from suit in that case.[119] The district court agreed and the case was dismissed in its entirety.[120]

Upon review, the Appellate Court supported most of the district court's rationale, but noted that the record reflected that several other Communist Bloc ships and crews were admitted to the Port of Norfolk within the same timeframe, creating an inference that the Coast Guard's

---

[114] Canadian Transport Co. v. United States, 663 F.2d 1081 (D.C. Cir. 1980).
[115] *Id.* at 1083
[116] *Id.* at 1084.
[117] Suits in Admiralty Act, 46 U.S.C. § 741 (2006).
[118] *Canadian Transport Co.*, 663 F.2d at 1083.
[119] *Id.* at 1085.
[120] Canadian Transport Co. v. United States, 430 F. Supp. 1168 (D.D.C. 1977), *aff'd in part, rev'd in part*, 663 F.2d 1081 (D.C. Cir. 1980).

actions were arbitrary.[121] The Appellate Court concluded that the Coast Guard's practice of admitting some Communist Bloc vessels while excluding others created a genuine issue of material fact as to whether it was truly performing a discretionary function.[122] Thus, the Appellate Court reversed the judgment of the District Court and the case remanded for further proceedings.[123] *Canadian Transport Co.* demonstrates that similar challenges may arise where MTSA regulations are employed to restrict entry of foreign shipping into U.S. ports.

8. Unique Challenges to Adjudicatory Process in International Port Security Law

In theory, the rapid expansion of international port security law could go so far as influencing adjudicative processes by affecting the application of procedural and evidentiary rules. For example, if a terrorist tucks himself away on a ship with a foreign-approved security plan and then wreaks havoc in the destination port, the terror victims could conceivably seek redress against the ship's operator for failing to implement all requisite security measures to prevent the attack. Plaintiff's counsel will naturally seek the ship's security plan with an eye toward building the case, but they may not get it.

Under the ISPS Code, a ship's security plans must be protected from "unauthorized access or disclosure."[124] U.S. law is in accord with this precept and goes even further to designate such documents as "sensitive security information."[125] In the United States, foreign and domestic vessel owners, operators, and charterers are charged with safeguarding sensitive security information[126] and are forbidden to release such documents except to persons with a "need to know."[127] Violation could subject the vessel operator to civil penalties and "other enforcement or corrective action" by the U.S. Department of Homeland

---

[121] Canadian Transport Co. v. United States, 663 F.2d 1081, 1088 (D.C. Cir. 1980).
[122] *See id.* at 1089 (noting that the Suits in Admiralty Act's discretionary function exemption is limited to the exercise of discretion in formulating governmental policy).
[123] *Id.* at 1093.
[124] ISPS Code, *supra* note 3, part A, 9.7.
[125] 33 C.F.R. § 104.400(c) (2011); 49 C.F.R § 1520.5(b) (2006).
[126] 49 C.F.R. § 1520.7 (2011).
[127] 49 C.F.R. § 1520.9 (2011).

Security.[128] Unfortunately for our hypothetical litigants, such information is not releasable under the Freedom of Information Act ("FOIA").[129] [130] Access to the sensitive information is specifically granted to attorneys only for the purpose of providing legal advice to the vessel operator or representing the vessel operator in judicial or administrative proceedings regarding those requirements.[131] This exception lies in the allowance that the U.S. Coast Guard may authorize the release of sensitive security information, provided that the requestor can demonstrate the "need to know."[132]

As a rule, the U.S. Coast Guard itself avoids receipt of foreign ship security plans and discourages the international transfer of such documents.[133] The U.S. Coast Guard cites lack of resources as the primary reason for not demanding receipt of global shipping's estimated 40,000 ship security plans.[134] It is worth noting that, as a practical matter, U.S. Coast Guard review of foreign ship security plans could open U.S. ship owners to undesirable reciprocal demands by the U.S.'s maritime trading partners. Due to this consideration, any request for U.S. Coast Guard authority to release vessel security plans will likely be evaluated through the lens of the foregoing regulations and procedure, thus inevitably requiring judicial intervention and substantially protracting the discovery process and litigation in general.

9. Criminal Law

Meaningful analysis of the international avalanche of criminal regulations defining port security-related offenses and penalties is far

---

[128] 49 C.F.R. § 1520.17 (2011).
[129] 5 U.S.C. § 552 (2006).
[130] 49 C.F.R. § 1520.15 (2011).
[131] 49 C.F.R. § 1520.11 (2011).
[132] 49 C.F.R. § 1520.15 (2011).
[133] Coast Guard Vessel Security, 68 Fed. Reg. 60,483, 60,488 ("Foreign flag vessels need not submit their Vessel Security Assessments or Vessel Security Plans to the Coast Guard for review or approval. . . . [O]wners and operators of foreign flag vessels that meet the applicable requirements of SOLAS Chapter XI will not have to submit their assessments or plans to the Coast Guard for review or approval.").
[134] *Port Security: Hearing Before the Subcomm. on Coast Guard and Mar. Transp. of the H. Comm. on Transp. and Infrastructure*, 108th Cong. (2003) (statement of Admiral Thomas H. Collins, Commandant, U.S. Coast Guard).

beyond the scope of this paper. However, it is worth noting that, as with any untried body of law, it is conceivable that circumstances may arise when the implementation of one rule causes the responsible party to violate another. Take, for instance, the time-honored precept of the Master's discretion. As set forth in the ISPS Code, the Master's discretion allows the Master to abrogate any law which conflicts with the Master's belief of what is necessary to maintain ship safety.[135] Simultaneously, international law as reflected in the ISPS Code requires ships in port to comply with the security requirements stated by that particular port authority.[136] In some countries, non-compliance of such directives may constitute a criminal offense,[137] which gives rise to conflicts between international standards and local implementation of port security.

To illustrate this point, consider that a passenger ship may frequent a heavily regulated port where the authority limits pier-side access to a single point of entry for security reasons. Violation of such a requirement could constitute a criminal offense under the laws of the port state. If a fire breaks out in the engine room, threatening passengers and crew, the captain may disregard this security requirement and open all access points to allow for emergency response. By opening additional entry points the captain is also potentially permitting unauthorized access to the ship from criminal elements. In such circumstances, the conflict between safety and security could give rise to criminal charges. In the alternative, where the captain neglects safety in favor of enforcing ship and port security measures, injured parties could pursue damages in tort. Although such a result may seem improbable, the burgeoning, but untested, body of international port security legislation could be rife with such conflicts.

---

[135] See SOLAS, supra note 2, ch. XI-2, reg. 8 ("The master shall not be constrained by the Company, the charterer or any other person from taking or executing any decisions which, in the professional judgment of the master, is necessary to maintain the safety and security of the ship. . . . If, in the professional judgment of the master, a conflict between any safety and security requirements applicable to the ship arises during its operations, the master shall give effect to those requirements necessary to maintain the safety of the ship.").
[136] SOLAS, supra note 2, ch. XI-2, reg. 4, 3.
[137] See, e.g., Cambodia, Annex A, supra note 35.

B. *Private Liability*

Private law defines, regulates, enforces, and administers relationships among individuals, associations, and corporations.[138] In the maritime context, such dispute could materialize along the well-traveled paths of contract and tort litigation, but as in the public realm, the impact of international port security law development on private disputes is likely to be wide reaching. While it is difficult to assess exactly how evolving international port security law will impact private law, the body of existing jurisprudence in other areas of transportation law may hint at the trajectories that resulting litigation may follow.

1. Marine Insurance

Marine insurance is arguably one of the most prevalent issues in private maritime law, touching at least tangentially on almost every aspect of the practice. As noted above, when a country which fails to effectively implement anti-terrorism measures in its port facilities, it may be publically identified, named in a PSA in the federal register, and have its vessels subjected to conditions of entry to U.S. ports. Marine insurers will note the adverse action and will likely increase premiums or terminate coverage. This compounds the negative implications arising from the country's failure to implement effective anti-terrorism measures. When policies are issued and claims arising from security incidents come to fruition, the legal scholar should expect to see significant legal debate concerning the precise meaning of "war risks" and other insured or excluded perils.[139]

---

[138] BLACK'S LAW DICTIONARY 830 (6th ed. 1995).
[139] "War risks" are generally defined as hostile acts or warlike operations. *See* Standard Oil Co. v. United States, 340 U.S. 54 (1950). The U.S. Supreme Court has found that, within the marine insurance context, the term "war risks" includes adventures and perils involving "restraints and detainments of all kings, princes, and people". 345 U.S. 427 (1953) (citation omitted). In contrast, lower courts have expanded the concept of "war risks" to include the use of offensive weapons such as mines, torpedoes, and bombs. North Branch Resources, L.L.C. v. M/V MSC CALI, 132 F. Supp. 2d 293 (S.D.N.Y. 2001). A hostile act need not necessarily involve the overt use of a weapon, but may include operations such as the extinguishment of a navigational light or the outfitting of a ship, if

2. Contractual Liability for Violating Port Security Measures

The exercise of port state control measures by a maritime trading nation can conceivably give rise to contractual disputes over liability for lost time and extra expenses incurred by shipping companies trying to comply with conditions of entry. Marine shipping contracts or "charter parties" typically define the terms of the shipping obligation and penalties for non-performance. Such charter parties allow for a specified period of time to load or discharge cargo, known as laytime. After agreed laytimes expire, the charterer may become liable for a specified rate of liquidated damages, known as demurrage.[140] Thus, to interpret the effect of charter parties, one must determine if laytime commenced. The answer to this hinges upon a factual determination as to whether the voyage was completed or, in maritime parlance, whether the vessel in question is an "arrived ship."[141] Theoretically, if a ship is detained at the end of a voyage for enhanced security consideration by the port state, a dispute may arise between the parties as to whether the vessel was an arrived ship, which would commence laytime and expose the charterer to liability for demurrage charges.[142]

Separate contractual liability related to port security implementation may also be found under the general maritime law warranty of seaworthiness. Stated simply, the warranty of seaworthiness requires that the ship be "reasonably fit for the use intended."[143] Under maritime law, this warranty is implied in all contracts.[144] It is arguable

---

done for hostile purposes. Int'l Dairy Eng'g Co. v. Am. Home Assurance Co., 352 F. Supp. 827 (N.D. Cal. 1970).

[140] Trans-Asiatic Oil Ltd., S.A. v. Apex Oil Co., 804 F.2d 773, 775 (1st Cir. 1986); Gloria Steamship Co. v. India Supply Mission, 288 F. Supp. 674, 675 (S.D.N.Y 1968).

[141] Fukaya Trading Co., S.A. v. E. Marine Corp., 322 F. Supp. 278, 283 (E.D. La. 1971); *see also* St. Ioannes Shipping Corp. v. Zidell Explorations, Inc., 336 F.2d 194, 196 (9th Cir. 1964) ("It is concededly the law that under a charter such as the one here, where the lay time is calculable beforehand, delays in the securing of the berth for a discharge of cargo, once the ship has arrived at port, are chargeable to the charterer.").

[142] *BIMCO ISPS/MTSA Clause for Voyage Charter Parties 2005*, BIMCO SPECIAL CIRCULAR (Baltic and Int'l Mar. Council, Bagsvaerd, Den.), June 15, 2005.

[143] Amerada Hess Corp. v. S/T Mobil Apex, 602 F.2d 1095, 1097 (2d Cir. 1979).

[144] Aaby v. States Marine Corp., 181 F.2d 383, 385 (2d Cir. 1950).

that the warranty of seaworthiness includes an assurance that the ship is administratively prepared to enter the destination port and deliver the cargo as intended by the parties.[145] A shipping company's failure to implement personnel, security plan, and documentation requirements required by the ISPS Code[146] could render those ships unseaworthy under general maritime law, enabling parties to sue for contract violations under the warranty of seaworthiness.

3. Tort Liability

Shipping companies could conceivably incur tort liability for failure to properly implement ISPS Code and MTSA security measures. Absent specific precedent, tort claims arising from port security incidents will likely reflect the line of jurisprudence occurring in aviation security claims. After the September 11th attacks, a class action claim was filed against the involved airlines and airport operators.[147] The class included injured claimants, survivors, and entities suffering property damage.[148] The suit alleged that the defendants failed to fulfill their assigned security responsibilities.[149] The district court rejected a Motion to Dismiss, holding that while an intervening intentional or criminal act generally severs the liability of the original tort-feasor,[150] the requirement for causation "has no application when the intentional or criminal intervention of a third party or parties is reasonably foreseeable."[151] The court reasoned that the airlines and airport operators were uniquely positioned to protect the plaintiffs from harm and were aware of the history of terrorist suicide missions and hijackings.[152] Due to this, an

---

[145] *See In re* Complaint of Delphinus Maritima, S.A., 523 F. Supp. 583, 595 (S.D.N.Y. 1981) (holding, *inter alia*, that a ship owner's failure to check crew credentials, furnish proper navigational charts, and other administrative failures rendered the ship unseaworthy).

[146] *See, generally*, mandatory provisions of ISPS Code, Part A, Section 9 (ship security plans), Section 10 (ship security records), Section 12 (ship security personnel) and Section 19 (International Ship Security Certificates).

[147] *In re* Sept. 11 Litig., 280 F. Supp. 2d, 279, 287 (S.D.N.Y. 2003).

[148] *Id.*

[149] *Id.*

[150] *Id.* at 302 (citation omitted).

[151] *Id.*

[152] *In re* Sept. 11 Litig., 280 F. Supp. 2d, 279 at 294-95 (S.D.N.Y. 2003).

obligation existed to take reasonable aviation security measures that would deter terrorist attacks.[153] Similarly, the duty to take reasonable security measures is well codified in maritime law.[154]

If terrorists attack a U.S. port or deliver weapons and operatives using security regulated vessels that are later used in an attack, claims against the ship owner will likely mirror those against the airlines. The plaintiffs can argue that any ISPS Code or MTSA requirement is a reasonable security measure and that the failure to follow it automatically demonstrates a breach of duty, exposing ship owners to the liability seen in aviation security cases.[155]

III. THE FUTURE OF INTERNATIONAL PORT SECURITY

While many port security-related legal dilemmas remain untried, significant diplomatic, political, and regulatory developments are already reducing much of the jurisdictional uncertainty surrounding the implementation of the MTSA. Through the U.S. Coast Guard, the United States is promoting an aggressive program of bi-lateral security development and international consensus building aimed to satisfy MTSA mandates and improve the overall integrity of the global maritime system, notably through the IPS Program.

---

[153] *Id.* at 307.
[154] International Convention for the Unification of Certain Rules Relating to Bills of Lading, Signed at Brussels, Aug. 25, 1924, T.S. No. 931, 120 U.N.T.S. 155 (entered into force Dec. 29, 1937).
[154] Id., Art. III, Rule 1
[155] Although the ship owner could file for limitation of liability protections, such a defense would only be effective if the ship was compliant with all applicable laws and regulations. *See* 46 U.S.C. App. §§ 181-188 (2006) (discussing that a vessel owner may limit tort liability to the amount of interest the owner holds in the vessel and freight pending, provided that the loss is incurred without their privity or knowledge). The discovery needed to determine compliance will hinge on the ship's records, including the security plans, which is problematic because U.S. policy prevents the easy disclosure of security plans. This also puts the ship owner in a difficult spot because the failure to keep complete administrative records or to follow training requirements will limit the ship owner's ability to demonstrate sufficient duty to establish a limited liability defense. *See generally* ISPS Code, *supra* note 3.

The effectiveness of the U.S. approach to regulatory coordination reflects the cooperative global sentiment that has given rise to the rapid expansion of international port security law. Naturally, this coordination is only successful if maritime nations share unified interest in safeguarding their combined port infrastructure. Some countries are inevitably less advanced in the field of port security than others, regardless of their sincerity. While the United States, the European Union, Canada, and Australia were politically and professionally situated following the September 11th attacks to fully regulate their port security processes, many coastal countries lacked the governmental capacity or political will to address port security beyond a cursory recognition of the fundamental international obligations of the SOLAS Convention.[156] Since the ISPS Code avoids critical elements such as incident response, enforcement, or application beyond the limited scope of the ship to port interface, countries which adopt the regime verbatim or by reference also adopt its built-in limitations.[157]

The challenge for the community of maritime nations is to find a way to elevate the global port security regulatory discussion above the ISPS Code's minimum standards. Unfortunately, the MTSA and its Canadian and European counterparts are useless in this context because they are crafted to address specific, complex port security issues that result in unduly convoluted marine security policies in comparison to the port security regimes commonplace in many African, South American, and Asian maritime nations. Since the particularized Western security approach does not translate easily into a general system, a uniform template or guideline does not yet exist to develop improved international port security regulations.

---

[156] SOLAS, *supra* note 2, resolution 5 ("[I]n some cases, there may be limited infrastructure, facilities and training programmes for obtaining the experience required for the purpose of preventing acts which threaten the security of ships and of port facilities . . . .").

[157] The international community is aware of the built-in limitations and tries to address them in cooperative resolutions. *See* SOLAS, *supra* note 2, resolution 5 (strongly urging contracting governments and member states to "provide, in co-operation with the Organization, assistance to those States which have difficulty in implementing or meeting the requirements of the adopted amendments or the ISPS Code . . . .").

A. Developing a New International Port Security Code

The need for further development of more specific port security standards was reiterated in the 2002 amendment to the SOLAS Convention and its associated resolutions.[158] More than a decade later, no further progress has been made to achieve this. In the absence of such detailed guidance, many developing nations are left directionless in their quest to achieve the port security standards enjoyed by the world's more advanced nations. Considering this, the IMO should commence development of an advanced SOLAS port security regulatory model to assist developing countries, promote international cooperation, facilitate information sharing, and elevate the global port security regulatory discussion, emphasizing that the standard must be above and beyond the current ISPS Code minimums.

A review of international port security law reveals that the substance of such a template is emerging. In the years following the September 11th attacks, many countries recognize the value of enhanced port security regulatory standards and seek them out. Nations that transcend the ISPS Code do so by addressing meaningful enforcement, incident response, and conducting compliance evaluation. Although unavoidably piecemeal in nature, the efforts of individual nations to improve on respective legislative and regulatory schemes reflect genuinely innovative port security implementation developments and trend toward bridging ISPS Code gaps, particularly with regard to facility administration, prohibitions, procedures, personnel duties, and adjudication. This suggests a common benchmark for maritime nations to coordinate their port security expectations may be identified.[159]

How can one identify the common benchmark, coalescing these independent regulatory advances into a viable port security regulatory model? For comparative analysis, it is useful to rethink the concept of port security regulation, exchanging the ISPS Code's multi-layered, cross-referenced approach for simplicity. Though disparate in form and legal tradition, international port security regulations tend to group

---

[158] *See* SOLAS, *supra* note 2, resolution 2; ISPS Code, *supra* note 3, preamble para. 5.
[159] *See* Annex A, *supra* note 35.

around three common themes: (1) the controlling authority,[160] (2) the primary port security objectives,[161] and (3) the means utilized by the controlling authority to enforce the regulatory objectives.[162] Compiling the essence of these into a collection of legislative best practices will create a tool to allow maritime nations to share their innovations and learn from their trading partners. This compilation will serve as a comprehensive international model port security code, creating a new uniform standard.

B. *International Model Port Security Code*

Developing a code that is internationally comprehensible is a challenge. By design, such a model must be concise and straightforward enough to be widely accessible. The model code must be thorough enough in scope to serve capacity building and developmental assistance applications. Since nations of disparate legal tradition and governance wish to coordinate port security measures, it should be sufficiently detailed for use as an analytical checklist. Meanwhile, the model should avoid terms of art and cross-references and permit universal consideration as an *à la carte* menu of stand-alone port security regulatory options.

At minimum, a model code should define the duties and powers of port and shipping authorities and the general, physical, and operational security requirements for both ships and ports. The model code should explain the role of enforcement, prosecutorial, and judicial elements in the implementation of the requirements. The model code should incorporate a broad survey of existing laws and regulations defining offenses and penalties. Lastly, it should remain flexible to address the changing doctrines of port security law as the field continues to evolve in response to the persistent threat of international terrorism. To create this model code, the international maritime community should take steps to supplement existing port security guidance under SOLAS

---

[160] 33 C.F.R. § 103 (2011).
[161] 33 C.F.R. § 104 (2011).
[162] 46 U.S.C. § 70110(a) (2006).

with a Model Port Security Code that will provide developmental assistance beyond the current limited standard of the ISPS Code.[163]

IV. CONCLUSION

Prompted by the early twenty-first century surge in international terrorism, the international community recognizes the need to safeguard the global shipping industry by regulating and coordinating international ship and port security. The world's coastal nations demonstrated unprecedented levels of cooperation to craft the field of international law that is embodied in the ISPS Code. Although the ISPS Code serves as the current standard for international port security discussions, it was intentionally limited by its drafters, rendering it effectively unenforceable as a stand-alone document. Several nations have enacted measures to bridge these gaps, but the United States has taken its regulatory approach a step further, conceptually pushing the boundaries of port security back to the shores of the nation's foreign trading partners. The need for a uniform international port security code to enhance and protect international security is unmistakable.

From its inception, the efficacy of port security law has drawn from the unity of purpose of coastal states in promoting the integrity of the global shipping system. Recognizing this dynamic, the IMO entrusts the evolution of port security law to the international community itself, tasking SOLAS signatory states with mutual assistance in the development of effective port security laws and regulations.[164] As maritime and port security law continues to develop and mature, maritime trading partners find it increasingly important to continue to improve the port security infrastructure, elevating the port security discussion beyond ISPS Code minimum standards and establishing legislative means for effective response and enforcement.

To support this pursuit, the community of maritime nations should create an advanced port security regulatory model. Such a model will serve as both an analytical and capacity building tool, and will enable

---

[163] The author proposes the following Model Port Security Code substance and structure included in Annex B.
[164] SOLAS, *supra* note 2, resolution 5.

developing nations to consider and discuss the legislative and regulatory means by which their trading partners define governmental duties and authorities. Critically, a model international port security code will specify ship and port security requirements and empower law enforcement officers, prosecutors, and judges to protect their respective sectors of the international maritime trade. A model port security code will add much needed support to achieving the international community's goal of safe and secure ports.

ANNEX A: COMPREHENSIVE LIST OF LEGISLATION FOR ISPS CODE IMPLEMENTATION

Algeria	Executive Decree re: Matters of ship and port installation security; Executive Decree inscribing the designation of qualified authorities.
Angola	Decreto No. 48/05 Diario Da Republica August 8, 2005.
Angola	Decreto No. 66/07 Diario Da Republica August 15, 2007.
Antigua & Barbuda	Antigua and Barbuda Merchant Shipping Act, 2006, Official Gazette Vol. XXVI No. 19 dated 6th April, 2006, Part VI Maritime Security.
Argentina	Presidential Decree 1241/03 (Regimen de la Navegacion Maritima, Fluvial Y Lacustre, Decreto 1241/2003, No. 138.536/03 del registro del Ministerio de Justicia, Seguridad Y Derechos Humanos, 12/12/2003.
Aruba	AB 1993 No. GT 18, 17 August 2007; AB 2004 no. 40, 09 May 2007; Ministeriele Regeling 2009 no. 81, 16 September, 2009; Schepenbesluit 2004 Decree on Shipping 2004-B.
Australia	Maritime Transport and Offshore Facilities Security Act 2003 (Act no. 131 of 2003, amd Act no. 81 of 2010), 6 July 2010; Maritime Transport and Offshore Facilities Security Regulations 2003 (Statutory Rules 2003 no. 366 amd SLI 2010 no. 178), 1 July 2010.
Austria	230th Regulation of the Minister of Transport, Innovation and Technology a national program to increase the security of Austrian ships, No. 387/1996, 21 June 2006.
Bahrain	Law 48/2009, 8 July 2009.
Bangladesh	Merchant Shipping (Ship and Port Facility Security) Rules 2008, November 2008.
Belgium	Regulation (EC) No 725/2004, 31 March 04; Directive 2005/65/EC of the European Parliament and of the Council of 26 October 2005 on enhancing port security; Royal Decree on the State Control of the Port, Number: 2010014271/Docket number: 2010-12-22/19, 22 December 2010; Royal Decree Establishing Rules and Common Standards for Ship Inspection and Survey Organizations and Relevant Activities of Maritime Administrations, Number: 2011014041/Docket number: 2011-03-13/03, 13 March 2011.
Belize	Registration of Merchant Ships (Ship Security) Regulations, 2004, Statutory Instr. No. 90 of 2004, 30 April 2004; Port Facility Security Regulations, Statutory Instr. No. 101 of 2004, 12 June 2004.
Brazil	Plano Nacional De Segunca Publica Portuaria, December 2002.
Brunei	Merchant Shipping (Safety Convention) (Amendment) Regulations, 2004, 23 September, 2004.

Bulgaria	Regulation (EC) No 725/2004, 31 March 04; Directive 2005/65/EC of the European Parliament and of the Council of 26 October 2005 on enhancing port security.
Cambodia	Sub-Decree on Ship and Port Facility Securities, no. 40 SD/PK, 9 May 2006.
Cameroon	Decree No. 2008/237 of 7/17/08; Arrette No. 410 of 7/17/08.
Canada	Marine Transportation Security Act, S.C. 1994, c.40, December 15, 1994; Marine Transportation Security Regulations, SOR/2004-144, 21 May 2004.
Chile	Reglamento General de Orden, Seguridad Y Disciplina en las Naves Y Litoral de la Republica, 10 September 2009; Instrucciones Para Entidades Que Cuentin Con Sistemas De Seguridad Privada Maritimo-Portuaria, 30 November 1997.
China	International Ship Security Code, 2008; Port Facility Security Code, 2007; Gangkou Sheshi Bao'an Gongzuo Zhinan (Guidelines for Port Facility Security Practice); International Ship Security Code, 2008.
Colombia	Decreto 730 De 2004, Diario Oficial 45.488, 12 March 2004; Resolucion numero 354 Dimar-Digen de 2003, 13 November 2003; Resolucion numero 339 Dimar-Digen de 2003, 28 October 2003.
Congo	Arrete No. 276.
Congo, Dem Republic of the	Ordonnance portant Creation et Fonctionnement du Comite National de Surete Maritime (CNSM) No. 410/CAB/SGT/2009; Direction No, 041/16-10.c-10/2009, 24/03/2009.
Cook Islands	Shipping (Maritime Security) Regulations 2004, Act No. 13;2004, 16 June 2004.
Costa Rica	Decretos No. 31845-MOPT, Alcance No. 27 a La Gaceta No. 119, 18 June 2004.
Croatia	Regulation (EC) No 725/2004, 31 March 04; Directive 2005/65/EC of the European Parliament and of the Council of 26 October 2005 on enhancing port security; The Protection of Commercial Vessels and Ports Open to International Maritime Traffic Code (ISPS Code) (Zakon o sigurnosnoj zastiti trgovackih brodova i luka otvorenih za medunarodni promet), Broj: 01-081-04-1357/2; Port Security Act 2004 (Official Gazette 48/04); Maritime Code (Pomorski zakonic).
Cuba	Resolucion No. 251/05, Gaceta Oficial, 1 March 2006, p. 179.
Cyprus	Regulation (EC) No 725/2004, 31 March 04; Directive 2005/65/EC of the European Parliament and of the Council of 26 October 2005 on enhancing port security.

Denmark	Regulation (EC) No 725/2004, 31 March 04; Directive 2005/65/EC of the European Parliament and of the Council of 26 October 2005 on enhancing port security; Announcements from DMA B. Ship Building and Equipment of B Chapter XI-2 Special Measures to Enhance Maritime Security, Executive Order No. 9423, 7 June 2004; Order on the Security of Port Facilities, Executive Order No. 144, 8 March 2004; Announcement of Port Security Features, Ordinance No. 414, 08 May 2012.
Dominica	Marine Safety Circular, MSC 01-04.
Dominican Republic	Presidential Decree 1082-03, 25 November 2003; Comision Portuaria PBIP, 10 March 2004.
Ecuador	Executive Decree 1.111, 27 November 2003; Instruction Oficio No. DIGMER-244/2003 (Pt A); Instruction Oficio No. DIGMER-257/2004; Instruction Oficio No. DIGMER-264/2004 (Pt B); DIGMER-SPM-119-R, 13 December 2005; DIGMER-SPM-924-O, 04 March 2004.
El Salvador	Ley General Maritimo Portuaria, No. 994, Official Gazette 182, Vol. 357, 1 October 2002.
Equatorial Guinea	Ministerial Order No. 16/2008, 7 March 2008.
Eritrea	The Eritrean Port Regulations, Legal Notice No. 103/2005, Gazette Vol. 14/2005, No. 8, 30 October 2005.
Estonia	Regulation (EC) No 725/2004, 31 March 04; Directive 2005/65/EC of the European Parliament and of the Council of 26 October 2005 on enhancing port security.
Fiji	Maritime & Ports Authority Standard Operational Procedures for Security Officers; Marine (ISPS Code) Regulations 2008, Act No. 35, 2008.
Finland	Regulation (EC) No 725/2004, 31 March 04; Directive 2005/65/EC of the European Parliament and of the Council of 26 October 2005 on enhancing port security.
France	Regulation (EC) No 725/2004, 31 March 04; Directive 2005/65/EC of the European Parliament and of the Council of 26 October 2005 on enhancing port security; Ordonnance No. 2005-898, 2 August 2005; Decret No. 2007-476, 29 March 2007; Decret No. 2007-937, 15 May 2007; Order on the Safety of Ships, Official Gazette No. 0304/Text No. 17, 31 December 2008; Decree on the Safety of Ships, Official Gazette No. 142/Text No. 34, 20 June 2004; Amendments to the Annex to the 1974 International Convention for the Safety of Life at Sea, Together an International Code for the Security of Ships and Port Facilities (ISPS Code), Official Gazette No. 75/Text No. 5, 28 March 2004.

Gambia	Ports Act, Act No. 21 of 1972 (Amd 2009), Chapter 68:01, 1 September 2009.
Germany	Regulation (EC) No 725/2004, 31 March 04; Directive 2005/65/EC of the European Parliament and of the Council of 26 October 2005 on enhancing port security; Regulation of Self-protection of Ships to Defend Against External Threats, 2787, 19 September 2005.
Ghana	Ghana Maritime Security Act, 2004, Act 675, 1 November 2004.
Greece	Regulation (EC) No 725/2004, 31 March 04; Directive 2005/65/EC of the European Parliament and of the Council of 26 October 2005 on enhancing port security.
Grenada	Statutory Rules and Orders of 2004, June 2004 (Ships and Port Facilities Security Regulations 2004).
Guatemala	Resolucion de la Conferencia - Codigo Internacional Para La Proteccion de Los Buques Y De Las Instalaciones Portuarias, Diario de Centro America No. 82, p. 20, 31 July 2006.
Guyana	Guyana Shipping (Ship and Port Facility Security) Regulations 2004, Reg. no. 2 of 2004, The Official Gazette, 8 May 2004.
Honduras	Decreto Ejecutivo No. PCM-002-2004, La Gaceta, No. 30,378, 30 April 2004; Acuerdo No. 09-DT, La Gaceta, No. 30,686, 3 May 2005.
Hong Kong	Merchant Shipping (Security of Ships and Port Facilities) Rules, Gazette No. 13 of 2004, 29 June 2004.
Iceland	Act on Maritime Security No. 50/2004, cf. amd. No. 18/2007.
India	Merchant Shipping Act 1958; Amd 2002; Amd 2003; India Ports Act.
Indonesia	Regulations Implementing ISPS Code.
Iraq	Law of Ports 21/1995.
Ireland	Regulation (EC) No 725/2004, 31 March 04; Directive 2005/65/EC of the European Parliament and of the Council of 26 October 2005 on enhancing port security; European Communities (Port Security) Regulations 2007, Iris Oifigiuil, 15 June 2007; European Communities (Ship and Port Facilities) Regulations 2004, S.I. No. 413 of 2004.
Israel	Ports Order of 1972.
Italy	Regulation (EC) No 725/2004, 31 March 04; Directive 2005/65/EC of the European Parliament and of the Council of 26 October 2005 on enhancing port security.
Jamaica	Harbors Act; Shipping Act.
Japan	Law for the Security of Ships and Port Facilities Law No. 31, 4/14/04.
Jordan	Law No. 46 of 2006/Law of Jordan Maritime Authority; Resolution No. 1 of 2004.

Kenya	Merchant Shipping Act of 2009.
Kiribati	Sec. 16 of Shipping Act of 1990; Amd 2006; Kiribati Ports Authority Act 1990 (Amd 1999).
Kuwait	Ministeriel resolution No. 90, 2004.
Latvia	Regulation (EC) No 725/2004, 31 March 04; Directive 2005/65/EC of the European Parliament and of the Council of 26 October 2005 on enhancing port security; Cabinet Minister Reg. 682; Procedure for Providing Networking Activities Vessel Traffic Monitoring and Information System of Data Exchange Within, Cabinet Regulation No. 857, 4 August 2009.
Liberia	Marine Notice ISP-001 09/04; Monrovia Security Plan 21 MAR 05.
Lithuania	Regulation (EC) No 725/2004, 31 March 04; Directive 2005/65/EC of the European Parliament and of the Council of 26 October 2005 on enhancing port security; Res. 490, 30 Apr 01; MoTC Order no. 3-614, 6 Nov, 03; Gov. Decree No. 90, 28 Jan 04; MoTC Order No. 3-108, 25 Feb 04; MoTC Order No. 3-370, 29 Jun 04; LMSA Order No. V-37, 1 Mar 05; MoTC Order No. 3-254, 1 Jun 05Gov. Decree no. 485, 29 May 06; MoTC Order No. 3-234, 8 Jun 06; MoTC Order No. 3-2, 23 Jun 0662; International Ship and Port Facility (Terminal) Security Code, Nr.138-503, 9 December 2002.
Malaysia	Act A1316 Merchant Shipping Act 2007.
Maldives	Draft Port Security Regulation.
Malta	Regulation (EC) No 725/2004, 31 March 04; Directive 2005/65/EC of the European Parliament and of the Council of 26 October 2005 on enhancing port security; Malta Maritime Authority Act, Subsidiary Legislation 352.21 2004.
Marshall Islands	MTSA; Title 22; Port Security Regulations; Marine Notice 2-011-16.
Mauritania	Decree 2006-016.
Mauritius	GN/03; 28/04; Ports Regulations 2005.
Mexico	Resolution no. 117; Ley de Navigacion; Reg. 5 Jul 2004.
Montenegro	Zakon O Sigurnosti Pomorske Plovidbe, February 2012.
Mozambique	Resolution No. 25/2004 of 14 July 2004.
Myanmar	Myanmar Merchant Shipping Act 1/2007 (7 Feb 07); The Burma Merchant Shipping Act.
Namibia	Namibia Ports Authority Act, No. 2 of 1994.
Nauru	Port Security Plan (Non-sig/recent coup).
Netherland Antilles (BES)	Landsbesluit havenbeveiling (Ao 2004 No. 51); Eilandsbesluit havenbeveiling (Ao 2004 No. 51); Lansverordening 29 Dec 2009; Ministeriele Beschikkink (PB 2004, No. 51).

Netherlands	Regulation (EC) No 725/2004, 31 March 04; Directive 2005/65/EC of the European Parliament and of the Council of 26 October 2005 on enhancing port security; Havenbeveiligingswet [Port Security Law] 7/6/04 & 7/7/10; Schepenbesluit 2004.
New Zealand	Maritime Security Act, March 31, 2004; Maritime Security Regulations, 2004.
Nicaragua	SOLAS Adopted by reference: Nat'l Law 399 (La Gazeta 9/13/04); Regs 2004/153.
Oman	Sultani Decree 98/81 Law for Organization of Sea Trade in Territorial Waters; Decree 12/93; Decree 35/81.
Pakistan	Karachi Port Security Force Ordinance, LXXXIV of 2002; Maritime Security Agency Act, 1994; Coast Guards Act, 1973.
Palau	Executive Order 221; Maritime Security Regulations.
Panama	Ley de Migracion (Ley No. 3 22 Feb 08); Ley 56 (6 Aug 08); Ley 57- General de marine Mercante, 6 August 2008; Ley 57 - General de Marine Mercante, 6 August 2008.
Papua New Guinea	Decision 217/2005; Merchant Shipping Regulation 2004.
Peru	Resolución Ministerial (Ministerial Resolution) 300-2004-MTC/02; 329-2004-MTC/02.
Philippines	Executive Order No. 311; Dept Order No. 2005-05; Senate Bill S.No. 970 (2010); RA No. 9993 (2011).
Poland	Regulation (EC) No 725/2004, 31 March 04; Directive 2005/65/EC of the European Parliament and of the Council of 26 October 2005 on enhancing port security.
Portugal	Regulation (EC) No 725/2004, 31 March 04; Directive 2005/65/EC of the European Parliament and of the Council of 26 October 2005 on enhancing port security.
Qatar	Law 8/2004 Protection of Maritime Facilities; Dec. 1966/29 Decree for the Organization of Qatari Seaports.
Romania	Regulation (EC) No 725/2004, 31 March 04; Directive 2005/65/EC of the European Parliament and of the Council of 26 October 2005 on enhancing port security.
Russia	Document No. 16-03, 9 Feb 07. RF Gov't Reg. 324 (4/11/00); RF Inst. BP-177-p (8/12/03); RF Inst. BP-29-p (2/25/04).
Samoa	Maritime Security Act, 2004; Shipping Act 1998
Sao Tome & Principe	Law Decree 2/1994, 13/2007, 32/2007, 30/2009; PF Access regulations March 2009; Decreto-Lei No. 4/2010.
Saudi Arabia	2006 GCC Rules & Regulations for Seaports (Partial).
Senegal	Decree 2006.322; Decision 2004.565; Decision 2004.1037.
Singapore	Maritime and Port Authority of Singapore Act of 1996 (S 215/2004 Amended) & Merchant Shipping Act of 1995. (Amended).

Slovenia	Reg (EC) No 725/2004, 31 Mar 05; Dir. 2005/65/EC, 26 Oct 05; 884/2005.
Solomon Islands	National Merchant Shipping Act, 1998.
Somalia	Maritime Security Bill 2011; Administrative Activity, Police and Service in Ports.
South Africa	Merchant Shipping Act 1951; Regulations, 2004; National Ports Act No. 12 2005.
South Korea	Ship and Port Facility Security Regulation No. 2003-65; Act for the Security of International Ship and Port Facilities; Enforcement Decree of the Act for the Security of International Ship and Port Facilities, February 4, 2008.
Spain	Reg (EC) No 725/2004, 31 Mar 05; Dir. 2005/65/EC, 26 Oct 05; 884/2005; Real Decreto 1617/2007, 7 Dec.; 2005 Amendments to the International Code for the Security of Ships and Facilities (ISPS Code), 196 (80), 20 May 2005; Resolution 1 of the Conference of Government Contracting International for the Safety of Life at Sea, Resolution 1, 12 December 2002; Resolution 2 of the Conference of Government Contracting International for the Safety of Life at Sea, Resolution 2, 12 December 2002; Ministry of Development Order, FOM/2381/2008 ORDER 13708, 30 July 2008; Annex to the Convention for the Safety of Life at Sea, 12 December 2002.
St. Kitts Nevis	Merchant Shipping (Ships and Port Facility Security) Regulations, 2004.
St. Lucia	Shipping (Ship and Port Facility Security) Regulations No. 46 of June 29, 2004.
St. Vincent	Ship and Port Facility Security Regulations, 2004 (Gazette of Statutory Rules and Orders, 2004 No. 18 6/29/04).
Sudan	Ministerial Decree 9/2003.
Suriname	Maritime Security Law, 2004 (SB 2004 No.90).
Sweden	Regulation (EC) No 725/2004, 31 March 04; Directive 2005/65/EC of the European Parliament and of the Council of 26 October 2005 on enhancing port security.
Syria	Unified Investments in Syrian Ports.
Taiwan	Commercial Port Law, 2005/02/05.
Tanzania	Merchant Shipping Act (No. 21 of 2003).
Thailand	Untranslated Legislation.
Timor-Leste	Draft Regulations.
Togo	Arrette No. 008/MTPTUH/SG/DAM; Arrette No. 009/MTPTUH/SG/DAM; Ministerial Order 9 Apr 10 (Prescriptions); Ministerial Order 2 Feb 10 (Report).
Tonga	Shipping Act Section (CAP 136); International Ship and Port Facility Security Regulation of 2004; Maritime Security SOP.

Trinidad & Tobago	Port Authority Procedures; Shipping Regs Ch. 50:10.
Tunisia	Maritime Safety Acts (Amd) 1976, 1999.
Turkey	Law 618/1925; Law 2692/1982.
Tuvalu	Merchant Shipping Act (Rev. 2008).
Ukraine	2 Shovtnya 2008, Sec. 16:10; 16:11; 16:18; 17:08; 17:13; 17:25; 17:50; 18:08; 18:03; 18:16.
United Arab Emirates	Port of Fujirah Ordinance of 1982.; NTA Strategic Plan 2011-2013.
United Kingdom	Regulation (EC) No 725/2004, 31 March 04; Directive 2005/65/EC of the European Parliament and of the Council of 26 October 2005 on enhancing port security; The Port Security Regulations 2009, No. 2048, 1 September 2009; The Ship and Port Facility (Security) Regulations 2004, No. 1495, 1 July 2004; The Ship and Port Facility (Security) (Amendment) Regulations 2005, No. 1434, 1 July 2005.
Uruguay	Instructivo De Proteccion Maritima; Decreto 181/2004.
Vanuatu	Port Security Regulation Order No. 17 of 2004.
Vietnam	PM Decision 125/2004; PM Decision 11/2009; Ministry of Transport Circular No. 27/2001/TT-BGTVT 4/14/11; Prime Minister Decision No. 191 9/16/2003.
Yemen	PFSP in file; Ministry of Transport Decision 108/2009 Rules & Instructions for Yemeni Ports.

ANNEX B: PROPOSED MODEL PORT SECURITY CODE SUBSTANCE AND STRUCTURE REVISIONS

MODEL PORT SECURITY CODE

Preamble

Part I – Authority

Chapter 1	**GENERAL PROVISIONS**
ARTICLE 1	Purpose
ARTICLE 2	Applicability
ARTICLE 3	Definitions
ARTICLE 4	Ship to Port Interface
ARTICLE 5	Force of Law
ARTICLE 6	Convention Authority
ARTICLE 7	Equivalent Security Arrangements
ARTICLE 8	Alternative Security Agreements

Part II – Maritime Security Organization

Chapter 1	**NATIONAL PORT SECURITY AUTHORITY (DESIGNATED AUTHORITY)**
ARTICLE 9	National Port Security Authority (NPSA)
ARTICLE 10	NPSA Duties
ARTICLE 11	NPSA Investigative Authority
ARTICLE 12	NPSA Enforcement Authority
ARTICLE 13	NPSA Adjudication Authority
ARTICLE 14	NPSA Security Level/Governance Authority
ARTICLE 15	NPSA Regulatory Authority
ARTICLE 16	NPSA Delegation Authority
Chapter 2	**PORT SECURITY ORGANIZATION**
ARTICLE 17	Port Security Officer (PSO)
ARTICLE 18	PSO Duties
ARTICLE 19	PSO Authority
ARTICLE 20	PSO Delegation Authority
ARTICLE 21	Port Facility Security Officer (PFSO)
ARTICLE 22	PFSO Duties
ARTICLE 23	PFSO Authority
ARTICLE 24	Port Security Committee (PSC)
ARTICLE 25	PSC Duties
ARTICLE 26	PSC Authority
Chapter 3	**SHIP SECURITY ORGANIZATION**
ARTICLE 27	Company Security Officer (CSO)
ARTICLE 28	CSO Duties

ARTICLE 29	CSO Authority
ARTICLE 30	Ship Security Officer (SSO)
ARTICLE 31	SSO Duties
ARTICLE 32	SSO Authority
Chapter 4	**RECOGNIZED SECURITY ORGANIZATIONS**
ARTICLE 33	Recognized Security Organizations (RSO)
ARTICLE 34	Recognized Security Organization Restrictions
ARTICLE 35	Recognized Security Organization Qualifications

Part III – General Security Provisions

Chapter 1	**SECURITY DOCUMENTATION**
ARTICLE 36	Security Assessments
ARTICLE 37	Security Plans
ARTICLE 38	Security Plan Integrity
ARTICLE 39	Statement of Compliance
ARTICLE 40	Declarations of Security
Chapter 2	**SECURITY LEVELS**
ARTICLE 41	Security Levels - General
ARTICLE 42	Security Level 1
ARTICLE 43	Security Level 2
ARTICLE 44	Security Level 3
Chapter 3	**TRAINING, DRILLS, AND EXERCISES**
ARTICLE 45	Training
ARTICLE 46	Drills
ARTICLE 47	Exercises
Chapter 4	**SECURITY PERSONNEL**
ARTICLE 48	Screening requirements
ARTICLE 49	Basic Port Security Knowledge
Chapter 5	**PROHIBITIONS**
ARTICLE 50	Conflicts of interest
Chapter 6	**RECORDS AND AUDITS**
ARTICLE 51	Record Keeping
ARTICLE 52	Audit Requirements

Part IV – Port Facility Security Procedures

Chapter 1	**PHYSICAL SECURITY**
ARTICLE 53	Restricted Areas
ARTICLE 54	Fixed and Moving Security Zones
ARTICLE 55	Restricted Access
ARTICLE 56	Perimeter

ARTICLE 57	Signage
ARTICLE 58	Access Points
ARTICLE 59	Communications
ARTICLE 60	Surveillance
Chapter 2	**ACCESS CONTROL**
ARTICLE 61	Access Control
ARTICLE 62	Identification Requirements
ARTICLE 63	Access Control – Regular users
ARTICLE 64	Access Control – Service providers
ARTICLE 65	Access Control – Ship's crew
ARTICLE 66	Access Control – Visitors
ARTICLE 67	Access Control – Vehicles
ARTICLE 68	Access Control – Law Enforcement/Emergency Responders
ARTICLE 69	Unauthorized Access Procedures
Chapter 3	**SHIP CONTROL**
ARTICLE 70	Ship Control Measures
ARTICLE 71	Conditions of Entry
ARTICLE 72	Communications/Reporting Procedures
Chapter 4	**PORT FACILITY OPERATIONS**
ARTICLE 73	Cargo Operations
ARTICLE 74	Ship's Stores
ARTICLE 75	Passenger Procedures
Chapter 5	**INCIDENT RESPONSE**
ARTICLE 76	Port Security Incidents
ARTICLE 77	Security Threats
ARTICLE 78	Incident Reporting Requirements
ARTICLE 79	Major Incident Response
ARTICLE 80	Minor Incident Response
ARTICLE 81	Weapons of Mass Destruction Response

Part V – Ship Security Procedures

Chapter 1	**PHYSICAL SECURITY**
ARTICLE 82	Security Zones
ARTICLE 83	Restricted Access
ARTICLE 84	Access Points
ARTICLE 85	Signage
ARTICLE 86	Lighting
ARTICLE 87	Surveillance
ARTICLE 88	Key Control
ARTICLE 89	Communications
ARTICLE 90	Defensive Security Equipment

ARTICLE 91	Ship Security Alert System (SSAS)
ARTICLE 92	Automated Identification System (AIS)
ARTICLE 93	Long Range Identification and Tracking (LRIT)
Chapter 2	**OPERATIONAL SECURITY**
ARTICLE 94	Master's Discretion
ARTICLE 95	Port Control Compliance
ARTICLE 96	Manning Requirements
ARTICLE 97	Security Sweeps
ARTICLE 98	Access Control
ARTICLE 99	Cargo Operations
ARTICLE 100	Ship's Stores
ARTICLE 101	Passenger Procedures
ARTICLE 102	International Ship Security Certificate (ISSC)
Chapter 3	**INCIDENT RESPONSE**
ARTICLE 103	Security Incidents
ARTICLE 104	Unauthorized Access/Breach Procedures
ARTICLE 105	Stowaway Procedures

Part VI - Enforcement

Chapter 1	**ENFORCEMENT AUTHORITIES**
ARTICLE 106	Administrative Enforcement Authority
ARTICLE 107	Security Guards - Defined
ARTICLE 108	Security Guard Authority
ARTICLE 109	Law Enforcement - Officers
ARTICLE 110	Law Enforcement Authority
ARTICLE 111	Quick Response Team
ARTICLE 112	Master's Power to Detain
Chapter 2	**INQUIRIES AND PROSECUTIONS**
ARTICLE 113	Administrative Inquiries
ARTICLE 114	Criminal Prosecutions
Chapter 3	**ADMINISTRATION ADJUDICATION**
ARTICLE 115	Administrative Jurisdiction
ARTICLE 116	Administrative Adjudication Authority
ARTICLE 117	Administrative Adjudication Procedure
ARTICLE 118	Administrative Remedies – Vessels
ARTICLE 119	Administrative Remedies – Facilities
ARTICLE 120	Administrative Remedies – Persons
ARTICLE 121	Administrative Appeals
Chapter 4	**CRIMINAL ADJUDICATION**
ARTICLE 122	Criminal Jurisdiction
ARTICLE 123	Venue

ARTICLE 124   Criminal Adjudication Procedure
ARTICLE 125   Criminal Appellate Procedure

Chapter 5   **OFFENSES & PENALTIES**
ARTICLE 126   Offenses – General
ARTICLE 127   Administrative Violations
ARTICLE 128   Criminal Violations

Appendix   Offenses and Penalties

COMMENT

EXECUTIVE PROCESS:
THE DUE PROCESS OF EXECUTIVE CITIZEN TARGETING BY THE COMMANDER-IN-CHIEF

Noah Oberlander[*]

INTRODUCTION

A group of insurgents attacked on September 11 in defiance against the United States Federal Government.[1] Fueled by foreign radical ideology and terror, the insurgents threatened the safety and well-being of the nation. The President issued an initial proclamation denouncing the insurgency and establishing procedures to defeat the insurgent group. As the United States' confrontation against the insurgency continued, the President's most trusted national security advisor, the Secretary of the Treasury, began meeting with intelligence and military officials to compile a list of high value insurgents for the military to target. One of

---

[*] George Mason University School of Law, J.D. 2014; Patrick Henry College, B.A. 2011. Thank you to Brandon Bierlein, Jeff Jennings, and Jessica Wagner for being healthy skeptics of Executive Power.

[1] The following scenario is based on a historical account of the Whiskey Rebellion. WILLIAM HOGELAND, THE WHISKEY REBELLION: GEORGE WASHINGTON, ALEXANDER HAMILTON, AND THE FRONTIER REBELS WHO CHALLENGED AMERICA'S NEWFOUND SOVEREIGNTY 215-36 (2006).

the insurgents at the top of the list, an American citizen, was believed to play an operational and support role in the insurgency.

The Secretary of the Treasury advised the President that while due process may require judicial process for prolonged detainment of the insurgents, initial military action to capture or kill the insurgents did not require court involvement. The President stressed the highest standards of legality ought to be followed when confronting the insurgents. Acting under general Congressional authorization and inherent constitutional power as Commander-in-Chief, the President approved the list and authorized military action.

The preceding scenario is not a description of the post-9/11 War on Terrorism or President Obama's targeting of Anwar al-Awlaki ("al-Awlaki"),[2] an American citizen and al Qaeda Arabian Peninsula leader.[3] Rather, the scenario describes the events of September 11, 1794 and George Washington's response to the Whiskey Rebellion.[4] Though separated by over two hundred years and quantum leaps in technological sophistication, the presidential response to this type of national crisis is largely unchanged. Today, the Executive Branch continues to grapple with the same normative and legal issues surrounding due process when responding to national security threats from American citizens. Yet, from George Washington's response in the Whiskey Rebellion, to President Obama's targeting of al-Awlaki, presidential action as Commander-in-Chief constitutes executive process.

This Comment argues that President Obama's targeting of American citizens like al-Awlaki complies with the Fifth Amendment's procedural requirement of due process[5] by affording those citizens

---

[2] Certain sources will alternatively spell "al-Awlaki" as "al-Aulaqi" consistent with its phonetic pronunciation. *See* Al-Aulaqi v. Obama, 727 F. Supp. 2d 1 (D.D.C. 2010).
[3] President Barack Obama, Remarks by the President at the "Change of Office" Chairman of the Joint Chiefs of Staff Ceremony (September 30, 2011) (transcript), *available at* http://www.whitehouse.gov/the-press-office/2011/09/30/remarks-president-change-office-chairman-joint-chiefs-staff-ceremony.
[4] *See* HOGELAND, *supra* note 1, at 208-09; THOMAS P. SLAUGHTER, THE WHISKEY REBELLION: FRONTIER EPILOGUE TO THE AMERICAN REVOLUTION (1986).
[5] U.S. CONST. amend. V ("No person shall . . . be deprived of life, liberty, or property, without due process of law . . . .").

executive process. Part I of this Comment explains that while judicial process is the most common form of due process, the omission of judicial procedure does not automatically violate due process. The Obama Administration argues the targeting process gave al-Awlaki sufficient due process to satisfy the constitutional requirement necessary for the killing of an American citizen. Specifically, the Obama Administration has established specific procedures for targeting American citizens like al-Awlaki. While critics argue targeting al-Awlaki violated due process, they overlook two alternative theories of due process: fairness and separation of powers. Part II of this Comment traces the progression of executive process under both theories of due process; fairness and separation of powers Necessity warrants executive process under a theory of due process as fairness. Discretion as Commander-in-Chief warrants executive process under a theory of due process as separation of powers. Part III of this Comment gives a rationale for targeting American citizens like al-Awlaki under both theories of due process. Under the *Mathews v. Eldridge*[6] balancing test, the Executive's targeting of al-Awlaki protected national security and President Obama's regularized procedure adequately minimized risk of error. Under the separation of powers theory, the Commander-in-Chief Clause confers on the President the discretion to act consistent with Congressional statute to ensure national security.

I. DUE PROCESS IS NOT MERELY JUDICIAL PROCESS

Judicial process is the most visible and commonly afforded type of due process, yet since the early days of the republic, the Supreme Court has recognized executive process as a real and meaningful species of due process.[7] Executive process is most often present when the President is acting under his authority as Commander-in-Chief against a national security threat.[8]

---

[6] 424 U.S. 319, 333-36 (1976).
[7] Martin v. Mott, 25 U.S. (12 Wheat.) 19, 30 (1827).
[8] *Id.*

A. *The Obama Administration's Executive Citizen Targeting Program*

While the Obama Administration has established a program that can target U.S. citizens who are senior operational leaders of al Qaeda or associated forces,[9] the only known American targeted to date is Anwar al-Awlaki.[10]

1. The Executive's Targeting of American Citizen al-Awlaki

In April 2010, the Obama Administration authorized the Central Intelligence Agency ("CIA") to target al-Awlaki, an American citizen born in New Mexico living in the Arabian nation of Yemen.[11] Although al-Awlaki allegedly met two of the 9/11 hijackers while serving as an imam at a mosque in San Diego;[12] following the September 11, 2001 terrorist attacks, al-Awlaki communicated a message of moderate mutual understanding to a congregation at the Dar al Hijrah Islamic Center located in the Washington, D.C. metropolitan area.[13] Yet, when

---

[9] U.S. Dep't of Justice, Lawfulness of a Lethal Operation Directed Against a U.S. Citizen Who Is a Senior Operational Leader of Al-Qa'ida or an Associated Force (Nov. 8, 2011) (released Feb. 3, 2013), http://www.fas.org/irp/eprint/doj-lethal.pdf.

[10] *See* Charlie Savage, *Secret U.S. Memo Made Legal Case To Kill a Citizen*, N.Y. Times, Oct. 8, 2011, at A1 (explaining while U.S. citizen Samir Khan was also killed by a drone strike he was not the target and merely collateral damage); Tom Finn & Noah Browning, *An American Teenager in Yemen: Paying for the Sins of His Father?*, Time (Oct. 27, 2011), http://www.time.com/time/world/article/0,8599,2097899,00.html ("A U.S. official said the young man 'was in the wrong place at the wrong time,' and that the U.S. was trying to kill a legitimate terrorist—al-Qaeda leader Ibrahim al-Banna, who also died—in the strike that apparently killed the American teenager."); Dana Priest & William M. Arkin, *Inside the CIA's "Kill List"*, PBS Frontline (Sept. 6, 2011), http://www.pbs.org/wgbh/pages/frontline/iraq-war-on-terror/topsecretamerica/inside-the-cias-kill-list/ ("[A]nother American al-Qaeda member, Adam Gadahn, was never considered for execution because in the judgment of intelligence analysts he was all talk, a Tokyo Rose.").

[11] Scott Shane, *U.S. Approves Targeted Killing of American Cleric*, NYTimes.com, Apr. 6, 2010, http://www.nytimes.com/2010/04/07/world/middleeast/07yemen.html.

[12] Mark Mazzetti, Eric Schmitt, and Robert F. Worth, *Two-Year Manhunt Led to Killing of Awlaki in Yemen*, N.Y. Times, Sept. 30, 2011, http://www.nytimes.com/2011/10/01/world/middleeast/anwar-al-awlaki-is-killed-in-yemen.html.

[13] *See NewsHour with Jim Leher, Fighting Fear: Ray Suarez Examines How Life Has Changed for one American Muslim Community Since Sept. 11* (PBS television broadcast

al-Awlaki left the United States for Yemen in 2004, his message shifted to anti-Americanism[14] and encouraging attacks against the United States.[15]

Once in Yemen, al-Awlaki became the "leader of external operations for al Qaeda in the Arabian Peninsula."[16] In 2010, the United States determined al-Awlaki was involved with the killing of thirteen persons at Fort Hood in Texas and linked to the plot to detonate explosives on an airliner in Detroit on Christmas Day 2010.[17] Al-Awlaki's confirmed his involvement with Nidal Hasan in the Fort Hood attack in a propaganda video.[18]

In April 2010, the New York Times reported that the National Security Council approved placing al-Awlaki on the CIA's list of terrorists targeted for killing with a drone strike.[19] In August 2010, al-Awlaki's father filed a lawsuit in the United States District Court for the District of Columbia seeking relief under the Alien Tort Statute and an injunction preventing the Executive from using lethal force against al-Awlaki.[20] The District Court found "the political question doctrine bar[red] judicial resolution" of the case, and therefore no injunction was issued.[21] On September 30, 2011, President Obama announced al-Awlaki was successfully killed in an American drone strike in Yemen, dealing "a major blow to al-Qaeda's most active operational affiliate."[22]

Oct. 30, 2001), http://www.pbs.org/newshour/bb/religion/july-dec01/fear_10-30.html.

> The fact that the U.S. has administered the death and homicide of over one million civilians in Iraq, the fact that the U.S. is supporting the deaths and killing of thousands of Palestinians does not justify the killing of one U.S. civilian in New York City or Washington, D.C., and the deaths of 6,000 civilians in New York and Washington, DC, does not justify the death of one civilian in Afghanistan.

[14] Mazzetti, Schmitt, and Worth, *supra* note 13.
[15] *Al-Awlaki Threatens Americans* (CNN.com broadcast Nov. 9, 2010), http://www.cnn.com/video/#/video/world/2010/11/09/todd.al.awlaki.threat.cnn.
[16] Obama, *supra* note 3.
[17] Shane, *supra* note 12.
[18] *Message to the American People by Sheikh Al-Awlaki* (2010), http://archive.org/details/AwlakiToUsa.
[19] Shane, *supra* note 12.
[20] Al-Aulaqi v. Obama, 727 F. Supp. 2d 1, 12 (D.D.C. 2010).
[21] *Id.* at 52.
[22] Obama, *supra* note 3.

2. The Obama Administration Agrees al-Awlaki Was Entitled to Due Process

Although the Department of Justice has composed a roughly fifty page memorandum explaining the legal rationale for targeting al-Awlaki, the memorandum is classified and remains secret despite Freedom of Information Act requests.[23] Despite the memorandum's secrecy, the Obama Administration acknowledged the importance of publically explaining the rationale for the targeted killing of citizens. Several senior White House officials give a handful of speeches that generally explained the program.[24] Additionally, in the Department of Justice released a White Paper summarizing its legal rationale for targeting U.S. citizens who are senior operational leaders of al Qaeda.[25] These Administration speeches, the DOJ White Paper, along with scattered press articles,

---

[23] On October 27, 2011, the Department of Justice denied the New York Times' two requests and the American Civil Liberties Union's one request for release of documents regarding the al-Awlaki memorandum under the Freedom of Information Act. The ACLU's first request has been partially stayed by the United States District Court for the Northern District of California. *See* First Amendment Coal. v. U.S. Dep't of Justice, No. C 12-1013, 2012 WL 3027460 (N.D. Cal.). The ACLU's second request was denied on January 3, 2013 by the United States District Court for the Southern District of New York. *See* N.Y. Times Co. v. U.S. Dep't of Justice, Nos. 11 Civ. 9336 & 12 Civ. 794, 2013 WL 50209 (S.D.N.Y.).

[24] *See, e.g.*, Attorney Gen. Eric Holder, Speech at Northwestern University School of Law (Mar. 5, 2012) (transcript available at http://www.justice.gov/iso/opa/ag/speeches/2012/ag-speech-1203051.html); John O. Brennan, Assistant to the President for Homeland Security and Counterterrorism, Speech at Harvard Law School: Strengthening Our Security by Adhering to Our Values and Laws (Sept. 16, 2011) (transcript available at http://www.whitehouse.gov/the-press-office/2011/09/16/remarks-john-o-brennan-strengthening-our-security-adhering-our-values-an); Harold Hongju Koh, Legal Advisor, U.S. Dep't of State, Speech at Annual Meeting of the American Society of International Law: The Obama Administration and International Law (March 25, 2010) (transcript available at http://www.state.gov/s/l/releases/remarks/139119.htm); Jeh Charles Johnson, Gen. Counsel, U.S. Dep't of Def., Dean's Lecture at Yale Law School: National Security Law, Lawyers and Lawyering in the Obama Administration (Feb. 22, 2012) (transcript available at http://www.cfr.org/national-security-and-defense/jehjohnsons-speech-national-security-law-lawyers-lawyering-obama-administration/p27448).

[25] U.S. DEP'T OF JUSTICE, LAWFULNESS OF A LETHAL OPERATION DIRECTED AGAINST A U.S. CITIZEN WHO IS A SENIOR OPERATIONAL LEADER OF AL-QA'IDA OR AN ASSOCIATED FORCE (Nov. 8, 2011) [hereinafter D.O.J. WHITE PAPER], *available at* http://www.fas.org/irp/eprint/doj-lethal.pdf.

provide enough details to piece together an evaluation of Executive Citizen Targeting.[26]

To the surprise of many of the program's critics, the legal rationale for Executive Citizen Targeting does not rely on emergency circumstances to justify bypassing the strictures of procedural due process.[27] Rather, the program affirms that even United States citizens who try to kill innocent Americans are entitled to the Fifth Amendment's procedural guarantee that the government may not deprive a citizen of his or her life without due process of law.[28] On the contrary, the central tenant of Executive Citizen Targeting is that "'due process' and 'judicial process' are not one and the same, particularly when it comes to national security."[29]

3. The Process Used to Target al-Awlaki

Evaluation of the Executive's action against al-Awlaki first requires a detailed understanding of the procedures already in place. The CIA and the military's Joint Special Operations Command ("JSOC") both keep lists of non-citizen terrorists who may be lawfully targeted.[30] The CIA list requires that potential targets must pose a "current and ongoing threat to the United States."[31] This requires evidentiary proof that is greater than a "some evidence" standard and is more like a "reasonable

---

[26] Savage, *supra* note 10.
[27] Amos Guiora, *Targeted Killing: Lawful if Conducted in Accordance with the Rule of Law*, in PATRIOTS DEBATE: CONTEMPORARY ISSUES IN NATIONAL SECURITY LAW 162-67 (2012); Toren G. Evers-Mushovic & Michael Hughes, *Rules for When There Are no Rules: Examining the Legality of Putting American Terrorists in the Crosshairs Abroad*, 18 NEW ENG. J. INT'L & COMP. L. 157 (2012); Michael Epstein, *The Curious Case of Anwar Al-Aulaqi: Is Targeting a Terrorist for Execution by Drone Strike a Due Process Violation when the Terrorist is a United States Citizen?*, 19 MICH. ST. J. INT'L L. 723 (2011).
[28] Holder, *supra* note 25; D.O.J WHITE PAPER, *supra* note 25, at 5 ("The Department assumes that the rights afforded by the Fifth Amendment's Due Process Clause . . . attach to a U.S. citizen even while he is abroad.").
[29] Holder, *supra* note 25.
[30] Mark Hosenball, *Secret Panel Can Put Americans on Kill List*, REUTERS (Oct. 5, 2011 7:59 PM), http://www.reuters.com/article/2011/10/05/us-cia-killlist-idUSTRE79475C20111005.
[31] Priest, *supra* note 10.

suspicion" or "probable cause standard."[32] The JSOC list requires the government to show potential targets are an enemy terrorist based on "two verifiable human sources", along with "substantial additional evidence." [33] Both lists include an unambiguous and unqualified preference to take custody of terrorists rather than kill them.[34]

For an American citizen to be targeted, the intelligence community must get approval and "specific permission"[35] through a two-tiered process at the National Security Council (NSC).[36] First, mid-level NSC officials,[37] likely the NSC Deputies Committee,[38] must recommend an American citizen terrorist for targeting. After this initial process, the

---

[32] *See* D.O.J WHITE PAPER, *supra* note 25 (stating that for a citizen to be targeted there must be "no evidence suggesting that he has renounced or abandoned such [terrorist] activities"). *Compare* Tara Mckelvey, *Inside the Killing Machine*, NEWSWEEK (Feb. 13, 2011), http://www.thedailybeast.com/newsweek/2011/02/13/inside-the-killing-machine.html:

> The CIA cables are legalistic and carefully argued. . . . The dossier, he says, "would go to the lawyers, and they would decide. They were very picky." Sometimes . . . the hurdles may have been too high. . . . Sometimes . . . the evidence against an individual would be thin, and high-level lawyers would tell their subordinates, "You guys did not make a case. . . ." "Sometimes the justification would be that the person was thought to be at a meeting" "It was too squishy." The memo would get kicked back downstairs.

with Hamdi v. Rumsfeld, 542 U.S. 507, 527 (2004) (explaining that a some evidence standard focuses "exclusively on the factual basis supplied by the Executive to support its own determination" and "does not require a weighing of the evidence, but rather calls for assessing whether there is any evidence in the record that could support the conclusion").

[33] S. COMM. ON FOREIGN RELATIONS, 111TH CONG, AFGHANISTAN'S NARCO-WAR: BREAKING THE LINK BETWEEN DRUG TRAFFICKERS AND INSURGENTS (Comm. Print 2009).

[34] Brennan, *supra* note 24.

[35] Shane, *supra* note 11.

[36] *Id.*

[37] Hosenball, *supra* note 30.

[38] The National Security Council Deputies Committee is chaired by the Assistant to the President and Deputy National Security and includes the Deputy Secretary of State, the Deputy Secretary of the Treasury, the Deputy Secretary of Defense, the Deputy Attorney General, the Deputy Secretary of Energy, the Deputy Secretary of Homeland Security, the Deputy Director of the Office of Management and Budget, the Deputy to the United States Representative to the United Nations, the Deputy Director of National Intelligence, the Vice Chairman of the Joint Chiefs of Staff, and the Assistant to the Vice President for National Security Affairs. *See* National Security Presidential Directive/PPD-1: Organization of the National Security Council System 3-4 (2009), http://www.fas.org/irp/offdocs/ppd/ppd-1.pdf.

NSC Principals Committee[39] reviews the target recommendations under the criteria outlined below.[40] Finally, the National Security Advisor notifies the President of the NSC's targeting decision and the President can unilaterally nullify the NSC's targeting decision for any reason.[41] Consistent with the constitutional system of checks and balances, the Executive Branch regularly informs appropriate members of Congress[42] and the public[43] about lethal force used against American citizens consistent with the constitutional system of checks and balances.

When reviewing an American terrorist target recommendation, Executive officials carefully determine whether (1) the citizen poses an imminent threat of violent attack against the United States, (2) capture is not feasible, and (3) the operation will be conducted in a way consistent with applicable law of war principles.[44] First, the Executive Branch determines a threat is imminent by weighing the relevant window to act, the possible harm to civilians by waiting, and the likelihood of future disastrous attacks against the United States.[45] For instance, the Executive Branch determined American citizen al-Awlaki's operational role was an imminent threat, whereas American citizen Adam Gadahn's anti-American rhetoric and al Qaeda membership was not an imminent threat.[46] While this view of imminence is more flexible than in the law enforcement context, it is consistent with the understanding of imminence under the international laws of war.[47] Second, the Executive

---

[39] Hosenball, *supra* note 30. The National Security Council Principals Committee is the senior interagency forum for consideration of policy issues affecting national security since 1989 and is chaired by the President's National Security Advisor and its members include the Secretary of State, the Secretary of the Treasury, the Secretary of Defense, the Attorney General, the Secretary of Energy, the Secretary of Homeland Security, the Director of the Office of Management and Budget, the Representative of the United States of America to the United Nations, the Chief of Staff to the President, the Director of National Intelligence, and the Chairman of the Joint Chiefs of Staff. *See* National Security Presidential Directive/PPD-1, *supra* note 38, at 4.
[40] Hosenball, *supra* note 30.
[41] *Id.*
[42] Holder, *supra* note 30.
[43] Shane, *supra* note 11.
[44] Holder, *supra* note 30.
[45] *Id.*
[46] Priest, *supra* note 10.
[47] Brennan, *supra* note 24.

Branch determines feasibility by examining the specific facts, time considerations, location of the targeted person,[48] the presence of hostile allies,[49] danger to civilians, risk to U.S. personnel, and the availability and willingness of local authorities to capture rather than kill the target.[50] Lastly, the program derives its ultimate authority from applicable law of war principles, including the 9/11 Authorization of Use of Military Force ("AUMF");[51] which authorized the President "to use all necessary and appropriate force against those nations, organizations, or persons he determines planned, authorized, committed, or aided the terrorist attacks that occurred on September 11, 2001.[52] However, the President does not have the authority to target Americans who are outside the scope of Presidential war power that is congressionally authorized[53] or inherent.[54]

In evaluating these criteria, the NSC debates, scrutinizes, and reviews the evidence before it while recognizing the seriousness of their decision to use lethal force.[55] While the exact evidentiary standard applied is classified, a "substantial evidence" standard or greater is likely the evidentiary standard.[56] After being placed on the list, the government

---

[48] Savage, *supra* note 10.
[49] *Id.*
[50] *Id.*
[51] Johnson, *supra* note 24.
[52] Authorization for Use of Military Force, PUB. L. NO. 107-40, § 2(a), 115 Stat..224, 224 (2001).
[53] Letter from Eric H. Holder, U.S. Attorney Gen., to Rand Paul, U.S. Sen. (March 7, 2013), *available at* http://www.washingtonpost.com/blogs/post-politics/files/2013/03/Senator-Rand-Paul-Letter.pdf ("'Does the President have the authority to use a weaponized drone to kill an American not engaged in combat on American soil?' The answer to that question is no.").
[54] Nat'l Comm'n on Terrorist Attacks upon the U.S., The 9/11 Commission Report 40-41 (2004),
available at http://www.gpoaccess.gov/911/index.html (explaining that President Bush authorized the shootdown of domestic commercial flight United 93); *see* The Brig Amy Warwick (The Prize Cases), 67 U.S. (2 Black) 635, 669 (1863) ("The President was bound to meet it in the
shape it presented itself, without waiting for Congress to baptize it with a name; and no name
given to it by him or them could change the fact.").
[55] Johnson, *supra* note 24.
[56] Priest, *supra* note 10.

must renew the target's approval every six months to ensure the threat remains imminent and not outdated.[57]

B. Critics of Executive Citizen Targeting Argue Due Process is Only Judicial Process

While critics vary in the amount of judicial process required, all critics of Executive Citizen Targeting argue the Fifth Amendment's Due Process Clause requires a U.S. citizen be given a certain level of judicial process.[58] Interestingly, even scholars who defend Executive Citizen Targeting acknowledge that due process is judicial process, but argue that wartime exigency creates an exception to applying due process to the battlefield.[59]

Generally, those who believe due process only refers to judicial process argue that courts must employ common law judicial procedure in the tradition of Magna Carta.[60] According to Judge Easterbrook, the Fifth Amendment's Due Process Clause merely requires following certain

---

[57] *Id.*
[58] Michael D. Ramsey, *Meet the New Boss: Continuity in Presidential War Powers?*, 35 HARV. J.L. & PUB. POL'Y 863, 868 (2012) (arguing that while al-Awlaki received some process within the Executive Branch, this process was not due process of law because the Fifth Amendment requires pronounced guilt by a court); Mike Dreyfuss, Note, *My Fellow Americans, We Are Going To Kill You: The Legality of Targeting And Killing U.S. Citizens Abroad*, 65 VAND. L. REV. 249, 282-83 (2012) (arguing that the Fifth Amendment entitled al-Awlaki to some level of trial process before an Article III court); Epstein, *supra* note 27 (arguing that the Fifth Amendment requires al-Awlaki be formally charged and be given a pre-deprivation judicial hearing); Richard Murphy & Afsheen John Radsan, *Due Process and Targeted Killing of Terrorists*, 31 CARDOZO L. REV. 405, 409-10 (2009) (arguing that Executive Citizen Targeting requires a minimal level of judicial intervention analogous to the "due process model of Hamdi/Boumediene" in the detention context); Kristen E. Eichensehr, Comment, *On Target? The Israel Supreme Court and the Expansion of Targeted Killings*, 116 YALE L.J. 1873, 1879 (2007) (arguing al-Awlaki is entitled to post-deprivation judicial review of a Bivens-style action); Jane Y. Chong, Note, *Targeting the Twenty-First-Century Outlaw*, 122 YALE L.J. 724 (2012) (arguing that persons such as al-Awlaki should be given the same judicial procedural protections given to outlaws under centuries of English common law).
[59] William C. Banks & Peter Raven-Hansen, *Targeted Killing and Assassination: The U.S. Legal Framework*, 37 U. RICH. L. REV. 667, 679 (2003) ("Necessity gives rise to the constitutional authority in both cases, and also justifies the President in exercising it without awaiting legislation").
[60] Frank H. Easterbrook, *Substance and Due Process*, 1982 SUP. CT. REV. 85, 95-98 (1982).

judicial procedures as they existed in 1791 common law.[61] To support this view, scholars frequently quote Alexander Hamilton's speech to the New York legislature that "[t]he words 'due process' have a precise technical import, and are only applicable to the process and proceedings of courts of justice; they can never be referred to an act of the Legislature."[62] The public's experience[63] and the black letter rule of Civil Procedure from *Mullane v. Central Hanover*[64] make this view, that due process is judicial process, almost instinctual. Even Justice Jackson explained the Due Process Clause's "cryptic and abstract words" were no more than the plain assurance of adjudication with prior notice and the opportunity to be heard.[65]

But while due process may often refer to judicial process, "[d]ue process is not necessarily judicial process."[66] Although various courts in the 1830's, 1840's and even in the 1870 Confiscation Act Cases held that due process was only judicial process, this movement was short lived.[67] After a thorough examination of the common law, courts largely reverted to their prior view that due process is a procedural function relating to inherent justice, fairness, and restraint on government generally.[68] By the turn of the twentieth century, the legal community returned to the

---

[61] *Id.* at 98.
[62] 8 THE WORKS OF ALEXANDER HAMILTON 29 (Henry Cabot Lodge ed., G.P. Putnam's Sons 1904). Some scholars argue Hamilton's statement is ambiguous at best and does not support Due Process as only judicial procedure. Since Hamilton's statements were given on the floor of the New York legislature, it would seem schizophrenic to argue passing the bill would violate Due Process while arguing Due Process is strictly judicial and not legislative. However, if Hamilton was arguing that Due Process is only judicial procedure, scholars argue Hamilton is plainly wrong. *See* Douglas Laycock, *Due Process and Separation of Powers: The Effort to Make the Due Process Clauses Nonjusticiable*, 60 TEX. L. REV. 875, 890-91 (1982).
[63] Ann Woolhandler, *Judicial Deference to Administrative Action–A Revisionist History*, 43 ADMIN. L. REV. 197, 238 (1991) ("Such direct exactions are those for which we tend to think that due process is judicial process. Thus criminal prosecutions remained under the de novo model, as did the civil actions against officials that fit most squarely into the common-law forms of action.").
[64] Jack H. Friedenthal, Arthur R. Miller, John E. Sexton & Helen Hershkoff, CIVIL PROCEDURE: CASES AND MATERIALS, 199-265 (10th ed., 2009).
[65] Mullane v. Cent. Hanover Bank & Trust Co., 339 U.S. 306, 313 (1950).
[66] Reetz v. Michigan, 188 U.S. 505, 507 (1903).
[67] RODNEY L. MOTT, DUE PROCESS OF LAW, 214 (1926).
[68] *Id.* at 217-19.

consensus that "legislative, executive, or administrative process may be due process."[69]

C. Two Alternative Theories of Due Process

The nature and meaning of due process is controversial and widely disputed even among scholars who maintain that due process is more than merely judicial process.[70] Scholars' various views of due process largely divide into two dominant theories of the phrase: those who view due process as fairness and those who view due process as a question of separation of power.[71]

1. Due Process as Fairness

Legal scholars developed the theory of due process as fairness out of frustration from nearly a century of ambiguity caused by the Supreme Court's questionable historic link between due process and Magna Carta.[72] The Supreme Court adopted the fairness theory and explained that the Due Process Clause's ambiguous text is unlike other specific provisions in the Bill of Rights because fairness is inherently less rigid and more fluid than other rights.[73] Fairness involves examining "contrary experiences, standards, and precedents to determine what is due."[74]

Justice Frankfurter's concurrence in *Joint Anti-Fascist Refugee Committee v. McGrath* develops the theory of due process as "[f]airness of procedure."[75] Due process is not a fixed "technical conception,"

---

[69] Thomas P. Hardman, *Judicial Review as a Requirement of Due Process in Rate Regulation*, 30 Yale L.J. 681, 689 (1921).

[70] *See* Keith Jurow, *Untimely Thoughts: A Reconsideration of the Origins of Due Process of Law*, 19 Am. J. Legal. Hist. 265 (1975).

[71] Nathan S. Chapman & Michael W. McConnell, *Due Process as Separation of Powers*, 121 Yale L.J. 1672, 1676 (2012).

[72] Edward Corwin's frustration with the Due Process Clause's ambiguity and historical inaccuracies led him by 1938 to end his long quarrel with the Supreme Court over the interpretation of the Due Process Clause and instead to find Due Process to constitute basic fairness. *See* Jurow, *supra* note 70, at 265.

[73] Betts v. Brady, 316 U.S. 455, 462 (1942).

[74] Andrew T. Hyman, *The Little Word "Due,"* 38 Akron L. Rev. 1, 2 (2005).

[75] Joint Anti-Fascist Refugee Comm. v. McGrath, 341 U.S. 123, 161 (1951) (Frankfurter, J., concurring).

"yardstick," or "mechanical instrument," but rather a "process" tailored to fairness given the particular circumstances.[76] To aid in balancing the interests of fairness, due process considers "history, reason, [and] the past course of decisions."[77] While Frankfurter acknowledged due process as fairness gives great flexibility, he also acknowledged, as Justice Brandeis had earlier, that due process also requires regularity.[78] The regular procedural safeguards of fairness are notice and hearing.[79] Yet, fairness "sanctioned by history or obvious necessity" may dictate "rare" and "isolated instances" where notice and hearing may be dispensed with altogether.[80] For Frankfurter, the exception to notice and hearing required examining the "precise nature of the interest . . . adversely affected" as well as existing protections, and alternatives to balance the "hurt complained of and good accomplished."[81]

After *McGrath*, the Supreme Court looked for a regularized framework to evaluate the costs and benefits of minimized notice and hearing to result in fair procedure.[82] When evaluating the various interests, the Supreme Court in *Goldberg v. Kelly* gave great weight to the "overpowering need[s]" of the individual's interest.[83] The deference given to individual interest by the Supreme Court in *Goldberg* placed a heavy, and perhaps unsustainable, procedural burden on the government.[84]

Later, the Supreme Court, in *Fuentes v. Shevin*, acknowledged the government's interest may demand minimized procedure in "extraordinary situations" while still satisfying the due process fairness requirement.[85] For example, historically weighty government interests

---

[76] *Id.* at 162-63.
[77] *Id.*
[78] *Id.* at 164; *see* Burdeau v. McDowell, 256 U.S. 465, 477 (Brandeis, J., dissenting).
[79] Joint Anti-Fascist Refugee Comm. v. McGrath, 341 U.S. 123, 165 (1951) (Frankfurter, J., concurring).
[80] *Id.* at 168.
[81] *Id.* at 163.
[82] *See* Goldberg v. Kelly, 397 U.S. 254 (1970); Fuentes v. Shevin, 407 U.S. 67 (1972).
[83] *Goldberg* 397 U.S. at 261 (1970).
[84] RHONDA WASSERMAN, PROCEDURAL DUE PROCESS: A REFERENCE GUIDE TO THE UNITED STATES CONSTITUTION 66 (2004).
[85] Fuentes v. Shevin, 407 U.S. 67, 90 (1972).

demanding minimized procedure include the government seeking to "collect the internal revenue of the United States, to meet the needs of a national war effort, to protect against the economic disaster of a bank failure, and to protect the public from misbranded drugs and contaminated food."[86] *Fuentes* focused on the directness and necessity of the government's interest, the need for special and prompt government action, and the assurances of strict control by narrowly drawn standards.[87]

On the foundation of *McGrath*, *Goldberg*, and *Fuentes*, the Supreme Court finally arrived at a regularized balancing test in *Mathews v. Eldridge* that evaluates both the individual and government interests in a particular instance.[88] The balancing test includes three factors: (1) the private interest affected, (2) the risk of erroneous deprivation, and (3) the government's interest involved.[89] While the holding in *Mathews* involved termination of social security disability benefits,[90] the Supreme Court continues using the *Mathews* balancing test in nearly every area of procedural due process to assess the appropriate level of fairness required to this day.[91] The *Mathews* balancing test meets the approval of those in the Law and Economics Movement because the "purpose of legal procedure is . . . the minimization of the sum of two types of costs: "error costs" and "direct costs."[92] The *Mathews* balancing test ensures fairness because it "maximize[s] efficiency."[93]

---

[86] *Id.* at 92.
[87] *Id.* at 91.
[88] Mathews v. Eldridge, 424 U.S. 319, 334-35, (1976).
[89] *Id.*
[90] *Id.*
[91] WASSERMAN, *supra* note 84, at 71.
[92] Richard A. Posner, *An Economic Approach To Legal Procedure and Judicial Administration*, 2 J. LEGAL STUD. 399, 399-400 (1973). ("'[E]rror costs' [are] the social costs costs generated when a judicial system fails to carry out the allocative or other social functions assigned to it [and] . . . "direct costs" [are those costs] such as lawyers', judges', and litigants' time. . . .").
[93] *Id.*

2. Separation of Powers

The theory of due process as separation of powers originated with Sir Edward Coke's linkage of due process and Magna Carta's "law of the land" constraint on the King.[94] Between 1613 and 1615, King James sought to expand his will as law an expansion of royal prerogative to extend his will as law through and through executive courts, which were not bound by the common-law.[95] Yet according to Coke, due process required separation of power ensuring "the Crown . . . coordinate governance involving deprivations of rights with Parliament and the common law courts."[96] Specifically, Coke maintained Magna Carta limited the King's authority to deprive citizens of certain rights "only according to existing law" as defined by custom and parliamentary declaration.[97] Coke's view became the accepted view organic to English law. During the American Revolution, American colonists quoted Coke and argued Parliament violated due process and abused its power by not acting under the "law of the land."[98] During the Constitution's ratification, anti-federalists such as George Mason sought to codify due process in a Bill of Rights to ensure separation of powers and avert "legislative as well as judicial and executive tyranny."[99] In 1791, the First Congress considered the Fifth Amendment to ensure separation of powers by applying due process "to all government action"[100] to serve as a "limit on the powers of all three branches."[101] While the Constitution left in place "limited prerogative powers of the President and inherent powers of the judiciary," the Due Process Clause ensured that the executive and judicial branches were limited to "executing and interpreting the law."[102] The Framers understood due process as dividing

---

[94] Chapman, *supra* note 71, at 1681-82.
[95] David W. Raack, *A History of Injunctions in England Before 1700*, 61 IND. L.J. 539, 573-75 (1986).
[96] Chapman, *supra* note 71, at 1692.
[97] *Id.* at 1681.
[98] *Id.* at 1699.
[99] MOTT, *supra* note 67, at 147.
[100] Chapman, *supra* note 71, at 1717.
[101] *Id.* at 1721.
[102] *Id.* at 1723.

"the authority to deprive subjects of life, liberty, or property between independent political institutions."[103]

The Supreme Court's first major case involving the Fifth Amendment Due Process Clause, *Murray's Lessee*, cited Coke and Magna Carta to support their holding that due process is "a restraint on the legislative as well as on the executive and judicial powers of the government."[104] Since *Murray's Lessee*, separation of powers remains an integral element of due process jurisprudence.[105] The rise of the modern political question doctrine, however, limits the number of cases the Supreme Court actually decides on the merits of due process under the theory of separation of powers.[106]

Most vividly, in *Nixon v. United States*, the Supreme Court left unanswered the question of whether due process required the Senate to grant a federal district judge a full evidentiary hearing before the entire

---

[103] *Id.* at 1681; Charles M. Hough, *Due Process of Law – to – Day*, 32 HARV. L. REV. 218 (1919) ("For present purposes it makes no difference whether Coke was right or wrong in identifying due process with the law of the land . . . . [I]t is accepted legal history, and lies at the bottom of all our classic legal writing.").

[104] Murray's Lessee v. Hoboken Land & Improvement Co., 59 U.S. (18 How.) 272, 276 (1855).

[105] *See* United States v. Montalvo-Murillo, 495 U.S. 711, 723-24 (1990) ("[T]he fundamental separation of powers among the Legislative, the Executive and the Judicial Branches of Government—all militate against this abhorrent practice [of detention prior to trial]."); Buckley v. Valeo, 424 U.S. 1, 124 (1976) ("The principle of separation of powers was not simply an abstract generalization in the minds of the Framers: it was woven into the document that they drafted in Philadelphia in the summer of 1787."); In re Winship, 397 U.S. 358, 380 (1970) (Black, J., dissenting) ("The article is a restraint on the legislative as well as on the executive and judicial powers of the government, and cannot be so construed as to leave congress free to make any process 'due process of law,' by its mere will."); Brinkerhoff-Faris Trust & Savings Co. v. Hill, 281 U.S. 673, 680 ("The federal guaranty of due process extends to . . . [the] legislative, executive, or administrative branch of government."); Wilson v. New, 243 U.S. 332, 366 (1917) ("The due process clause restrains alike every branch of the government, and is binding upon all who exercise Federal power, whether of an executive, legislative, or judicial character.") (Day, J., dissenting).

[106] James M. McGoldrick, Jr., *The Separation of Powers Doctrine: Straining Out Gnats, Swallowing Camels?*, 18 PEPP. L. REV. 95, 98 (1990) ("The Court's use of the political question doctrine to avoid resolution of foreign affairs issues has left us without any clear line of authority as to ultimate responsibility for making life and death decisions about use of military force in addressing international conflict.").

Senate prior to impeaching Judge Walter Nixon[107] Rather than examine the due process issue, the Supreme Court found the issue a nonjusticiable political question.[108] The Supreme Court explained for impeachment there is a "textually demonstrable constitutional commitment of the issue to a coordinate political department or a lack of judicially discoverable and manageable standards for resolving it."[109] Allowing judiciary involvement in the impeachment proceedings would "eviscerate" the Constitution's limit on the Judiciary imposed by separation of powers.[110] While the Supreme Court ultimately did not evaluate the merits of Nixon's claim, their rationale supports the concept that former Judge Nixon was given appropriate legislative process and therefore sufficient Fifth Amendment Due Process.[111]

Despite a robust modern political question doctrine, the Supreme Court has on rare occasion injected itself into the merits of separation of powers disputes. In *United States v. Nixon*, a unanimous Supreme Court determined President Nixon must comply with a subpoena because to hold otherwise would "cut deeply into the [Fifth Amendment's] guarantee of due process of law and gravely impair the basic function of the courts."[112] Essentially, the President's immunity claim failed to constitute sufficient due process, because the function of criminal adjudication is a judicial, as opposed to an executive process.[113]

II. THE EXECUTIVE PROCESS OF THE COMMANDER-IN-CHIEF

When acting under the authority granted in the Constitution's Commander-in-Chief Clause, both the fairness and separation of powers theories of due process establish a rich foundation of executive process grounded in history and reason.[114]

---

[107] Nixon v. United States, 506 U.S. 224 (1993).
[108] *Id.* at 228.
[109] *Id.* (quoting Baker v. Carr, 369 U.S. 186, 217 (1962)).
[110] *Id.* at 235.
[111] *Id.* at 237-38.
[112] United States v. Nixon, 418 U.S. 683, 712 (1974).
[113] *Id.* at 713.
[114] U.S. CONST. art. II, § 2.

A. *Necessity, Executive Process, and Due Process as Fairness*

Under the theory of due process as fairness, executive process is founded on the basis of necessity. In the early decades of the twentieth century, the Supreme Court heard a series of Gubernatorial Insurrection Cases where necessity warranted executive process. In *Moyer v. Peabody*, Justice Holmes explained the necessities of insurrection warranted the Colorado Governor, as Commander-in-Chief of state forces, to substitute his own discretion on whether to kill citizens inciting insurrection and resisting peace, rather than follow ordinary judicial procedure.[115] Necessity required the "ordinary rights of individuals" yield to what the governor "deems the necessities of the moment."[116] As Commander-in-Chief, the governor, not a court, is the final judge in determining the use of soldiers, those who may be killed, those who may be "seized, and other methods of quelling insurrection and restoring peace.[117] Holmes concluded that "[p]ublic danger warrants the substitution of executive process for judicial process."[118] Only where the governor fails to act in "good faith" or with no "reasonable ground(s) for his belief" may the judiciary interfere.[119] But even then, the governor's subjective view of the facts control, rather than an objective view of those facts.[120]

In a later gubernatorial insurrection case, the Supreme Court again noted that when a governor acts as Commander-in-Chief, his discretion "whether an exigency . . . has arisen" is "conclusive."[121] The nature of the Commander-in-Chief power "necessarily implies that there is a permitted range of honest judgment."[122] Despite this limit, the outer "allowable limits of military discretion" are "judicial questions" when considering good faith.[123] Consistent with Chief Justice Evan Hughes decision in *Blaisdell*, these gubernatorial insurrection cases do not "create

---

[115] Moyer v. Peabody, 212 U.S. 78, 85 (1909).
[116] *Id.*
[117] *Id.* at 84-85.
[118] *Id.* at 85.
[119] *Id.*
[120] *Id.* at 78, 85.
[121] Sterling v. Constantin, 287 U.S. 378, 399 (1932).
[122] *Id.*
[123] *Id.* at 401.

power"[124] in an emergency, but rather necessity "furnish[es] the occasion for the exercise of power" as Commander-in-Chief.[125]

While the necessity of domestic insurrection warrants executive process, the Supreme Court's recent terrorist detention cases show the narrow scope of executive process. In *Hamdi v. Rumsfeld*, the President's finding that Yaser Esam Hamdi was an enemy combatant did not provide sufficient due process.[126] While the Supreme Court ultimately gave Hamdi a type of judicial process, the Supreme Court recognized such process was only due "when the determination is made to *continue* to hold those who have been seized."[127] For battlefield captures, the President's discretion through his military officers is sufficient due process.[128] The Supreme Court employed the *Mathews* balancing test to conclude fairness required Hamdi receive "notice" and hearing "before a neutral decisionmaker."[129] Justice Souter explained in his concurring opinion that there was no "actual and present" necessity since Hamdi had been "locked up for over two years."[130] Therefore, under *Mathews*, the government's national security interest was limited because "emergency power of necessity must at least be limited by the emergency."[131]

B. *Presidential Discretion, Executive Process, and Due Process as Separation of Powers*

The theory of due process as separation of powers also establishes a strong foundation for executive process. While codified only in history and not in the annals of a case reporter, President Washington's response in the Whiskey Rebellion constitutes the first exercise of executive process as Commander-in-Chief. The 1792 Militia Act required a federal judge notify the President when insurgents were "too powerful to be suppressed by the ordinary course of judicial

---

[124] Home Bldg. & Loan Ass'n v. Blaisdell, 290 U.S. 398, 425 (1934).
[125] *Id.* at 426.
[126] Hamdi v. Rumsfeld, 542 U.S. 507, 509 (2004).
[127] *Id.* at 534.
[128] *Id.*
[129] *Id.* at 533.
[130] *Id.* at 552 (Souter, J., concurring).
[131] *Id.*

proceedings."[132] Instead, President Washington "went directly to Justice Wilson for a finding of insurrection" so he could respond to the insurrection quickly.[133] Using Hamilton's compiled list of top rebel leaders, President Washington led his forces to quell the rebellion in Pennsylvania.[134] Consistent with President Washington's restrained and judicious character, President Washington's had Richard Peters, a federal judge, accompany the forces to help "coordinate civil process with the military authority."[135] The President made clear the judge was under instruction of the military arm, and "not the other way round."[136] The Executive Branch used force and made arrests independent of any judicial process, while acknowledging due process required charges for prolonged detention.[137] After President Washington's successful Whiskey Rebellion campaign, Congress in 1795 amended the 1792 Militia Act by removing the "requirement that the President seek judicial approval before calling out the militia—all that was required now was a presidential proclamation."[138]

Under the revised 1795 Militia Act, the Supreme Court twice affirmed the President's authority as Commander-in-Chief to determine when to use military force and what methods to use to preserve the peace.[139] In *Martin v. Mott*, Justice Story noted the President "exclusively" had the authority to determine whether an exigency invoking the 1795 Militia Act had arisen.[140] Subjecting the President's discretionary judgment to judicial review would subject the military to "ruinous litigation" and place in the hands of the judiciary questions lacking "strict technical proof" and "important secrets of the state."[141] Justice Story explained that where a statute gives the President discretionary power, the President is the "sole and exclusive judge of the

---

[132] Act of May 2, 1792, ch. 28, § 2, 1 Stat. at 264.
[133] John Yoo, *George Washington and the Executive Power*, U. ST. THOMAS J.L. & PUB. POL'Y 1, 14 (2010).
[134] HOGELAND, *supra* note 1, at 208-09.
[135] *Id.* at 219.
[136] *Id.*
[137] *Id.*
[138] Yoo, *supra* note 133, at 15.
[139] CLINTON ROSSITER, THE SUPREME COURT AND THE COMMANDER IN CHIEF 17 (1976).
[140] Martin v. Mott, 25 U.S. (12 Wheat.) 19, 30 (1827).
[141] *Id.* at 31.

existence of those facts."[142] While it is true that "such a power may be abused,"[143] all power is "susceptible of abuse."[144] Under the Constitution, the President's "public virtue" and honesty, frequent elections, and "watchfulness of the representatives" guard against "usurpation or wonton tyranny."[145]

Similarly in *Luther v. Borden*, Justice Taney noted no court of the United States is justified in contravening the President's factual determination as Commander-in-Chief.[146] While any branch may abuse power, the Constitution places Commander-in-Chief discretion solely in the hands of the President because his "elevated office," high responsibilities, and public expectations are the strongest safeguard "against a willful abuse of power as human prudence and foresight could well provide."[147] Quite plainly, "[t]he ordinary course of proceedings in courts of justice" would be utterly unfit for the crisis."[148] As Federalist 78 echoes, "[t]he Executive . . . holds the sword . . . [while] [t]he judiciary, on the contrary, has no influence over either the sword or the purse."[149]

Likewise, in *The Prize Cases*, the Supreme Court determined President Lincoln's proclamation blockading various southern ports constituted "official and conclusive evidence to the Court that a state of war existed."[150] The President's determination of a citizen's belligerency binds the courts because the Commander-in-Chief Clause entrusts the President, not the judiciary, to "determine what degree of force the crisis demands."[151]

The development of the political question doctrine has largely prevented the Supreme Court from addressing the executive process of

---

[142] *Id.* at 31-32.
[143] *Id.* at 32.
[144] *Id.*
[145] *Id.* at 19, 32.
[146] *Luther v. Borden*, 48 U.S. (7 How.) 1, 44 (1849).
[147] *Id.*
[148] *Id.*
[149] THE FEDERALIST No. 78 (Alexander Hamilton).
[150] The Brig Amy Warwick (The Prize Cases), 67 U.S. (2 Black) 635, 670 (1863).
[151] *Id.*

the President's Commander-in-Chief discretion.[152] Yet Justice Thomas' dissent in *Hamdi* shows that if the Supreme Court reached the merits of an executive process case, it would likely employ the nineteenth century rationale outlined in *Mott* and *Borden*.[153] This is due to the court's lack of "aptitude, facilities, [and] responsibility" to appropriately exercise Commander-in-Chief discretion.[154] Conversely, the President has discretion as Commander-in-Chief because the information is often "delicate, complex, and . . . prophe[tic]."[155] Consequently, due process requires deference to the President's determination of "all the factual predicates" and requires judicial intervention only where there is "the clearest conviction" the President's determination "cannot be reconciled with the Constitution and the constitutional legislation of Congress."[156]

C. *The Good Faith Limit to Executive Process*

Under the necessity and separation of power theories of executive process, good faith and consistency with the Constitution and Congressional authorization limit the scope of executive process. For example, the Supreme Court has consistently applied these limits to executive process. In *Little v. Barreme*, President Adams' determination that the *Flying Fish* vessel violated a non-intercourse law was reversed because the President seized the vessel in exact contradiction to the statute.[157] In *Youngstown Sheet & Tube v. Sawyer*, President Truman's seizure of the steel mills lacked good faith relationship to the Korean conflict given appropriate understanding of the "theater of war."[158] Under Justice Jackson's concurring rationale in *Steel Seizure*, the legislative history of the Taft-Hartley Act meant President Truman's directly contradicted the statute through his seizure.[159] Dissenting in *Korematsu*, Justice Murphy explained that the President's national

---

[152] McGoldrick, *supra* note 106.
[153] Hamdi v. Rumsfeld, 542 U.S. 507, 582-83 (2004) (Thomas, J., dissenting).
[154] *Id.* at 585.
[155] *Id.* at 582 (quoting Chicago & Southern Air Lines, Inc. v. Waterman S.S. Corp., 333 U.S. 103, 111 (1948)).
[156] *Id.* at 584 (quoting Ex parte Milligan, 4 Wall. 2, 133 (1866) (Chase, C.J., concurring in judgment)).
[157] Little v. Barreme, 6 U.S. (2 Cranch) 170, 176-77 (1804).
[158] Youngstown Sheet & Tube Co. v. Sawyer (Steel Seizure), 343 U.S. 579, 587 (1952).
[159] *Id.* at 639-40 (Jackson, J., concurring).

security claims justifying Japanese internment lacked good faith relationship to national security threats from Japan and instead was obvious racial discrimination.[160] These cases show that even though executive process is a meaningful species of due process, executive process is not immunized from constitutional scrutiny by the judiciary.[161]

III. THE EXECUTIVE PROCESS OF EXECUTIVE CITIZEN TARGETING

The rich tradition in American jurisprudence of executive process under both the fairness and separation of powers theories provides two independent and robust legal rationales for the Obama Administration's Executive Citizen Targeting program.

A. *Targeting al-Awlaki Satisfies* Mathews *Balancing*

Under the theory of due process as fairness, the circumstantial nature of the *Mathews* balancing test only allows examining the specific circumstances of President Obama's targeting of al-Awlaki.[162] The Department of Justice's legal memorandum defending the President's action limits itself to the particular factual situation surrounding al-Awlaki and therefore cannot make a programmatic argument for Executive Citizen Targeting.[163]

Under the first prong of the *Mathews* balancing test, the President's targeting of al-Awlaki implicated the nation's security given al-Awlaki's leadership in al Qaeda Arabian Peninsula and his repeated attempts to orchestrate terrorism in the United States. Unlike *Hamdi*, al-Awlaki posed an actual and present security risk, implicating the true necessity of national security.[164] However, under the second prong of *Mathews*, al-Awlaki's interest in his own life is one of the most important

---

[160] Korematsu v. United States, 323 U.S. 214, 234 (1944) (Murphy, J., dissenting).
[161] *See* Marbury v. Madison, 5 U.S. (1 Cranch) 137, 177 (1803) ("It is emphatically the province and duty of the judicial department to say what the law is.").
[162] See *supra* text accompanying note 88.
[163] Savage, *supra* note 10 ("The memo, however, was narrowly drawn to the specifics of Mr. Awlaki's case and did not establish a broad new legal doctrine to permit the targeted killing of any Americans believed to pose a terrorist threat.").
[164] See supra text accompanying note 130.

interests protected by due process.[165] Indeed, preservation of one's life is the foundation of social contract and a core responsibility of government.[166] Even though al-Awlaki's life interest was at stake, as *Moyer* and *Sterling* note, necessity may empower the Commander-in-Chief to kill or arrest citizens. Furthermore, President Obama and the NSC also sought to capture rather than kill al-Awlaki, but capture proved infeasible. Moreover the Supreme Court's recent Fourth Amendment seizure analysis in *Scott v. Harris* shows that under certain circumstances deadly force constitutes reasonable seizure.[167] While the police used deadly force in *Harris*, for purposes of the reasonableness analysis, the Supreme Court viewed the deadly force as a type of seizure given the danger posed by the motorist's reckless behavior to the public.[168]

While the necessity of national security is grave, the appropriateness of President Obama's action against al-Awlaki largely stems from the third prong of *Mathews* requiring minimized risk of erroneous deprivation. Al-Awlaki's targeting required approval by the NSC's Deputies Committee, approval by the NSC's Principals Committee, and ultimate approval from the President himself. Much like the Administrative Procedure Act regularizing due process in the Executive, "the National Security Act of 1947 formalized the principle of centralized presidential *management* of those officials' external acts."[169] In addition to the regularized process of the NSC, the Executive Branch informed appropriate members of Congress and the public about the use of lethal force against al-Awlaki. While the specific evidentiary standard is classified, the standard is certainly robust and weighty enough for the President to publically disclose al-Awlaki's involvement in the 2010 Fort Hood attack and attempted 2010 Christmas Day attack.[170] President Obama could have merely relied on his demonstration of good faith, but instead relied on these additional procedures to minimize the risk of

---

[165] D.O.J White Paper, supra note 25, at 6 ("An individual's interest in avoiding erroneous deprivation of his life is 'uniquely compelling.' . . . No private interest is more substantial.").

[166] *See* THOMAS HOBBES, LEVIATHAN 112 (Michael Oakeshott ed., 3d ed. 1966) (1651).

[167] Scott v. Harris, 550 U.S. 372, 382 (2007).

[168] *Id.* at 373.

[169] Harold Hongju Koh, *Why the President (Almost) Always Wins in Foreign Affairs: Lessons of the Iran-Contra Affair*, 97 YALE L.J. 1255, 1281 (1988).

[170] *See supra* text accompanying note 3 and 17.

error when targeting al-Awlaki. Satisfying *Mathews*, the necessity of national security coupled with President Obama's robust procedures, ensure the President's actions constitute a form of executive process that harmonizes with the fairness of due process.

B. *Executive Citizen Targeting is Within the Executive's Authority*

Under a theory of due process as separation of power, not only is President Obama's targeting of al-Awlaki warranted, but programmatic Executive Citizen Targeting is also warranted to combat terrorism. The 9/11 AUMF approved by Congress specifically confers on the President the authority to use all necessary and appropriate force against those "he determines" are responsible for 9/11 or to prevent future terrorism.[171] While the AUMF uses some qualifying language, ultimately the authorization leaves to the President, as Commander-in-Chief, the final determination of when military force is targeted against citizens. The AUMF is similarly structured to the amended 1795 Militia Statute giving the President discretion to determine the existence of an insurrection.

Consistent with the executive precedent of President Washington's judiciousness and restraint during the Whiskey Rebellion, President Obama's Executive Citizen Targeting program also shows restraint. The use of a two-tier approval from the NSC, consulting with Congress, and communicating with the public, when approving citizen targets all show restrained executive process. Additionally, the President himself must approve citizen targets. This level of accountability in the President is consistent with the rationale of *Luther v. Borden*.[172] Indeed, all power is subject to abuse, but there is no greater accountability than the President himself bearing direct political responsibility for his actions as Commander-in-Chief.

C. *Extending Justiciability to Executive Citizen Targeting Cases*

While the United States District Court's invocation of the political question doctrine in *Al Aulaqi v. Obama* gave the President a

---

[171] Authorization for Use of Military Force Pub. L. No. 107-40 § 2(a) 115 Stat.C224, 224 (2001).
[172] See *supra* text accompanying notes 146-47.

victory, courts should consider extending justiciability to executive process cases, particularly Executive Citizen Targeting cases.[173] Unless courts pierce the veil of the political question doctrine, application of good faith, statutory contradiction, and constitutional overreach will not meaningfully limit executive process. Rendering a decision on the merits will strengthen the legal legitimacy of Executive Citizen Targeting as a constitutional program employed by the President as Commander-in-Chief in good faith and consistent with statute. Though executive process is a form of due process, the Fifth Amendment also demands that the judiciary play a critical role in "judgment" while having "neither FORCE nor WILL."[174]

IV. CONCLUSION

Due process is not limited to merely judicial process, but rather is a check on all three branches from abusing power. Executive process is a type of due process that ensures the President can accomplish those duties conferred on him by the Constitution. Even in the midst of enormous national security necessities, due process as fairness requires the President minimize the risk of error. Fairness also requires judicial checks on presidential judgments lacking a good faith relationship to asserted impending necessities. Similarly, due process as separation of powers requires the President bear the political responsibility of Commander-in-Chief himself. Separation of powers also demands that the judiciary check presidential actions when they contravene statutory or constitutional provisions. To strengthen the legitimate exercise of executive process and to protect against abuse, the judiciary should extend justiciability to cases involving presidential wartime actions. The concept of due process meaningfully checks abuses of power and undergirds the core ideals of American constitutional governance. From the early actions of President Washington to the present actions by President Obama, executive process demands the President exercise restraint while exhibiting the discretion necessary to ensure our nation's safety.

---

[173] See *supra* text accompanying note 20.
[174] THE FEDERALIST NO. 78 (Alexander Hamilton).

NOTE

HINGING ON HABEAS?
THE GUANTANAMO MEMORANDUM OF UNDERSTANDING AND THE DETAINEES' CONTINUED RIGHT TO COUNSEL

Amy M. Shepard[*]

I. INTRODUCTION

Eleven years ago, in the wake of the terrorist attacks of September 11, 2001, the first detainees[1] captured in the Global War on

---

[*] George Mason University School of Law, J.D. Candidate, May 2014; Editor-in-Chief, GEORGE MASON NATIONAL SECURITY LAW JOURNAL, 2013-2014; Middlebury College, B.A., Political Science, *cum laude*, May 2008. I would like to thank my family, Cindy Shepard, Gary Shepard, Laurie Shinaman and Eric Shinaman for their support, thoughtful comments, and humor throughout this process. Thank you Joshua Stern for encouraging me to go to law school and Professor Jeffrey Pokorak for advice once I got there. Finally, thank you Michael O'Brien for never, ever going to law school.

[1] The United States Government intentionally refers to people captured and imprisoned at Guantanamo as "detainees" instead of "prisoners" to avoid the implication that those being held could benefit from the prisoner of war status under the Geneva Conventions. *See* Brendan M. Driscoll, Note, *The Guantanamo Protective Order*, 30 FORDHAM INT'L L.J. 873, 873 n.1 (2007) (citing Joseph Margulies, *Guantanamo and the Abuse of Presidential Power* 255 n.3 (2006), and Stephen Grey, *Ghost Plane: The True Story of the CIA Torture Program* (2006)); *see also* Draft of a Memorandum from Alberto R. Gonzales to the President (Jan. 25, 2002) *available at* http://www.torturingdemocracy.org/documents/20020125.pdf (finding there are "reasonable grounds," which includes *inter alia*, preserving flexibility, to conclude that

Terrorism arrived at the U.S. Naval base at Guantanamo Bay, Cuba ("Guantanamo").[2] Nine days after their arrival, attorneys filed the initial legal challenge to the detention of detainees at Guantanamo in the form of a petition for habeas corpus.[3] Today, of the 799 men who have been held at Guantanamo,[4] 166 remain.[5] Throughout the past decade, not a single detainee has been fully tried or convicted of any crime.[6] Despite this, the United States Government (the "USG") has taken multiple measures to deny detainees the ability to challenge their indefinite detentions.[7] Most recently, the USG changed long-standing rules over attorney-client relations at Guantanamo by charging the executive branch, not the judicial branch, with protecting habeas petitioners' right to access their counsel.[8]

The new rules issued by the Department of Justice (the "DOJ") in May 2012, restrict lawyers' access to detainees who no longer have a

---

al Qaeda and Taliban detainees are not prisoners of war under the Geneva Convention III on the Treatment of Prisoners of War (GPW)); Memorandum from the U.S. President to the Vice President, the Sec'y of State, the Sec'y of Defense, the Att'y Gen., Chief of Staff to the President, Dir. of Cent. Intelligence, Ass't to the President for Nat'l Sec. Affairs, and Chairman of the Joint Chiefs of Staff on Humane Treatment of al Qaeda and Taliban Detainees (Feb. 7, 2002), *available at*
http://www.torturingdemocracy.org/documents/20020207-2.pdf (declaring the GPW does not apply to Taliban or al Qaeda detainees).
[2] Steve Vogel, *U.S. Takes Hooded, Shackled Detainees to Cuba*, WASH. POST, Jan. 11, 2002, at A10.
[3] *See* Driscoll, *supra* note 1, at 873 n.2 (citing *Coalition of Clergy v. Bush*, 189 F. Supp. 2d 1036 (C.D. Cal. 2002) (dismissing petition for want of standing and jurisdiction), *aff'd* 310 F.3d 1153 (9th Cir. 2002)).
[4] Jane Sutton & Josh Meyer, *Insight: At Guantanamo Tribunals, Don't Mention the "T" Word*, REUTERS (Aug. 20, 2012),
http://www.reuters.com/assets/print?aid=USBRE87J03U20120820.
[5] *Guantanamo by the Numbers*, HUMAN RIGHTS FIRST,
http://www.humanrightsfirst.org/wp-content/uploads/pdf/USLS-Fact-Sheet-Gitmo-Numbers.pdf (last updated Oct. 3, 2012).
[6] *See In re* Guantanamo Bay Detainee Continued Access to Counsel, No. 12-398, 2012 U.S. Dist. LEXIS 126833, at *24 (D.D.C. Sept. 6, 2012).
[7] *Id.*
[8] *See* Mike Scarcella, *DOJ Pushes Changes in Attorney-Client Relationships at Gitmo*, NAT'L L.J. (Aug. 7, 2012) [hereinafter *DOJ Pushes Changes*],
http://www.law.com/jsp/nlj/PubArticleNLJ.jsp?id=1202566524069.

habeas corpus petition before the court.[9] In this context, habeas corpus petitions seek a legal and factual explanation for the detainees' detention, or alternatively, release from Guantanamo.[10] While habeas corpus petitions make up the majority of suits filed by Guantanamo detainees,[11] currently a number of detainees at Guantanamo do not have active habeas petitions.[12] Under the new rules, enforced through an attorney signed Memorandum of Understanding (the "MOU")[13] that replaced a 2008 Protective Order,[14] the Navy base Commander at Guantanamo ("Commander") would have sole veto power over attorney access, as well as access to classified material.[15] The military, not the courts, are given "the final and unreviewable discretion" for settling any arising disputes.[16] The effect of the new rules is to remove attorney-client access from the court's discretion and, instead, entrust the military to determine when attorneys may visit detainees, what information may be gathered, and how it may be used.[17] In *In re* Guantanamo Bay Detainee Continued

---

[9] Baher Azmy, *Obama Backtracks on Guantanamo*, WASH. POST, Aug. 17, 2012, at A19 [hereinafter *Obama Backtracks on Guantanamo*].

[10] *See* BLACK'S LAW DICTIONARY 778 (9th ed. 2009) (defining "habeas corpus" as "[a] writ employed to bring a person before a court, most frequently to ensure that the person's imprisonment or detention is not illegal").

[11] Driscoll, *supra* note 1, at 888.

[12] *See* Respondents' Motion to Refer the Counsel-Access Issue for Decision by a Single District Court Judge and to Hold in Abeyance Former Petitioners Esmail's and Uthman's Motions for Order Concerning the Protective Order at 2, Abdah v. Obama, No. 04-CV-01254 (RCL) (D.D.C. July 26, 2012) (referencing over 20 cases where the issue of continued counsel access has been raised after detainees' habeas cases have been dismissed).

[13] *See* Motion Concerning the Protective Order Entered by Judge Hogan on Sept. 11, 2008 at 9, Abdah v. Obama, No. 04-1254 (D.D.C. July 9, 2012), *available at* http://www.lawfareblog.com/wp-content/uploads/2012/07/Motion-re-Protective-Order-Esmail-July-9-2012-ALL-AS-FILED.pdf.

[14] *In re* Guantanamo Bay Detainee Litig., 577 F. Supp. 2d 143 (D.D.C. 2008).

[15] Bill Mears, *Military Limiting Guantanamo Detainee Access to Lawyers*, CNN SECURITY CLEARANCE (Aug. 7, 2012, 6:23 PM), http://security.blogs.cnn.com/2012/08/07/military-limiting-guantanamo-detainee-access-to-lawyers/?hpt=hp_tl.

[16] Jack King, *New Attack on Counsel Access at GTMO To Be Heard Friday*, NAT'L ASS'N OF CRIM. DEF. LAWS. (Aug. 17, 2012), http://www.nacdl.org/NewsReleases.aspx?id=24936.

[17] *Obama Backtracks on Guantanamo*, *supra* note 9.

Access to Counsel, the District Court for the District of Columbia struck down these rules as an "illegitimate exercise of Executive power."[18]

This Note analyzes the MOU through the court case of *In re Guantanamo Bay Detainee Continued Access to Counsel*.[19] This Note aims to facilitate broader public awareness of a narrow issue that underlies the fundamental problem at Guantanamo - indefinite detention without charge or trial. To do this, this Note will demonstrate that the USG unconstitutionally attempted to restrict detainees' access to legal representation. Part I provides a brief background on the unique posture of Guantanamo and the development of the detainees' rights to be heard in federal court. Tracing the detainees' rights to counsel pre-MOU, Part I closes with a discussion of the 2008 Protective Order which governed all attorney-client relations at Guantanamo just prior to the MOU. Part II considers the MOU in detail. This section examines the language of the MOU, how it differs from the Protective Order, what these differences mean for attorney-client relations at Guantanamo, and the arguments of its proponents and critics. Part III of this Note details the District Court for the District of Columbia's analysis of the MOU and its holding in *In re Guantanamo Bay Detainee Continued Access to Counsel*. Finally, Part IV of this Note argues the District Court's ruling was legally correct and sound for public policy purposes.

II. BACKGROUND

A. *Historical Legal Background*

In response to the terrorist attacks of September 11, 2001, Congress enacted the Authorization of Use of Military Force ("AUMF") permitting the President of the United States to "use all necessary and appropriate force against those nations, organizations, or persons he determines planned, authorized, committed, or aided the terrorist attacks that occurred on September 11, 2001, or harbored such organizations or

---

[18] *In re* Guantanamo Bay Detainee Continued Access to Counsel, No. 12-398, 2012 U.S. Dist. LEXIS 126833, at *74 (D.D.C. Sept. 6, 2012).
[19] *Id.* at *18-24.

persons" in order to prevent future acts of terrorism.[20] With this authority, the United States military detained many suspected al Qaeda and Taliban fighters at Guantanamo absent criminal charges.[21] In 2004, a plurality of the Supreme Court upheld the President's authority to detain such individuals, when augmented by congressional authorization through the AUMF as "necessary and appropriate."[22] The same year, the Supreme Court rejected the USG's argument that federal courts had no jurisdiction to hear detainee habeas petitions,[23] the first of which were filed in 2002.[24] In its initial attempt to overturn the Supreme Court's ruling, Congress amended the federal habeas statute,[25] with the Detainee Treatment Act of 2005 ("DTA").[26] The DTA deprived the courts jurisdiction over habeas petitions brought by Guantanamo detainees.[27] But the Supreme Court in *Hamdan v. Rumsfeld* held the DTA not applicable to petitioners with cases pending when the statute was enacted.[28] Congress again countered by passing the Military Commissions Act of 2006 ("MCA").[29] Section 7 of the MCA stripped

---

[20] Authorization for Use of Military Force, Pub. L. No. 107-40, § 2(a), 115 Stat. 224 (2001) (codified at 50 U.S.C. § 1541 (2006)).

[21] Tung Yin, *President Obama's First Two Years: A Legal Reflection: "Anything but Bush?": The Obama Administration and Guantanamo Bay*, 34 HARV. J.L. & PUB. POL'Y 453, 456 (2011).

[22] *Id.* at 456 (citing Hamdi v. Rumsfeld, 542 U.S. 507 (2004)).

[23] Rasul v. Bush, 542 U.S. 466, 484 (2004). *See Obama Backtracks on Guantanamo, supra* note 9 (discussing the implications of *Rasul* and crediting the case with laying the groundwork for the discovery of abuse inflicted upon detainees and their unwarranted detention with reports that more than 600 of the 800 Muslim men once held at Guantanamo have been released since *Rasul*).

[24] Jennifer L. Milko, *Separation of Powers and Guantanamo Detainees: Defining the Proper Roles of the Executive and Judiciary in Habeas Cases and the Need for Supreme Guidance*, 50 DUQ. L. REV. 173, 177 (2012) [hereinafter *SOP and Guantanamo Detainees*] (explaining that the first habeas corpus petitions filed in 2002 were initially dismissed for lack of jurisdiction until the Supreme Court confirmed the district courts had jurisidiction Boumediene v. Bush, 553 U.S. 723, 734 (2008)).

[25] 28 US.C. § 2241 (2000).

[26] Detainee Treatment Act of 2005, Pub. L. No. 109-148, 119 Stat. 2739 (codified as amended in scattered sections of 10, 28, and 42 U.S.C.).

[27] *SOP and Guantanamo Detainees, supra* note 24, at 177.

[28] Hamdan v. Rumsfeld, 548 U.S. 557, 576-77 (2006).

[29] Military Commissions Act of 2006, Pub. L. No. 109-366, 120 Stat. 2600 (2006) (codified in part at 28 U.S.C. § 2241).

jurisdiction from all Guantanamo cases relating to detention, transfer, or other statuses.[30]

In the landmark case of *Boumediene v. Bush*,[31] the Supreme Court invalidated §7 of the MCA.[32] Recognizing that the MCA took away the power of the federal courts to hear habeas petitions, the Court concluded the privilege of the Suspension Clause[33] extended to Guantanamo, and any denials of habeas corpus must comply with the Suspension Clause.[34] The purpose of the privilege of habeas corpus, as the Court discussed, was to provide the detainee with "a meaningful opportunity to demonstrate that he is being held pursuant to the erroneous application or interpretation of relevant law."[35] Upon review of the history of the writ of habeas corpus and the DTA's review processes, the Supreme Court found that § 7 of the MCA was an insufficient substitute for habeas corpus.[36] Therefore, the Court held § 7 of the MCA was an unconstitutional suspension of the privilege of the writ of habeas corpus for Guantanamo detainees.[37] Thus, the *Boumediene* decision reopened the courts to Guantanamo detainees and expressly granted detainees the constitutional right to petition for habeas relief.[38]

B. *Guantanamo Detainees Have a Right To Counsel*

1. Framework for Detainee Counsel-Access

In *Hamdi v. Rumsfeld*, the Supreme Court held a Guantanamo detainee "unquestionably has the right to access counsel in connection

---

[30] *SOP and Guantanamo Detainees*, *supra* note 24, at 178.
[31] Boumediene v. Bush, 553 U.S. 723 (2008).
[32] *Id.* at 739.
[33] The Suspension Clause provides: "The Privilege of the Writ of Habeas Corpus shall not be suspended, unless when in Cases of Rebellion or Invasion the public Safety may require it." U.S. CONST. art. I, § 9, cl. 2.
[34] *Boumediene* 553 U.S. at 771.
[35] *Id.* at 779 (internal quotation marks omitted).
[36] *SOP and Guantanamo Detainees*, *supra* note 24, at 179 (citing *Boumediene*, 553 U.S. at 792).
[37] *Id.* (citing *Boumediene*, 553 U.S. at 792).
[38] *Id.*; *see also Obama Backtracks on Guantanamo*, *supra* note 9.

with the proceedings."[39] In *Al Odah v. United States*, the District Court for the District of Columbia rejected the USG's argument that the petitioners, three Kuwaiti nationals detained at Guantanamo, have no right to counsel under the Constitution, treaties, or statutes.[40] Absent such a right, any attorney-client relationship is at the USG's "pleasure and discretion."[41] Citing the federal habeas statute,[42] the Criminal Justice Act,[43] and the All Writs Act,[44] the court held that detainees at Guantanamo are entitled to representation by counsel.[45] The court also held that the USG is not permitted to unilaterally rescind the attorney-client relationship and its accompanying attorney-client privilege covering communications.[46]

While detainees have the right to counsel, courts continue to weigh the USG's interest in restricting access to certain information about the detainees, the base, and other aspects of the Global War on Terrorism against the detainees' attorneys' need to access some of the same information to effectively represent their clients.[47] To deal with these oft-conflicting interests, the federal district courts of the District of Columbia have generally employed protective orders[48] to govern the access and use of confidential information by attorneys.[49]

The first proposed framework for detainee counsel-access appeared in *Al Odah v. United States* where the court recognized its

---

[39] Hamdi v. Rumsfeld, 542 U.S. 507, 539 (2004).
[40] Al Odah v. United States, 346 F. Supp. 2d 1, 5 (D.D.C. 2004).
[41] *Id.*
[42] 28 U.S.C. § 2241 (2006).
[43] Criminal Justice Act, 18 U.S.C. § 3006A (2006).
[44] All Writs Act, 28 U.S.C. § 1651 (2006).
[45] *Al Odah*, 346 F. Supp. 2d at 5.
[46] *Id.*
[47] *See* Driscoll, *supra* note 1, at 874.
[48] BLACK'S LAW DICTIONARY 1343 (9th ed. 2009) (defining a "protective order" as "[a] court order prohibiting or restricting a party from engaging in conduct (esp. a legal procedure such as discovery) that unduly annoys or harasses the opposing party or a third-party witness").
[49] Driscoll, *supra* note 1, at 874, 874 n.4 (explaining that petitions for habeas corpus by Guantanamo detainees have generally been filed in the U.S. District Court for the District of Columbia).

power "to fashion procedures by analogy to existing procedures, in aid of the Court's jurisdiction and in order to develop a factual record as necessary for the Court to make a decision on the merits of" detainee habeas claims.[50] The USG then moved for a Protective Order "to prevent the unauthorized disclosure or dissemination of classified national security information."[51]

Following the ruling in *Al Odah*, U.S. District Judge Joyce Hens Green coordinated and managed all Guantanamo proceedings and rules on common procedural and substantive issues.[52] With the exception of cases before Judge Richard J. Leon, all then-pending Guantanamo cases were transferred to Judge Green.[53]

2. The 2004 Protective Order: Setting the Stage, The Original Protective Order Governing Attorney-Client Relations at Guantanamo Bay

Since 2004, protective orders, issued by the U.S. District Court for the District of Columbia, guide an attorney's access to not only confidential information but also their clients.[54] On November 8, 2004, U.S. District Judge Joyce Hens Green issued a framework (the "Green Protective Order") for detainee counsel-access in order "to prevent the unauthorized disclosure or dissemination of classified national security information."[55] This order implements a set of procedures originally proposed by the Department of Defense (the "DoD").[56] The Green

---

[50] *Al Odah*, 346 F. Supp. 2d at *6.

[51] *In re* Guantanamo Detainee Cases, 344 F. Supp. 2d 174, 175 (D.D.C. 2004).

[52] *In re* Guantanamo Bay Detainee Continued Access to Counsel, No. 12-398, 2012 U.S. Dist. LEXIS 126833, at *27 (D.D.C. Sept. 6, 2012).

[53] *Id.*

[54] Zoe Tillman, *Lawyers for Gitmo Detainees Argue Against New Attorney-Client Rules*, BLT: THE BLOG OF LEGALTIMES (Aug. 17, 2012, 2:06 PM), http://legaltimes.typepad.com/blt/2012/08/lawyers-for-gitmo-detainees-argue-against-new-attorney-client-rules.html.

[55] *In re* Guantanamo Detainee Cases, 344 F. Supp. 2d at 175. The formal title of the Green Protective Order is: "Amended Protective Order and Procedures for Counsel Access to Detainees at the United States Naval Base in Guantanamo Bay, Cuba." *Id.*

[56] Driscoll, *supra* note 1, at 892 n.85 (explaining the Department of Defense's "Revised Procedures for Counsel Access to Prisoners at the U.S. Naval Base in Guantanamo Bay,

Protective Order was subsequently used in the vast majority of Guantanamo habeas cases before the District Court for the District of Columbia.[57]

The procedures enumerated in the Green Protective Order govern attorney access to clients, the logistics of attorney visits to Guantanamo, and correspondence between the attorney and the detainee.[58] Among its provisions, the Green Protective Order requires a detainee's attorney to possess a security clearance, conditions attorney access to clients and material upon a signed agreement binding them to the security provisions set forth in the order, and provides for access to classified information only at a secure facility established and managed by court appointed military personnel.[59]

Generally, the Green Protective Order is considered a success, as it efficiently balanced the goals of "protecting the legitimate and important national security interests of the United States while ensuring that attorneys representing detainee[s] are permitted effective access to their clients."[60] The Green Protective Order was enforced without objection for four years.[61]

3. The 2008 Protective Order: The Status Quo Prior to the MOU

Following the 2008 *Boumediene* decision, the District Court for the District of Columbia again appointed a single judge to rule on common procedural issues in order to maintain judicial consistency and

---

Cuba" modified an earlier set of procedures, the "Procedures for Counsel Access to Prisoners at the U.S. Naval Base in Guantanamo Bay, Cuba," that had been submitted to the court in another detainee matter).

[57] Adem v. Bush, 425 F. Supp. 2d 7, 19 (D.D.C. 2006).

[58] Driscoll, *supra* note 1, at 892.

[59] *Id.* at 893.

[60] *Id.* at 910 n.179 (internal citations omitted). Officials of the USG have also declared the Green Protective Order a success. *See supra* (internal citations omitted) (noting Commander McCarty characterized the Green Protective Order as generally successful).

[61] *In re* Guantanamo Bay Detainee Continued Access to Counsel, No. 12-398, 2012 U.S. Dist. LEXIS 126833, at *27 (D.D.C. Sept. 6, 2012).

facilitate an efficient resolution of Guantanamo habeas cases.[62] This time, Judge Thomas F. Hogan was designated "to coordinate and manage proceedings in all cases involving petitioners presently detained at Guantanamo Bay, Cuba."[63] This means all pending habeas cases and subsequent cases filed, with the exception of cases before Judge Richard Leon and *Hamdan v. Bush*, were transferred to Judge Hogan's docket.[64] Judge Hogan issued his own Protective Order (the "Hogan Protective Order") containing procedures for counsel access to detainees and to classified information.[65] This order is substantially similar to the Green Protective Order.[66] The Hogan Protective Order superseded the Green Protective Order and the District Court for the District of Columbia eventually adopted the Hogan Protective Order in all Guantanamo habeas cases.[67] For purposes of this paper, the relevant provisions of the order shall be consolidated and discussed in the following three parts: (a) counsel access to classified and protected information and documents; (b) access by counsel to Guantanamo detainees; and (c) penalties imposed for violating the protective order.

a. Requirements for Counsel Access to Classified and Protected Information

The Hogan Protective Order sets out procedures that detainees and their respective counsel[68] must follow in order to receive access to

---

[62] *Id.* at *27-28 (citing *In re* Guantanamo Bay Detainee Litig., Misc. No. 08-442 (TFH), Order [1] at 1-2, July 2, 2012).

[63] *Id.* at *28.

[64] *Id.* at *27-28.

[65] *In re* Guantanamo Bay Detainee Litig., 577 F. Supp. 2d 143 (D.D.C. 2008).

[66] *In re* Guantanamo Bay Detainee Continued Access to Counsel, No. 12-398, 2012 U.S. Dist. LEXIS 126833, at *28.

[67] Benjamin Wittes, *On Continued Counsel Access at Gitmo and the Government's Filing*, LAWFARE BLOG (July 27, 2012, 8:06 AM), http://www.lawfareblog.com/2012/07/on-continued-counsel-access-at-gitmo-and-the-governments-filing/.

[68] *See In re* Guantanamo Bay Detainee Litig., 577 F. Supp. 2d at 147 ("[P]etitioners' counsel includes attorneys . . . representing the petitioner in habeas corpus or other litigation in federal court in the United States, as well as co-counsel, interpreters/translators, paralegals, investigators and all other personnel or support staff employed or engaged to assist in the litigation.").

classified[69] or protected[70] national security information.[71] According to the Hogan Protective Order, without authorization from the USG, attorneys for the detainees shall not have access to any classified or protected information unless the attorney has received the necessary security clearance *and* signed the Memorandum of Understanding,[72] binding the attorney by the terms and conditions of the protective order.[73]

The Hogan Protective Order entrusts Court Security Officers ("CSO"), designated by the District Court for the District of Columbia, to protect against the unauthorized disclosure of any classified documents or information.[74] The CSO is responsible for governing the "secure area," the only location classified information shall be stored, maintained and used.[75] All documents prepared by detainees or their attorney that contain or may contain classified information, including notes and

---

[69] *See Id.* at 147, 146-48 (defining "classified information" to include any document or information designated by any Executive Branch agency as classified in the interest of national security pursuant to an Executive Order, any document or information currently or formerly in the possession of a private parry that was derived from USG classified information, verbal or non-documentary classified information known to petitioners or their counsel, or any document and information the petitioner or petitioner's counsel was notified of containing classified information). All classified documents or information remain classified until declassified by the agency or department that issued the original classified status. *Id.* at 147.

[70] *See id.* at 151 (designating "protected information" to include any document or information the District Court for the District of Columbia deems either *sua sponte*, upon the request of the USG and the consent of the petitioner's counsel formalized through a court order, or a grant of the USG's request over an objection by detainee's counsel by court order, not suitable for public filing).

[71] *Id.* at 145.

[72] *Id.* at 148 ("[T]he MOU is a condition precedent to a petitioner's counsel having access to, or continued access to, or continued access to, classified information for the purposes of these proceedings."); *see id.* at 164-65 (Exhibit A: Memorandum of Understanding Regarding Access to Classified National Security Information).

[73] *Id.* at 148, 151.

[74] *In re* Guantanamo Bay Detainee Litig., 577 F. Supp. 2d at 147 ("'Unauthorized disclosure of classified information' means any knowing, willful, or negligent action that could reasonably be expected to result in a communication or physical transfer of classified information to an unauthorized recipient.").

[75] *Id.* ("'Secure area' means a physical facility accredited or approved for the storage, handling, and control of classified information.").

memoranda, must stay in the secure area unless the CSO declassifies them in their entirety.[76] Attorneys may remove classified documents from the secure area only after receiving authorization by the CSO.[77]

In addition to limiting the location of classified and protected information, the Hogan Protective Order curtails discussion of the materials.[78] Attorneys must obtain CSO authorization before discussing classified information outside of the secure area, over the phone, or through electronic mail.[79] Attorneys for detainees who satisfy the necessary prerequisites may share and discuss, among themselves, classified or protected information on a need to know basis, "to the extent necessary for the effective representation of their clients."[80] However, attorneys may not make any public or private statements disclosing any classified or protected information.[81] Attorneys cannot even discuss classified information with their clients unless their clients provided the information to the attorneys.[82]

b. Requirements for Counsel Access to, and Communications with, Detainees

The DOJ controls whether attorneys may meet with a detainee.[83] Attorneys must submit a request to the DOJ in advance—typically no less than 20 days before the visit—and once access is granted, no more than two attorneys plus one interpreter/translator may meet with a detainee at one time unless otherwise approved by the Commander prior to the visit.[84] In order for attorneys to communicate and meet with detainees, the attorneys must agree, in writing, to comply fully with the Hogan Protective Order and they must hold a valid United States security

---

[76] *Id.* at 148-49.
[77] *Id.* at 148.
[78] *Id.* at 149.
[79] *Id.*
[80] *In re* Guantanamo Bay Detainee Litig., 577 F. Supp. 2d at 149-52.
[81] *Id.* at 150, 152.
[82] *Id.*
[83] *Id.* at 158.
[84] *Id.*

clearance at the Secret level or higher.[85] Attorneys must also provide the DoD with evidence that the detainee authorizes their assistance.[86]

In addition to the extensive requirements above, the Hogan Protective Order specifies additional procedures for correspondence between attorneys and detainees.[87] It establishes a "privilege team"[88] of DoD officials to review and confirm the legal mail status of incoming materials.[89] Correspondence not falling within the definition of legal mail, such as letters from the detainees' families, must be sent through the U.S. Postal Service, and may not be included with legal mail.[90]

Any information an attorney learns from a detainee is classified information, unless and until it is submitted to the privilege team and the privilege team or federal courts determine it to be otherwise.[91] Additionally, an attorney cannot communicate with his or her client by telephone unless the conversation is approved by the Commander- a permission that is not often granted.[92]

c. Penalties for Unauthorized Disclosure of Classified and/or Protected Information or Documents

The Hogan Protective Order aims to prevent the unauthorized disclosure of classified or protected documents or information to anyone who is not authorized to receive them.[93] Violators may be punished

---

[85] *Id.* at 157; *see id.* at 165 (Exhibit B: Acknowledgement).

[86] Attorneys must provide the DoD with a Notification of Representation form no later than ten days after the conclusion of a second visit with a detainee. *In re* Guantanamo Bay Detainee Litig., 577 F. Supp. 2d at 157.

[87] *Id.* at 158-59.

[88] *Id.* at 156 ("'Privilege team' means a team comprised of one or more DoD attorneys and one or more intelligence or law enforcement personnel who have not taken part in, and, in the future, will not take part in, any domestic or foreign court, military commission, or combatant status tribunal proceedings involving the detainee.").

[89] *Id.* (defining "legal mail" as legal documents and other letters related to the counsel's representation of that detainee).

[90] *See id.* at 159.

[91] *See id.* at 159, 163.

[92] *In re* Guantanamo Bay Detainee Litig., 577 F. Supp. 2d at 163.

[93] *Id.* at 156.

regardless of whether the unauthorized disclosure was made directly or indirectly, through retention, or negligence.[94] Violations of the terms of the Hogan Protective Order are to be brought before the District Court for the District of Columbia immediately under a potential Contempt of the Court charge.[95] Since an unauthorized disclosure of classified information violates United States criminal laws, criminal proceedings may ensue.[96] If violations do occur, the attorney's access to classified and privileged information is terminated.[97] These repercussions aim to protect the national security interests of the United States, its government personnel, and its facilities.[98]

III. THE MOU

In May 2012, the DOJ began issuing new rules governing attorney-client relations at Guantanamo.[99] Pursuant to the latest policies, the USG required attorneys for detainees whose habeas petitions had been dismissed or denied on the merits, to sign the MOU that will supersede the Hogan Protective Order.[100] While the USG asserted its new MOU provided "essentially the same"[101] provisions for counsel-access as the Hogan Protective Order, attorneys for the detainees, and one federal court, found sections of the MOU to significantly and adversely modify the prior protective order.[102] Attorneys could no longer

---

[94] *Id.* at 155-56.

[95] *Id.* at 155.

[96] *Id.*

[97] *Id.*

[98] *In re* Guantanamo Bay Detainee Litig., 577 F. Supp. 2d at 155.

[99] Baher Azmy, *Obama Turns Back the Clock on Guantanamo*, WASH. POST, Aug. 16, 2012, at A19.

[100] *See* Stephen I. Vladeck, Response, *Access to Counsel, Res Judicata, and the Future of Habeas at Guantanamo*, 161 U. PA. L. REV. PENNUMBRA 78, 88 (2012); *see also* Mike Scarcella, *Justice Department Drops Challenge of Gitmo Lawyer Rules*, NAT'L L.J. (Dec. 17, 2012) [hereinafter *Justice Department Drops Challenge of Gitmo Lawyer Rules*], http://www.law.com/jsp/nlj/PubArticleNLJ.jsp?id=1202581856395.

[101] *In re* Guantanamo Bay Detaine[e] Continued Access to Counsel, Misc. No. 12-0398 (RCL), 2012 WL 3193560 at 15 (D.D.C. Aug. 7, 2012).

[102] *See In re* Guantanamo Bay Detainee Continued Access to Counsel, No. 12-398, 2012 U.S. Dist. LEXIS 126833, at *30 (D.D.C. Sept. 6, 2012).

meet with their clients nor access classified or protected information pursuant to the terms of the Hogan Protective Order.[103]

Under the Hogan Protective Order, the "need to know" for attorneys is presumed, and attorneys are allowed to view classified information from their own case and related cases.[104] The Hogan Protective Order also expressly permits attorneys to discuss relevant information, including classified information with each other "to the extent necessary for the effective representation of their clients."[105] Additionally, the Hogan Order safeguards an attorney's continued access to certain classified information, including the attorney's work-product.[106]

Conversely, the MOU countermands the Hogan Protective Order by eliminating the "need to know" presumption and privilege.[107] Instead, an attorney is denied access to all classified documents or information, including their own work product that they had previously obtained or created regarding a detainee's habeas petition.[108] The attorney must petition the USG and justify a satisfactory need to use the previously obtained or created classified materials before the attorney is granted access to it.[109] Under the MOU, the DoD Office of the General Counsel, in consultation with the pertinent classification authorities within the DoD and other agencies, will make these new "need to know" determinations.[110] Additionally, the MOU no longer allowed attorneys to share information amongst themselves regarding their detainee's action

---

[103] *See generally In re* Guantanamo Bay Detaine[e] Continued Access to Counsel, 2012 WL 3193560.
[104] *In re* Guantanamo Bay Detainee Litig., 577 F. Supp. 2d 143, 149-52 (D.D.C. 2008).
[105] *Id.* at 150.
[106] *See id.* at 148-49.
[107] *See In re* Guantanamo Bay Detaine[e] Continued Access to Counsel, 2012 WL 3193560, at 10; *see also* Exhibit A, *In re* Guantanamo Bay Detaine[e] Continued Access to Counsel, Misc. No. 12-0398 (RCL), Doc. No. 12-1 ¶ 8(b) (Aug. 7, 2012).
[108] *See In re* Guantanamo Bay Detaine[e] Continued Access to Counsel, Misc. No. 12-0398 (RCL), Doc. No. 12-1 ¶ 8(b).
[109] *Id.*
[110] *Id.*

unless specifically authorized to do so by the "appropriate government personnel."[111]

While the District Court for the District of Columbia is empowered to enforce the Hogan Protective Order,[112] the MOU delegated "[a]ny disputes regarding the applicability, interpretation, enforcement, compliance with or violations of" the MOU to the "final and unreviewable discretion" of the Commander.[113] The Commander is also given complete "authority and discretion" over attorneys' continued access to classified or protected information as well as access to or communication with detainees.[114]

Although the MOU is binding on attorneys who have represented detainees under the Hogan Protective Order, the new MOU contained no provisions for the substitution of attorneys nor for the addition of new attorneys.[115] In fact, the USG advised detainees' attorneys that "[a]lthough not stated in the MOU itself, the Government . . . anticipates limiting the number of attorneys who may have continued access to a detainee under the MOU to two. Similarly, the Government also anticipates limiting the number of translators for each detainee to one" with the potential to change an unavailable post-habeas translator with the USG's blessing.[116]

Further, under the Hogan Protective Order, the USG may not unreasonably withhold approval for matters within its discretion.[117] No such standard appears in the MOU. Additionally, the MOU declared that the "operational needs and logistical constraints" at Guantanamo, as well as the "requirements for ongoing military commissions, Periodic

---

[111] *Id.* ¶ 8(a)(10).

[112] *In re* Guantanamo Bay Detainee Continued Access to Counsel, No. 12-398, 2012 U.S. Dist. LEXIS 126833, at *30 (D.D.C. Sept. 6, 2012).

[113] *See* Exhibit A, *In re* Guantanamo Bay Detaine[e] Continued Access to Counsel, Misc. No. 12-0398 (RCL), Doc. No. 12-1 ¶ 8(f).

[114] *See id.* at ¶ 6.

[115] *See id.* at ¶ 3.

[116] *In re* Guantanamo Bay Detaine[e] Continued Access to Counsel, Misc. No. 12-0398 (RCL), 2012 WL 3193560 at 11 n.3 (D.D.C. Aug. 7, 2012).

[117] *See* Exhibit A, *In re* Guantanamo Bay Detaine[e] Continued Access to Counsel, Misc. No. 12-0398 (RCL), Doc. No. 12-1 ¶ 8(c).

Review Boards, and habeas litigation" will take priority over attorney access.[118]

A. *The DOJ's Defense of the MOU*

James J. Gilligan, Assistant Director of the DOJ's Civil Division's Federal Programs Branch, wrote in court filings that the "Government does not contend [that detainees without habeas petitions before the court] have no entitlement thereafter to the assistance of counsel, or must fend for themselves in court if they file new habeas cases."[119] The DOJ proffered that detainees retain the right, in certain circumstances, to file successive habeas corpus petitions.[120] Mr. Gilligan further pointed out that detainees may maintain privileged and confidential communication with counsel pursuant to the MOU, which, he added, six attorneys for detainees had already signed.[121]

The USG argued that the executive branch is responsible for overseeing counsel access to detainees when a detainee does not have an active or an impending habeas petition, or where a renewed petition is "speculative."[122] When these situations are present, the DOJ contended that a ruling in favor of the detainees would violate the separation of powers principle because it would strip the executive branch of its authority to control access to military posts and classified information.[123] The USG also objected to a ruling in favor of the detainees because the court would then issue "what is in effect a permanent injunction" against the MOU.[124] A permanent injunction would result in the executive branch granting private counsel access to a military detention facility and access to classified national security information.[125] The USG further

---

[118] *In re* Guantanamo Bay Detainee Litig. 577 F. Supp. 2d 143, 149-52 (D.D.C. 2008).
[119] *DOJ Pushes Changes*, *supra* note 8.
[120] *Id.*
[121] *Id.*
[122] *In re* Guantanamo Bay Detaine[e] Continued Access to Counsel, Misc. No. 12-0398 (RCL), 2012 WL 3193560 at 3-4 (D.D.C. Aug. 7, 2012).
[123] *Id.* at 3; *see Justice Department Drops Challenge of Gitmo Lawyer Rules*, *supra* note 100.
[124] *See In re* Guantanamo Bay Detaine[e] Continued Access to Counsel, 2012 WL 3193560 at 3.
[125] *See id.*

argued that this issue was premature, and that unless and until the detainees demonstrate that the MOU has "impeded their ability to present new habeas petitions to the Court," which had not occurred in this case, the court had no power to address the counsel-access question.[126]

B. *Objections to the MOU*

Attorneys for the detainees argued that their clients were entitled to continued court-ordered counsel access in accord with the Hogan Protective Order for as long as their clients are detained at Guantanamo, regardless of the detainees' habeas status.[127] Attorneys for the detainees were perplexed as to why the USG was replacing the time-tested and workable provisions of the Hogan Protective Order with the MOU.[128] They argued that the MOU impeded on their clients' right to access counsel, and therefore, their clients' right to access the courts.[129]

Detainees' attorneys maintained that the MOU's provisions that depart from the Hogan Protective Order were "onerous and restrictive."[130] They were vehemently opposed to the provisions that gave the Commander absolute authority over attorney access to clients and classified material and that prioritized base operational issues over attorney-access.[131] Attorneys for the detainees took issue with the MOU's grant of "final and unreviewable discretion"[132] to the

---

[126] *Id.* at 15.

[127] Motion Concerning the Protective Order Entered by Judge Hogan on Sept. 11, 2008, Abdah v. Obama, No. 04-1254 (D.D.C. July 9, 2012), *available at* http://www.lawfareblog.com/wp-content/uploads/2012/07/Motion-re-Protective-Order-Esmail-July-9-2012-ALL-AS-FILED.pdf.

[128] *See id.* at 9 (indicating hundreds, if not thousands, of attorney-client visits have successfully taken place pursuant to the Hogan Protective Order); *see also DOJ Pushes Changes*, *supra* note 8.

[129] *See* Motion Concerning the Protective Order Entered by Judge Hogan on Sept. 11, 2008, *supra* note 126, at 7; *see also* Vladeck, *supra* note 100, at 78, 88.

[130] Motion Concerning the Protective Order Entered by Judge Hogan on Sept. 11, 2008, *supra* note 126, at 4.

[131] *See* Mears, *supra* note 15; King, *supra* note 16.

[132] Frederic J. Frommer, *Judge Skeptical of New Policy on Gitmo Access*, ASSOCIATED PRESS (Aug. 17, 2012, 2:26 PM), http://bigstory.ap.org/article/judge-skeptical-new-policy-gitmo-access.

Commander, instead of the courts, for settling any disputes that arise.[133] As one attorney commented, "[the USG is] essentially saying, 'trust us' . . . but there's no well of trust here."[134]

Attorneys for the detainees were opposed to the MOU's "numerous highly restrictive provisions" including, for example, the prohibitions on attorney access to their own work product in the event their client's habeas action is terminated, prohibitions against sharing information from different cases and between attorneys, and the prohibition against the presumption in favor of an attorney's "need to know."[135] Because of these provisions, attorneys for the detainees argued that the Hogan Protective Order must continue to apply to all detainees, regardless of their habeas status, in order to preserve the efficiencies and equities created through information-sharing.[136]

Rejecting the USG's claim that the detainees have not shown harm, William Livingston ("Livingston"), an attorney for two detainees at Guantanamo who were affected by the MOU, argued that his clients were already harmed when his team could not meet with them after refusing to sign the MOU.[137] Livingston expressed a fear amongst detainees' attorneys that the MOU would "open the door for future restrictions on access," and, as a consequence, future harm.[138] This fear was predicated on the language of the MOU and the USG's indication it may limit each detainee without a case pending to a maximum of two attorneys.[139] Livingston pointed out there is nothing in the MOU to prevent the USG from restricting representation to one lawyer or to prevent the USG from imposing other restrictions after the MOU is

---

[133] See Mears, *supra* note 15; King, *supra* note 16.

[134] Tillman, *supra* note 54 (quoting William Livingston, partner at Covington & Burling and counsel for two Guantanamo detainees).

[135] Motion Concerning the Protective Order Entered by Judge Hogan on Sept. 11, 2008 at 5-7, Abdah v. Obama, No. 04-1254 (D.D.C. July 9, 2012), *available at* http://www.lawfareblog.com/wp-content/uploads/2012/07/Motion-re-Protective-Order-Esmail-July-9-2012-ALL-AS-FILED.pdf.

[136] See id.

[137] Tillman, *supra* note 54.

[138] Id.

[139] Id.

signed.[140] Expressing the sentiment amongst attorneys representing detainees at Guantanamo, Livingston said, "The MOU guarantees nothing. . . . Why should we agree to such a thing?"[141] Attorneys for the detainees asked the court to rule that the USG violated the Hogan Protective Order by requiring attorneys to sign the MOU and that the court rule the Hogan Protective Order applies to all cases, regardless of a detainees' habeas status.[142]

IV. THE MOU IS UNCONSTITUTIONAL

On September 6, 2012, the United States District Court for the District of Columbia issued its opinion striking down the MOU and the USG's attempt to supersede the court's authority as an "illegitimate exercise of Executive power."[143] The court concomitantly upheld the governance of the Hogan Protective Order over detainee-counsel access "so long as detainees can bring habeas petitions before the Court."[144] The decision effectually gave the federal courts continued jurisdiction over current and future habeas petitions filed by Guantanamo detainees.[145]

Endorsing the mantra "if it ain't broke, don't fix it," Judge Lamberth focused on the fact that for eight years two protective orders under judicial oversight had, in his opinion, safely and effectively governed attorney-client relations at Guantanamo.[146] During these eight years, the USG never expressed an opposition to those orders nor did the USG bring any violations of those orders to the court's attention.[147]

---

[140] *See id.*

[141] Frommer, *supra* note 132.

[142] *See* Motion Concerning the Protective Order Entered by Judge Hogan on Sept. 11, 2008 at 9, Abdah v. Obama, No. 04-1254 (D.D.C. July 9, 2012), *available at* http://www.lawfareblog.com/wp-content/uploads/2012/07/Motion-re-Protective-Order-Esmail-July-9-2012-ALL-AS-FILED.pdf.

[143] *In re* Guantanamo Bay Detainee Continued Access to Counsel, No. 12-398, 2012 U.S. Dist. LEXIS 126833, at *74 (D.D.C. Sept. 6, 2012).

[144] *Id.* at *47, *74.

[145] Vladeck, *supra* note 100, at 81.

[146] *In re* Guantanamo Bay Detainee Continued Access to Counsel, 2012 U.S. Dist. LEXIS 126833 at *27, *29.

[147] *See id.* at *29.

The court took issue with many of the MOU's departures from the Hogan Protective Order.[148] For example, the court expressed concern about the MOU's lack of a reasonableness standard to prevent the USG from unilaterally and arbitrarily refusing to grant attorneys permission to access their client and protected materials.[149] The court observed that since the MOU is not operational until countersigned by the Commander, the Commander may deny a detainee access to counsel without being held accountable by refusing to countersign the MOU.[150] On a similar note, the court was apprehensive about the Commander's ability to prioritize the operational needs and logistical constraints of the base over counsel's need to access his or her client or information. The court said this provision "is particularly troubling as it places a detainee's access to counsel, and thus the detainee's constitutional right to access the courts, in a subordinate position to whatever the military commander of Guantanamo sees as a logistical constraint."[151] Further, the court was concerned about the MOU's provision that strips counsel of the "need to know" designations and instead requires counsel to justify their need to access any previously obtained or created classified documents to the satisfaction of specified government agents. The court had reservations that this requirement might lead to "lengthy, needless and possibly oppressive delays," all the while requiring counsel to disclose "some analysis and strategy to their adversary merely to obtain their past work-product."[152]

The court relied on the history of the Writ of Habeas Corpus to establish that the Judiciary, not the Executive, is responsible for "call[ing] the jailer to account," and therefore, ensuring detainees have access to the courts in a way that is "adequate, effective, and meaningful."[153]

The Court held that detainees with and without habeas petitions before the court have the same need to access counsel, and therefore the

---

[148] *See id.* at *29-33.
[149] *Id.* at *31.
[150] *See In re* Guantanamo Bay Detainee Litig., 577 F. Supp. 2d 143, 158 (D.D.C. 2008).
[151] *In re* Guantanamo Bay Detainee Continued Access to Counsel, 2012 U.S. Dist. LEXIS 126833 at *33.
[152] *Id.* at *31.
[153] *Id.* at *34-35, *40.

USG's unsubstantiated interest in a proposed two tiered regime that imposes different rules for detainees with and without active petitions could not be upheld.[154]

While it is uncontested that courts generally do not interfere with the oversight of prisons by the executive branch, the court disagreed that the executive branch should be free from judicial oversight in the determination of counsel-access to detainees.[155] The court aptly pointed out that even the USG concedes that Guantanamo is not a corrections facility.[156] The court indicated that even if Guantanamo was one, "it does not follow that the judiciary has secondary responsibility for ensuring [detainees] have adequate access to the courts."[157] In fact, the Supreme Court has expressly ruled against policies that threaten the ability of detainees to challenge their detention effectively.[158] In a 1996 case, the Supreme Court held that although the executive branch "may have the responsibility for regulating its facilities, the Court is charged with ensuring that [detainees] are 'provided with the tools . . . to challenge the conditions of their confinement.'"[159] This is especially true for detainees being held at Guantanamo.[160]

The court also rejected the USG's argument that the court was interfering with the Executive's power to control classified information.[161] In its justification for why the USG's argument does not pass the "smell test," the court reiterated the fact that the Hogan Protective Order was effectively in force for four years without

---

[154] *Id.* at *39-40.

[155] *Id.*

[156] *Id.* at *40-41.

[157] *In re* Guantanamo Bay Detainee Continued Access to Counsel, 2012 U.S. Dist. LEXIS 126833 at *40.

[158] *Id.* at *41 ("[The] state and its officers may not abridge or impair a prisoner's right to apply to a federal court for a writ of habeas corpus.") (quoting *Ex parte* Hull, 312 U.S. 546, 549 (1941)).

[159] *Id.* at *42 (citing Lewis v. Casey, 518 U.S. 343, 351 (1996)).

[160] *Id.* at *42.

[161] *Id.* at *73; *In re* Guantanamo Bay Detaine[e] Continued Access to Counsel, Misc. No. 12-0398 (RCL), 2012 WL 3193560 at 4 (D.D.C. Aug. 7, 2012).

incident.¹⁶² Not a single complaint about a leak of classified information was brought before the court.¹⁶³ Because the MOU barely alters the classified and protected provisions of the Hogan Protective Order (the MOU only stripped counsel of their need to know status), the court concluded that the USG is satisfied with the classified and protected provisions of the Hogan Protective Order, and therefore, that a ruling in favor of the detainees did not challenge the USG's right to protect classified information.¹⁶⁴

The court held that it is the Judiciary's responsibility to ensure detainees have access to habeas relief and not the Executive's, finding that the USG lacked legal authority to unilaterally impose new rules governing the detainees' continued access to counsel absent an active habeas action.¹⁶⁵ The court therefore declared the MOU "null *ab initio*," meaning the MOU was void from the beginning.¹⁶⁶ The court repudiated the USG's argument that a ruling against the MOU and for the Hogan Protective order would translate into a permanent injunction.¹⁶⁷ As part of the court's dismissal of the USG's argument, the court emphasized that the Hogan Protective Order is only effective for as long as detainees are held at Guantanamo and are able to petition for habeas and other relief before the federal courts.¹⁶⁸

The court also held that its review of the issue at hand is not premature as the USG promulgated.¹⁶⁹ The court cites *Lewis v. Casey*, a case that permits the use of past interference with detainees' presentation of claims in order to satisfy the actual harm requirement, to support its use of evidence of past abuses by the USG concerning attorney access to

---

¹⁶² *In re* Guantanamo Bay Detainee Continued Access to Counsel, No. 12-398, 2012 U.S. Dist. LEXIS 126833, at *73 (D.D.C. Sept. 6, 2012).
¹⁶³ *Id.*
¹⁶⁴ *Id.* at *73-74.
¹⁶⁵ *Id.* at *46-47.
¹⁶⁶ *Id.* at *47; BLACK'S LAW DICTIONARY 5, 1172 (9th ed. 2009) (defining "null" as "having no legal effect" and "*ab initio*" as "from the beginning").
¹⁶⁷ *See In re* Guantanamo Bay Detainee Continued Access to Counsel, 2012 U.S. Dist. LEXIS 126833, at *47-48.
¹⁶⁸ *Id.*
¹⁶⁹ *Id.* at *63-64; *In re* Guantanamo Bay Detaine[e] Continued Access to Counsel, Misc. No. 12-0398 (RCL), 2012 WL 3193560 at 16 (D.D.C. Aug. 7, 2012).

detainees.[170] These include issues pertaining to habeas representation and access to medical records.[171]

The court acknowledges it has an obligation:

> [T]o assure that those seeking to challenge their Executive detention by petitioning for habeas relief have adequate, effective and meaningful access to the courts. In the case of Guantanamo detainees, access to the courts means nothing without access to counsel . . . . The Court, whose duty it is to secure an individual's liberty from unauthorized and illegal Executive confinement, cannot now tell a [detainee] that he must beg leave of the Executive's grace before the Court will involve itself. This very notion offends separation-of-powers principles and our constitutional scheme.[172]

On December 6, 2012, the court struck down the MOU as "an illegitimate exercise of Executive Power," and upheld the Hogan Protective Order as the governing rules for attorney access to detainees as well as protected and classified information at Guantanamo whether a detainee has a habeas petition before the court or not.[173] On December 14, 2012, the deadline passed for the DOJ to file a statement of the issues to continue the case.[174] This effectively abandoned the USG's pursuit of the MOU.[175]

---

[170] *In re* Guantanamo Bay Detainee Continued Access to Counsel, 2012 U.S. Dist. LEXIS 126833, at *47-48 (referencing Lewis v. Casey, 518 U.S. 343, 349 (1996)).

[171] *In re* Guantanamo Bay Detainee Continued Access to Counsel, No. 12-398, 2012 U.S. Dist. LEXIS 126833, at *64-70 (D.D.C. Sept. 6, 2012) (citing Adam v. Bush, 425 F. Supp. 2d 7, 9 (D.D.C. 2006); Tumani v. Obama, 598 F. Supp. 2d 67, 70 (D.D.C. 2009); Al-Joudi v. Bush, 406 F. Supp. 2d 15-17, 21-22 (D.D.C. 2005); and Husayn v. Gates, 588 F. Supp. 2d 7, 9 (D.D.C. 2008)).

[172] *Id.* at *74-75.

[173] *Id.*

[174] *See Justice Department Drops Challenge of Gitmo Lawyer Rules, supra* note 100.

[175] *Id.*

V. ANALYSIS

More than a decade after September 11, 2001, many detainees have had their day in court and have lost their habeas cases.[176] Those that no longer have a habeas case before the court are subject to the terms of the MOU as the only means of challenging their detention going forward. In addition to the legal basis for striking down the MOU as discussed in the court's opinion above, several policy considerations support the governance of continued access to counsel for detainees by the Hogan Protective Order and not the MOU. The Hogan Protective Order better promotes judicial expediency and efficiency, it better encourages and facilitates pro bono practice, and it is another step in the right direction to shatter the image of Guantanamo as a "legal black hole."

A. *The Hogan Protective Order Better Promotes Judicial Expediency and Efficiency*

The Hogan Protective Order aims to provide detainees with the requisite tools to prosecute habeas petitions before the courts. By leaving counsel-access to the unrestrained discretion of the Commander in the MOU, detainees may decide to circumvent the Commander all together by proceeding pro se.[177] Detainees proceeding pro se may cause major headaches for themselves and the courts as many detainees speak limited or no English, have no legal training, and have no means to be kept up to date with new legal and political developments. Incoherent, legally unsound, and ill-prepared pleadings slow down the judicial system and prevent cases from moving forward in an expedient and efficient way.

Even if a detainee successfully receives permission from the Commander for continued access to counsel, the MOU does not provide for attorney substitutions or replacements. This predicament might prove an inefficient use of the court's time if an attorney is unable to continue representing his or her client mid-trial and another member of

---

[176] Clive Stafford Smith, *Guantanamo Bay: Statistics*, REPRIEVE (July 28, 2011), http://www.reprieve.org.uk/publiceducation/guantanamostats/ ("59 decided habeas cases: 38 prisoners granted habeas and 21 prisoners denied habeas.").

[177] BLACK'S LAW DICTIONARY 1341 (9th ed. 2009) (defining "pro se" as "[o]ne who represents oneself in a court proceeding without the assistance of a lawyer").

the team is not allowed to step in to continue the case with a seamless transition. Further, the USG has already indicated it may, in the future, limit the number of attorneys allowed to represent a detainee, adding to the likelihood that this dilemma could occur.

The MOU's prerequisite of Commander permission for continued access to counsel presents the scary notion that viable, judiciable cases may never be brought before the courts again because the Commander's decision is discretionary and unreviewable. As President Obama seeks to close the detention facilities at Guantanamo,[178] adjudicating claims for detainees seems one clear way to further that goal. The *Boumediene* decision reopened the courts to Guantanamo detainees and expressly granted detainees the constitutional right to petition for habeas relief.[179] The Hogan Protective Order, when compared to the MOU, is the most efficient and effective means for allowing detainees access to the courts, and an opportunity to navigate through the judicial system.

B. *The Hogan Protective Order Better Encourages and Facilitates Pro Bono Practice*

Adhering to the Hogan Protective Order already places many obstacles before attorneys representing detainees pro bono.[180] To mention just a few, attorneys for the detainees must obtain security clearances, prove permission from their client to represent them, only keep and discuss classified and protected materials and work product in a USG designated location, be given permission, which is rare, to speak

---

[178] Stephen Dinan, *Four Years After Obama's Signature Promise, Gitmo Is Still Open*, WASH. TIMES, (Jan. 20, 2013), http://www.washingtontimes.com/news/2013/jan/20/obamas-first-term-promise-close-gitmo-prison-still/.

[179] *See SOP and Guantanamo Detainees*, *supra* note 24 at 179; *Obama Backtracks on Guantanamo*, *supra* note 9.

[180] BLACK'S LAW DICTIONARY 1323 (9th ed. 2009) (explaining the word "pro bono" derives from Latin roots meaning "for the public good" or "[b]eing or involving uncompensated legal services performed esp[ecially] for the public good").

with their client over the phone, and clear the logistical arrangements for their visit with the USG well in advance of their arrival.[181]

Representing a detainee is incredibly time consuming and expensive. Over the course of a decade, many of these attorneys dedicate hundreds of hours of pro bono service representing a detainee and the costs of such representation are enormous. Attorneys are practically limited from flying down to Guantanamo for a few hours to meet with their client or access the protected area because only two flights fly in and out of Guantanamo.[182] Due to this, accessing a few key documents in the protected area can easily become a two-day affair. To accommodate the workload and offset the cost of performing this work pro bono, law firms often establish teams of attorneys to represent detainees so that attorneys may maintain their billable hours and their paying clients while representing the detainees. Additionally, a single lawyer or a team of lawyers often represents multiple detainees to streamline the work and the expense. Under the Hogan Protective Order, the team is not limited in number, nor is it restricted in substitutions or replacements. As long as each individual attorney or support staff complies with the Hogan Protective Order's provisions, including the requisite security clearance, they may assist in the representation. This allows attorneys more flexibility in their scheduling, as they may switch or take turns traveling to Guantanamo. This is not true under the MOU. As mentioned above, the USG indicates it may unilaterally amend the MOU to limit the number of attorneys representing any particular detainees to only two. The rigidity of the MOU makes an already difficult job practically impossible for attorneys who need to balance their pro bono practice with their other clients who pay the bills. Because the MOU does not provide any provisions for the substitution or addition of counsel, a detainee risks being left without any representation if their attorneys are unable to visit or need to remove themselves from the case due to health or other pressing matters.

---

[181] *In re* Guantanamo Bay Detainee Litig., 577 F. Supp. 2d 143, 148-49, 157-58, 163 (D.D.C. 2008).

[182] *In re* Guantanamo Bay Detainee Continued Access to Counsel, No. 12-398, 2012 U.S. Dist. LEXIS 126833, at *60-61 (D.D.C. Sept. 6, 2012).

For close to a decade, not a single violation of the Green or Hogan Protective Orders has come before the court. The MOU is more rigid than the Green and Hogan Protective Orders. Because the MOU did not allow for interchanging or adding attorneys, it placed a greater strain on those attorneys already representing detainees and acted as a deterrent to attorneys who would otherwise join ongoing cases. As the District Court for the District of Columbia so eloquently put it, "The Court would like to note that pro bono counsel in these cases have worked diligently to provide detainees with competent legal counsel. It would have been difficult and costly for the Court to manage its Guantanamo docket without the help of pro bono counsel."[183] The Hogan Protective Order best assures pro bono representation of the detainees can and will continue.

C. *The Hogan Protective Order Better Dispels the Image of Guantanamo as a "Legal Black Hole"*

The MOU's provision that the military, not the courts, are given the "final and unreviewable discretion" for settling any arising disputes is troubling because, as recent incidents indicate, the MOU is only the tip of the iceberg when it comes to USG abuses of counsel access to detainees.[184] A previous policy implemented by the USG at Guantanamo violated "both the letter and spirit of the attorney-client privilege" when letters from attorneys containing privileged attorney-client communications were intercepted and reviewed by the USG.[185] There were even reports that content from those letters were shared with the prosecution team.[186] Further, the District Court for the District of Columbia cites other abuses including issues pertaining to habeas representation and access to medical records.[187] Without judicial

---

[183] *Id.* at *61.

[184] *Id.* at *43, *47-48 (referencing Lewis v. Casey, 518 U.S. 343, 349 (1996)).

[185] Letter from Wm. T. (Bill) Robinson III, President, Am. Bar Ass'n, to Honorable Leon Panetta, Sec'y of Def. (Dec. 21, 2011), *available at* http://www.americanbar.org/content/dam/aba/uncategorized/2011/gao/2011dec21_guantanamoattcltpriv.authcheckdam.pdf.

[186] *Id.*

[187] *In re* Guantanamo Bay Detainee Continued Access to Counsel, No. 12-398, 2012 U.S. Dist. LEXIS 126833, at *64-70 (D.D.C. Sept. 6, 2012) (citing Adam v. Bush, 425 F. Supp. 2d 7, 9 (D.D.C. 2006); Tumani v. Obama, 598 F. Supp. 2d 67, 70 (D.D.C. 2009); Al-Joudi

oversight, the detention facilities at Guantanamo revert back to the image of a "legal black hole,"[188] which one journalist described as the impression of hypersecret, indefinite detention.[189] Judicial oversight, and not USG immunity, provides the vigilance necessary to prevent actions such as these from happening again.

Additionally, conditions and treatment of detainees at Guantanamo improved because of judicial oversight and attorney involvement.[190] Even after the USG decides their case cannot be prosecuted and that they should be transferred, many detainees remain at Guantanamo because the country they would be transferred to is deemed too dangerous.[191] Because of the work of human rights groups and the detainees' attorneys, most Guantanamo detainees are now permitted to eat, pray and exercise together.[192] The Hogan Protective Order provides a working balance of detainees' needs for unfettered access to counsel and the needs of the USG to protect classified and protected information and to ensure the safety of its people. The MOU dangerously tips the scales in favor of the USG, and brushes closely with the return of the "legal black hole."

For the policy reasons stated above, The Hogan Protective Order, not the MOU, should govern counsel-access for detainees regardless of their habeas status.

---

v. Bush, 406 F. Supp. 2d 15-17, 21-22 (D.D.C. 2005); and Husayn v. Gates, 588 F. Supp. 2d 7, 9 (D.D.C. 2008)).
[188] See Obama Backtracks on Guantanamo, supra note 9.
[189] See Baher Azmy, Op-Ed., *Guantanamo's Cost Hangs Heavy for Obama*, TIMESUNION.COM (Jan. 10, 2012, 11:46 PM), http://www.timesunion.com/opinion/article/Guantanamo-s-cost-hangs-heavy-for-Obama-2461105.php.
[190] See Obama Backtracks on Guantanamo, supra note 9.
[191] See DEP'T OF JUSTICE ET AL., FINAL REPORT: GUANTANAMO REVIEW TASK FORCE ii (2010), available at http://www.justice.gov/ag/guantanamo-review-final-report.pdf.
[192] Jennifer Daskal, Op-Ed., *Don't Close Guantanamo*, N.Y. TIMES (Jan. 10, 2013), http://www.nytimes.com/2013/01/11/opinion/dont-close-guantanamo.html.

VI. CONCLUSION

A decade has passed since the first detainees arrived at Guantanamo. The need for judicial oversight is as strong now as it was then. For detainees who do not speak English, are not familiar with the United States judicial system, and have no means to learn of judicial and political changes, access to the courts is meaningless without access to counsel. The Hogan Protective Order provides access to counsel and therefore, the courts, regardless of a detainee's habeas status. The Hogan Protective Order is time-tested and effective and justly continues to govern a detainee's continued access to counsel.